THE
INVENTION
OF SODOMY IN
CHRISTIAN
THEOLOGY

T0385871

THE
INVENTION
OF SODOMY IN
CHRISTIAN
THEOLOGY

MARK D. JORDAN

THE UNIVERSITY OF CHICAGO PRESS
Chicago and London

Mark D Jordan is professor at the Medieval Institute, University of
Notre Dame He is the author of *Ordering Wisdom The Hierarchy of
Philosophical Discourses in Aquinas* (1986) He is also an editor and
translator of *Thomas Aquinas, On Faith. summa theologiae 2a-2ae qq
1–6* (1990), the supervising editor of *Patrologia Latina Database*
(1993–95), managing editor of *Medieval Philosophy and Theology*
(1991–95), and coeditor of *Ad litteram Authoritative Texts and Their
Medieval Readers* (1992)

The University of Chicago Press, Chicago 60637
The University of Chicago Press, Ltd , London
© 1997 by Mark D Jordan
All rights reserved Published 1997
Printed and bound by CPI Group (UK) Ltd, Croydon, CR0 4YY
06 05 04 03 02 01 00 99 98 97 97   1 2 3 4 5
ISBN: 978-0-226-41039-5 (cloth)
ISBN: 978-0-226-41040-1 (paper)

CIP data to come

"In the stillness in the autumn moonbeams
his face was inclined toward me,
And his arm lay lightly around my breast—
and that night I was happy"

Contents

Acknowledgments

For some, disputes over the meaning of Catholic theology are historical exercises like any other. They have just the interest of disputes over the doctrines of other Mediterranean religions now generally disbelieved, say Mithraism or Manichaeism. For others of us, disputes over Catholic theology remain urgent. They are urgent not just because we chose to remain faithful for the present to the promise of a Catholic Christianity, but because we live under the power of institutions that claim to act on the teachings of Catholic theology. Some of us have spent years in the dimming, homophobic rooms of traditional Catholic theology not just because we wanted to know how much of it was true, but because it was always being used to wound us. The reader should know then that this book grew out of a double engagement with the history of Catholic theology—an engagement both with its truth and with its ideological abuses.

The book is an argument about the incoherence of the theological category "Sodomy." I wrote it at the University of Notre Dame as an openly gay (because safely tenured) member of the faculty. I wrote it also as a member of an outlawed lesbian and gay group and while publicly active on its behalf. By the prevailing standards of churchly persecution, I have not suffered particularly for my violation of the codes of permitted visibility. Others, who tried to remain invisible, have suffered much worse. I lift up in memory two men in particular. One was a colleague on the faculty, the other an undergraduate student. Both were hastened towards despair by Notre Dame, which is to say, by the local arm of the Catholic Church. Both killed themselves—all too invisibly. The religious order to which my colleague belonged denied everything. The family of the young man does not know to this day the motives of his death. So I count myself lucky. I am out; I am alive.

Still, I could not have survived the grinding prejudice of Notre Dame except for the support of remarkable friends. They have not only encouraged me to write this book, they have held on to me through cycles of despair and, more recently, of grief. Many of these friends I cannot safely name, for fear of imperiling their positions at Notre Dame or in the local community. Those I can name are John Blandford, David Burrell, Randy Coleman, David Foley, Bill Hecker, Marsha Kopacz, Ron Lee, Jim Lodwick, Jason Lynch, Nathan Mitchell, Hilary Radner, Philip Schatz, Bill Storey, John Van Engen, and Michael Vore. From outside the constricted, too often bitter world of Notre Dame, I have received the steadying support of Sally Dunn, Patrick Garlinger, Pam Hall, David Halperin, Greg Hutcheson, Peter Jordan, and Doug Mitchell. The other name that must be spoken has already figured in the dedication.

Easter A.D. 1996

Portions of chapter 7 originally appeared in *Constructing Medieval Sexuality*, edited by Karma Lochrie, Peggy McCracken, and James Schultz. Reprinted with the kind permission of the University of Minnesota Press.

A Prelude after Nietzsche
The Responsibilities of a History of Sodomy

HISTORIES AND WORDS

"The Invention of Sodomy" is a double pun.

A pun on "invention" first. I mean the word both in the common sense of building something new and in the rhetorical sense of finding ideas useful for composing speeches. Sodomy was invented by medieval theologians in the first sense so far as the name and the category were built with materials taken from older texts. Sodomy was invented in the second sense so far as the new name and its category were found to be very useful for pursuing well-established rhetorical programs.

Next a pun on "Sodomy." "Sodomy" is a medieval artifact. I have found no trace of the term before the eleventh century. It is also a medieval artifact as a category for classifying—for uniting and explaining—desires, dispositions, and acts that had earlier been classified differently and separately. But "Sodomy" is also a judgment. The judgment made in "Sodomy" has been as durable as any medieval artifact. So I speak of the invention of Sodomy for Christian theology as a whole: the medieval invention was the invention of Sodomy simply speaking. It was the invention that would be decisive for all later Christian theology in the West—hence for European or American legislation, medicine, natural science, and manners. The fearful abstraction in our use of the term is medieval, as are our prurient confusions over what the word really means.

In what follows, I mean to recover the medieval acts of invention that constituted Sodomy and prepared for its long-standing effects. I do not want to do this in the style of a history. Narrative history, that charming cousin of the novel, is as constrained by principles of verisimilitude and sequence as the sonnet by its rules of prosody. The historian is enabled to produce the beautiful effects of constraint but is also required to worry from page to page about constructing a narrative within the cramped space

1

of whatever passes for plausibility. The form of the laboriously wrought historical narrative displaces the forms of the old texts with which it claims to be concerned. Narrative historiography misleads by concealing or effacing the shapes of the documents, the character of the voices, from which it derives. The shapes, the voices, are the principal thing here.

I mean to recover the invention of Sodomy not in the form of a historical narrative, but by trying to represent it in a piece of modern, American English. It is impossible, of course, to represent the invention completely. Any representation in our English of the medieval Latin *sodomia* will necessarily fail to capture significant features of the original. But even a partial representation may be useful if it forces modern readers or speakers to reflect on what is concealed in their descriptions and valuations of Sodomy. The usefulness of incomplete representations of ancient things is, so far as I can see, the only reason for feeding scholars.

To represent the invention of a term is to show that it was made for specific purposes, that it was made from particular materials, and that it entered into use at certain points in individual conversations. The term is invented: it begins its history with a past. This past may be long or short, simple or complex, peaceful or contentious. Whatever it is, it must be displayed clearly by any account of the term's invention. This is done by showing what went into that past and how the term's meanings, its roles in discourses, are affected and perhaps determined by it. Can any account do so much?

METHOD AND INNOCENCE

One innocence remains a virtue for the scholar of medieval accounts of what we call "sexuality." It is not innocence of procedure. To ignore the now sophisticated disputes about how to proceed in recovering historical sexualities, disputes that go back at least to Nietzsche, is to risk a vicious maleducation. Foucault, Halperin, and Sedgwick may perhaps be countered, but not disdained. Nor is it a virtue to be innocent of the variety of human desires and practices. Any honest scholarship of sexuality is always in part what Nietzsche called a "natural history of morals." This kind of history begins by fracturing the assumption that the mores of our city, class, church, club, or climate are simply natural. It means to prevent any study of morality that is "poorly informed and not even very curious in regard to peoples, times, and pasts."[1] To be innocent of the variety of ways in

1 Nietzsche, *Beyond Good and Evil* 5 §186 (Colli-Montinari 5.106) Full bibliographic information for all cited works is found under Works Cited Unless otherwise indicated, translations are my own

which humans have mythologized or proscribed what they do with their genitals is to be unfit for being a moralist, much less a scholar of morals. Nor is it enough to speak about the object of historiography as "the Other" and then to write about it innocently on terms of utmost familiarity. To call something strange "strange" is not to understand it, much less to domesticate it.

One innocence does remain a virtue for the scholar of sexuality: innocence in the presence of speech. Nietzsche himself confesses that he found the origin of moral valuations only by attending innocently to language. "The signpost to the *right* road was given me by the question, What was the real etymological meaning of the signs for 'good' coined in the various languages?"[2] Indeed, he proposes as a topic for some learned academy's competition just this question, "What signposts does the science of language, and especially etymological investigation, provide for the history of development of moral concepts?"[3] The question is Nietzsche's first technique for unfolding the overly compressed and contradictory meanings concealed by the familiar surface of moral words. "All concepts in which an entire process has been semiotically gathered escape definition; only what is without history is definable."[4]

These questions and cautions should be applied most scrupulously in the scholarship of historical sexualities and their moral constructions. The central terms used by medieval Christian theologians to describe what we call "sexual activity" cannot be translated into modern English. They condense in themselves different and in some ways briefer histories of category formation. Consider the terms *luxuria, vitium sodomiticum,* and *peccatum* (or *vitium*) *contra naturam* as they figure in Scholastic texts. It might be permissible to transliterate the last two as "Sodomitic vice" and "sin (or vice) against nature," with appropriate warnings. But *luxuria,* the root term, cannot even be transliterated as "luxury" without provoking misunderstandings each time. We may have reasons for thinking that these terms are referentially and genetically connected to some terms that we use, such as "homosexual activity" or "Sodomy." I mean we may have reasons for thinking that the writers of some medieval texts would have used *vitium sodomiticum* to refer to actions or events that we would call "homosexual," and we have historical narratives that lead us to believe that their applications of terms became remote ancestors to ours. But even these reasons mislead us. There is no linear progress in the genealogies of Christian

2 Nietzsche, *On the Genealogy of Morals* 1 §4 (Colli-Montinari 5:261)
3 Nietzsche, *On the Genealogy of Morals* 1 note (Colli-Montinari 5·289)
4 Nietzsche, *On the Genealogy of Morals* 2 §13 (Colli-Montinari 5 317)

moral terms. The terms condense results of contests between opposing tendencies or programs—or else show how the contests had no coherent results. Whatever has been begotten between *sodomia* and "Sodomy," it will not give us a simple genealogy.

How to proceed in studying the genealogy of *sodomia* in medieval theology? Nietzsche's notion of etymology will not suffice. We can indeed begin by watching the coining of the term, and especially how its peculiarly sexual meaning is attached to it despite earlier, authoritative moralizations of the story of Sodom. But the tracing of etymologies is neither sufficiently sure nor sufficiently subtle. Innumerable interpretations are concealed in asserting that an ancient or medieval term had a certain meaning. Moreover, etymologies tend to project a single term across many texts, suppressing the ways in which precise meaning comes to that term through the vocabulary and rhetorical structure of a single text. Dictionaries consist of generalizations, hence of imprecisions. The grossest imprecisions are seen in contrasting dictionary definitions with the usage of a learned, sophisticated, and original author. Whatever else they are, the most prominent medieval theologians are learned, sophisticated, and—sometimes despite themselves—original. Their uses of key terms cannot be learned by turning to any dictionary, even a dictionary that attempts to generalize just their uses.

Nor can we recover the meanings of *sodomia* and terms adjacent to it by translating them all into some neutral superlanguage for comparison with translations of sets of moral terms from other historically instanced languages. There is no "culture-independent semantic meta-language, based on an 'alphabet of human thought': that is to say, on a non-arbitrary system of universal semantic primitives."[5] Attempts to perform such translations, to discover such a "meta-language," are exercises in self-deception—not to say of self-disclosure. If we can sometimes trick ourselves into thinking that we have captured the essence of a particular usage in medieval Latin with some phrases or sentences in modern English, we do so only by ignoring the largest, the most striking shifts of whole categories—say, of the category of the "moral" or the "sexual." The claim for a universal superlanguage covering moral terms and judgments is just the latest form of the positivist pretense, all too familiar for Nietzsche, that a true scholar can achieve "the greatest possible impartiality and 'objectivity' of treatment"—unless "greatest possible" is an irony.[6]

5 Wierzbicka, *Semantics, Culture, and Cognition*, p 200
6 The phrase comes from Sidgwick, *Outlines of the History of Ethics*, p vi.

Nor can we reconstruct the genealogy of Christian moral terms about genital activity by a kind of anthropological observation. Even if anthropology were more optimistic about its accuracy than it now is, its techniques could not be borrowed. Medieval theologians cannot act as informants in the way that Micronesian atoll dwellers have. They can neither correct our attempts to speak their languages nor tell us what oddities they encounter in trying to learn ours. Moreover, the languages of Scholastic theology were and are remote from everyday speech, medieval or modern. A Scholastic language was never learned in the recurring situations of daily life. It was always learned in complex textual structures meant not only to teach terms or rules, but to purify and to authorize them.

Nor can we uncover the genealogy of "Sodomy" by invoking a well-established "queer theory." I have already suggested that there are a number of writers to whom I am indebted for what I understand about the history of sexuality. Indeed, I judge that anyone who wants to undertake a history of sexuality must be indebted to them. But I do not think that these writers give or mean to give a completed science of queerness that can be applied as a cookie cutter to any possible historical dough. On the contrary, what is so admirable in the writing of Foucault, Halperin, and Sedgwick is precisely the refusal to take the question of same-sex desire as settled, as captured by theory. I myself tend to think that we have barely begun to gather evidence of same-sex desire. We are thus very far from being able to imagine having a finished theory.

How then to proceed? By beginning innocently to learn *sodomia* and its siblings from specific texts. We might, for example, regard the terms as protagonists in the plots of various classifications, arguments, or persuasions and the texts themselves as performances. We are to learn what kind of character each protagonist has by watching its actions in the performance. I do not mean to suggest that there are no difficulties in trying to do this. There are no presuppositionless readings—indeed, no pure beginnings in speech. I do mean to say that we can practice the innocence that good students have when learning. For example, we must not assume that *sodomia* or *luxuria* or other such terms have a constant meaning across texts. On the contrary, we should begin by supposing that the terms have to be learned anew with each author. But we can also suppose that a didactic text has its own resources for teaching readers how its central terms are to be used. We assume, in other words, that the texts are active teachers for us. They perform for us and in us. Of course, the texts will perform only if we do not immediately set aside the means by which they carry out the performance—I mean the rhetorical and pedagogical structures that are their largest features. We cannot follow a text's teaching if we begin by ignoring or exploding its teacherly plan.

I place roughly a dozen texts at the center of attention in what follows. The texts are enormously diverse in genre, achievement, theological acuity, and influence. Their diversity is an important part of my argument, because I mean to show that the category "Sodomy" will be problematic no matter where or how it is used. If my argument is right, it suggests that a parallel argument could be made from another selection of texts—indeed, from any selection of medieval theological texts on Sodomy. But I have wanted to make the argument from some of the most eminent texts, from authors who are taken to condemn Sodomy most vehemently or decisively. That principle makes obvious the choice of such figures as Peter Damian, Albert the Great, and Thomas Aquinas. No balanced reading of theological texts on Sodomy could ignore them. Nor could it ignore Alan of Lille's *Plaint of Nature,* even though I will argue that Alan's poem is in fact just the opposite of what it appears at first reading. I have then chosen less famous texts from less familiar genres—liturgical and pastoral texts, for example, or medical ones—on principles of accessibility. I continue to hold to the pious belief that a good reading is one that invites the reader to read for herself the text under consideration. I do not regard myself as a dispenser of an arcane science. I regard myself only as a practiced reader of certain texts that must be read if we want to undo the ideological damage they have provoked or passively authorized.

The pedagogy of great theological texts cannot be reduced to a set of regularities or rules. Their manners of teaching are idiosyncratic—that is part of what makes each of the texts notable. Each teaching has to be learned by study with the individual teacher. There can be no general method for reading them, no algebra of interpretation. It is not even clear whether theories of interpretation have any other use than to send one back to particular readings. Certainly in the face of medieval texts about *sodomia* there is no prescription for reading other than the exhortation to enter into the curriculum of each text in order to be taught by it how it uses its most important terms. Still, it may be important to be reminded of certain obvious features of the terms.

A First Grammar of "Sodomy"

On the face of it, *sodomita,* "Sodomite," is not a common noun, but the proper name for the inhabitant of a historical city. It is extended metaphorically to others, who are counted covert or honorary citizens. So too *sodomia* is the name for the characteristic activity or vice of those inhabitants. It functions in the same way as "Boston marriage" or "Castro clone." With time, the specific reference in such words and phrases wears away and the sedimented metaphor comes to seem a simple description. Since one point of this book is to wash off sediment in order to see underlying metaphors, I will typically capitalize "Sodomite" and related terms in English (though not in Latin).

Sexual vocabulary is particularly rich in metaphors, ironies, and allusions. This seems as true for medieval Latin as for modern English. Both use dozens of ways to speak about sexual things without speaking about them, to point without describing, to suggest without disclosing. Geographical metaphors are a small but particularly telling subset of the sexual vocabulary. They represent the maximum of indirection because they require a particular historical knowledge. Although an uninformed hearer can make some guess at the meaning of "blow job," she is unlikely to make much sense of "French" or "Greek" without specific instruction. The same is true in Latin.[7]

Some of the mechanisms of geographical metaphors in sexual language are not hard to analyze. The terms are perfectly opaque in the way most proper names are. They further suggest that the activity in question is not of local origin, that it comes from elsewhere. Its practitioners are foreigners or consorts of foreigners. These others are then easily likened to bearers of disease. A sexual practice originated elsewhere and imported is quickly enough described as contagion, as plague. Geographical names can call up medical ones. They also connect the sexual practice described to larger groups of cultural prejudices or stereotypes. To call a practice "Greek" is to call up whatever else one thinks about the inhabitants of Greece. So it is with "Sodomitic" and what is heard or imagined about the inhabitants of the city of Sodom.

Of course, displacing a sexual practice by naming it geographically has its consequences. It sets boundaries not only on a practice, but on explanations for it. If the practice was invented elsewhere and imported, then it ought to be controllable by controlling the importation. It cannot be a possibility or temptation widely available to human beings. It needs to be invented before being transported. And so on. In this and many other ways, geographical metaphors embedded in certain sexual terms carry specific presuppositions. Once these presuppositions are overlooked because of a

7 The evolution of geographical euphemisms associated with Sodom will be discussed in chapter 2, but doubters may want to see immediately the classical examples in Adams, *The Latin Sexual Vocabulary*, p 202

metaphor's familiarity, it becomes all too easy to insert the term in arguments with very different presuppositions. The result is instability—that is, one kind of instability. There are others more specifically connected with the social regulation of genital activity between persons of the same genitals. A number of concepts and terms become unstable when confronted with the secrecy surrounding homoerotic practices, with the difficulty of recognizing the "Sodomite." Other instabilities are produced in or around the sarcasms about effeminacy; others still, in asserting a special opposition to God in same-sex copulation.

A decisive responsibility for any genealogy of sexual terms is to represent their kinds of instability. So space will have to be found in English for displaying the gyrations of *sodomia* and its sibling terms. The space will then have to be extended by seeking the causes of their motions. The causes of instability are not to be found in mere variety of usage across a range of speakers, with one meaning over here and another over there. They are rather causes of terminological oscillation or conceptual reversal in a single speaker's discourse—which is to say, in the discourse of every speaker who inherits the histories embedded in the terms or concepts. The resulting instabilities are seen not in a survey or census, but in the careful reading of particular texts. They can be represented only by showing at least some of the details. The details of single speeches have to be gone over and gone over again. The deliberate pace of examination demands of the reader a willingness to settle for local insights rather than global fantasies.

The book that follows is not, then, an attempt to get at statistical generalizations about sexual behavior; it is not a social history of "medieval homosexuality." I doubt whether such a history is possible; I judge that it is not desirable. What is powerful in human thoughts is particular. Because the particularities of Scholastic treatments of same-sex pleasure have yet to be represented responsibly, the power of the surviving Scholastic categories has yet to be understood. It cannot be understood when looking for a cultural point of view or *mentalité*. At its best, Christian theology is an arduous intellectual discipline that requires roughly the technical competence of mathematical mechanics. You cannot get at Newton by extemporizing on the "mind-set" of his *Principia*. The same is true for Thomas Aquinas's *Summa*. To read Newton is to demonstrate the propositions with him, and to read Aquinas is to reenact his dialectical arguments in all their rigor, precision, and richness of learned reference.

I hold that it is impossible to reenact dialectical arguments in theology without "doing theology," that is, without beginning to think according to one or another of the clusters of habits that have been called "Christian theology." It is a disputed question how far someone who is not a Christian believer can think theologically. I do not mean to settle the question. In most of what follows, I speak as someone who is trying to think with and through certain Christian texts without raising the question of my own faith. Only in the postlude do I speak professedly as a Christian to other Christians. Whether or how far this makes the postlude inaccessible to non-Christian readers I must leave for them to decide.

This book is then an exercise in witnessing the theological invention of arguments for categorizing—that is, for uniting and reifying, for judging and punishing—genital acts between members of the same sex. The arguments are more than coining new terminology, of course, and it is the "more" that has made the terminology so durable and so powerful in European societies. Whether the exercise can be of help in the present strife over Christian teaching about homosexuality, I do not know. I believe, on the one hand, that the failure of many Christian churches to speak intelligently, much less prophetically, about sexuality brings discredit on the whole of their preaching. The churches could begin to repent of their failure by examining honestly the paradoxes embedded in their long traditions of moral teaching on sexuality. I believe, on the other hand, that most styles of Christian theology now fashionable require that theology's own past be repressed or abused. These styles of theology make it unlikely that any piece of medieval theology can be represented convincingly—much less a piece so encrusted, jagged, and threatening as the teaching about the sexes.

Whatever the limits of representation, I do mean to show in the following pages that the category "Sodomy" has been vitiated from its invention by fundamental confusions and contradictions. These confusions and contradictions cannot be removed from the category. They are the stuff from which it was made. That is why "Sodomy" has had such a long life in oppressive legislation and demagoguery. It is confused and contradictory in just the way that oppressors and demagogues find advantageous. If I am right, the category "Sodomy" cannot be used for serious thinking. It certainly cannot be used for rethinking what Christian theology has to say about human sex.

ONE

The Passions of St. Pelagius

With time, the martyr Pelagius would become younger, more eloquent, more desirable. In 925 or 926, when he was martyred, he was thirteen years old, precociously pious, and a prisoner in Cordoba with other Christians. According to the testimony of his fellow prisoners, his beauty was such that the caliph, 'Abd al-Rahmân III, desired to add him to his household as another sexual attendant. Pelagius refused to succumb to the king's desire, as he refused to renounce Christianity. And so, the witnesses say, he was first tortured and then dismembered.

In reading some medieval variations on this story, I do not mean to be cynical about whatever was suffered in fact by the boy behind it. Who can be cynical about torture, for whatever reason, or about the savageries of religions? But I do mean to examine what cynicism there is already in medieval tellings of the story of Pelagius. The appalling events, whatever they were, became early on the vehicle for increasingly overbearing lessons, both patriotic and religious. From the first, there is no disentangling the "facts" of Pelagius's suffering from the polemical uses of it. Nor is it possible to disentangle the retellings of the passions of Pelagius from the ambivalent relations of Iberian Christianity to the same-sex love it thought was preached and practiced by Islam.[1]

The dating and the interrelation of the earliest texts about Pelagius are not known, though it seems clear that three different kinds of texts were written within fifty years of his death. The first presents itself as a narrative

---

1 I will not treat the complicated questions about the discourses or hypothesized practices of same-sex desire in the Islamic regimes Much that is written about them is excessively general and too dependent on dubious secondary works An egregious example is Daniel, "Arab Civilization and Male Love," pp 59–65 Even John Boswell allows himself to remark that, in early medieval Spain, "every variety of homosexual relationship was common from prostitution to idealized love" (*Christianity, Social Tolerance, and Homosexuality*, p 196)

of his passion based on eyewitness accounts. It was written in Iberia before 967 by an otherwise unknown priest, Raguel.[2] The second text is a metrical life of Pelagius by the Saxon canoness Hrotswitha. It may also belong to 960s.[3] The third text is a Mozarabic liturgy, an office of St. Pelagius from León, written perhaps in or after 967 to mark the arrival of the saint's relics—or perhaps thirty years earlier to memorialize his wonders.[4] I am less interested in the precise dating of the works than in the ways their genres transmute the underlying account and deflect its dangers.

RAGUEL'S WITNESS

The first genre for the telling of Pelagius's death is a narrative constructed from the testimony of eyewitnesses.[5] The narrative does not pretend to be transcribed testimony. It is a well-crafted story of a martyrdom, beginning with an invocation of divine aid and ending with a claim on Pelagius as patron of the local church.[6] In between there are deft quotations of Scripture, moral applications, and classical allusions. The author is a priest, Raguel, who is identified in one manuscript as the "teacher of this passion."[7] Raguel is not without his teacherly pretensions. He begins with self-conscious reflections on beginning. He proceeds often through antitheses, which he uses in series to amplify or punctuate the basic narrative. Questions about the scope of Raguel's literary learning will soon become important, but his polished and polemical purposes in telling the story stand forth no matter how one decides them. Raguel is eloquent in order to condemn the religion, the morals, and the savagery of the young saint's Islamic captors.

Pelagius himself was not captured by them. He was given as a substitute

---

2. See the summary of scholarly conjecture in Díaz y Díaz, "La pasión de S Pelayo y su difusión," pp 106–110

3 See Dronke, *Women Writers of the Middle Ages*, pp 56–57

4. See Díaz y Díaz, "La pasión de S. Pelayo," pp 111–112.

5. For what follows, I use the critical edition in Rodríguez Fernández, *La pasión de S. Pelayo*, which will be cited by line numbers. The other most easily accessible editions are those in Díaz y Díaz, "La pasión de S. Pelayo," pp. 113–116, and in the *Acta sanctorum, Junii* 7 183C–184F The version in the *Acta* seems to have been "corrected" throughout to the standards of neo-Latin To my knowledge, the *Passion* has never been translated into English.

6 The last point leads some to think that the text was composed for liturgical use. Perhaps so, though it is clearly not part of the ordinary office of the saint, which follows it and may well depend on it See Díaz y Díaz, "La pasión de S Pelayo," p 110

7. From the second *Pasionario* of Cardeña, now Escorial MS b I 4, folio 127, "Raguel Presbyter doctor fuit huius Passionis Cordubensis," as reported in Rodríguez Fernández, p 17; see also *Acta sanctorum*, 181B, and Díaz y Díaz, "La pasión de S Pelayo," p. 106.

for a clerical relative, the bishop Hermoygius. Hermoygius had been taken prisoner after the rout of Christian forces at Valdejunquera in the summer of 920. He was at risk of death because of the hardships of imprisonment. So he arranged for his ten-year-old cousin to take his place, hoping all the while, our chronicler notes, that other captives would be sent in place of his young surrogate. Once in prison, Pelagius lived an exemplary life under divine guidance. He was able to overcome even those temptations that had afflicted him in the world. Principal among his virtues was chastity. He kept his body whole. He "purified the vessel" to prepare it as a fitting chamber in which to rejoice as the spouse (*sponsus*) of Jesus, to delight in the bloody embrace of martyrdom as marriage.

Jesus, teaching him inwardly, began to transform Pelagius outwardly. Raguel cannot find words enough for description. The boy's appearance "praised" the teacher within. He was "signally decorated" by the signs of his destination in paradise. His face took on a "lovelier beauty."[8] Indeed, word of this attractiveness reached the Muslim "king," who is not here named by Raguel. (The name is given only in a colophon.) The king sends for Pelagius to be brought to him at a banquet. Pelagius is dressed in royal robes and led into the hall, the attendants whispering that he is fortunate to have his beauty carry him so far. The king offers the boy much to renounce Christ and affirm Mohammed: wealth, opulent clothing, precious ornaments, life in the court. There is even the offer of the companionship of any of the court's young men (*tirunculi*), with whom Pelagius can do what he will.[9] The king further promises to free from jail a number of other Christians, including Pelagius's relatives.

All of this Pelagius refuses with a string of contrasts between the passing of temporal things and the eternity of Christ. Ignoring the refusal, the king reaches out to touch Pelagius *joculariter*. The adverb is odd. It could mean something like "humorously," but that meaning hardly fits here. In Ovid, who may well be on Raguel's mind, the root verb, *joco*, is used as a metaphor for copulation.[10] So *tangere joculariter* may mean at least "to touch sexually" and perhaps even "to fondle" in the quite sexual sense. How else can one explain Pelagius's reaction? He strikes the king and spits out a

8. Respectively, Raguel *Passio S Pelagu*, "foris erat inluminator" (Rodríguez Fernández lines 47–48), "celebraret magistrum specie tenus" (48), "species iam paradisigena prerogatiue decoraret" (46–47), and "uenustiorem uultus pulcritudinem" (62–63).

9 Raguel *Passio S Pelagu*, "Sumes preterea tibi qualem ex his tironunculis elegeris, qui tuis ad votum moribus famuletur" (Rodríguez Fernández lines 82–83)

10. For examples, see Adams, *The Latin Sexual Vocabulary*, pp 161–162 We will encounter a very sexual personification of Jocus in Alan of Lille (see chapter 4 below)

contemptuous question: "Do you think me like one of yours, an effeminate (*effeminatum*)?"[11]

Raguel's Pelagius may mean "effeminate" in the general sense that connects any form of sexual self-indulgence with womanliness. This would seem to go along with the martyr's choice of Paul as model.[12] But Pelagius may also have in mind the more specific sense that *effeminatum* has in one passage of the Vulgate. There, in a condemnation of the reign of Roboam, the "effeminate" are those who commit "all the abominations of the gentiles, which God destroyed before the face of the sons of Israel."[13] The reference would seem to be both to the destruction of Sodom and to the sexual abominations condemned in Leviticus. So the "effeminate" would seem to be those who "lie with a man as with a woman." Certainly Pelagius's next response emphasizes the sexual character of the king's touch. The martyr rips off the fine gown in which he has been dressed and he stands forth, naked, like a "strong athlete in the palaestra."[14]

The king does not immediately command Pelagius's destruction. He imagines rather that the boy might be changed by the "pimping persuasions" of the court's young men. It is only when these prove unsuccessful, when the king feels his own desires spurned, that the anger rises in him. He orders Pelagius to be seized with iron tongs and twisted about, until he should either renounce Christ or die. Pelagius does neither. So the king demands at last that the boy be cut to pieces with swords and thrown into the river. Raguel describes the dismemberment graphically. What is more, he likens the frenzy of Pelagius's executioners to the mad rites of the Bacchae: "they were turned into Bacchae (*debacchati sunt*) through the mad desires" unleashed in the hacking, so much so that one would have thought that they were sacrificing the boy rather than executing him.[15] Throughout

11 This is the reading of Rodríguez Fernández and Díaz y Díaz: "Numquid me similem tuis effeminatum existimas? (lines 93 and 92, respectively). The Bollandists read, more suggestively, "Numquid me similem tuis effeminatis existimas?" (184C), that is, "Do you think me like one of your effeminates?"

12. Raguel *Passio S Pelagii,* "Legerat enim magistrum sibi Paulum in doctrinis uigilantem" (Rodríguez Fernández lines 39–40).

13 3 Kings 14:24 (Vulgate), "Sed et effeminati fuerunt in terra feceruntque omnes abominationes gentium quas adtrivit Dominus ante faciem filiorum Israhel"

14. Raguel *Passio S Pelagii,* "Et ilico uestimenta ibi que indutus erat scidit et fortem in palestra se alletam constituit" (Rodríguez Fernández lines 93–94)

15 Raguel *Passio S Pelagii,* "tam inmania in eum exerto pugione ludibria debaccati sunt" (Rodríguez Fernández lines 107–108) Earlier editors read "devacati sunt," as in the edition by Florez, *España Sagrada,* 23.235 The Bollandists had already decided that this was Spanish dialect for "debacchati," especially since no alternative presents itself See *Acta Sanctorum* 181C

these torments the voice of Pelagius is heard calling out for God's help. The "athlete's" voice is stilled only after he is called to the martyr's crown by the Lord.

The reference to the Bacchae and the emphasis on the unstilled voice are striking, especially in a passage so rich in the customary images of Christian martyrdom. The verb *debacchor* is rare. Not just the allusion, but the archaizing word used to make it put the reader in mind of poetic learning, of expertise in pagan mythography. Poetic associations seem to be confirmed by what happens in Raguel's narration to the saint's speaking body. The martyr who would not be silent is to be cut apart and then drowned. So it is. His limbs come to rest on one shore, his severed heard on another. Any reader of Latin poetry will hear in these events echoes of the death of Orpheus. Orpheus too was cut apart by a tribe of Bacchae, who seized tools from terrified farmers in order to kill him. The voice that had charmed animals with its singing fell silent under the blades. Yet once thrown into the river, Orpheus somehow still sang, borne down towards the sea. Only this miracle is lacking in Pelagius to make the likeness complete.

Is the dismemberment of Pelagius meant by Raguel to call to mind the death of Orpheus? Certainly parts of the Orpheus myth had been allegorized for Christian purposes long before Raguel began to write. The allegory is presented in Boethius's *Consolation*, for example, and then appropriated by a number of his readers in both vernacular and Latin forms.[16] But the part of the myth that matters to the passion of Pelagius is not the already allegorized loss of Eurydice. It is rather Orpheus's dismembering because of his refusal to have sexual relations with women after Eurydice's second death. Indeed, Ovid begins his narration of the dismembering by noting that Orpheus taught Thracian men the love of boys.[17] The connection between Orpheus and same-sex love would be registered by later commentators, as it would pass into the vernacular traditions.[18] Now Ovid's *Metamorphoses* was known in Spain as Raguel wrote.[19] It may be that he means to Christianize this other part of the Orpheus myth by inverting it: Pelagius becomes the Christian Orpheus because he is dismembered not just for his purity, but for his explicit rejection of same-sex desire.

One could hear other mythic resonances. The martyrdom of Pelagius inverts or reclaims the well-known tale of Zeus and Ganymede. If Zeus

16 Boethius *Philosophiae consolatio* 3 met 12 (Bieler ed., lines 76–78) For some early examples of allegorizations of this passage, see Chance, *Medieval Mythography*, pp 211–230

17 Respectively, Ovid *Metamorphoses* 11 1–84 and 10 83–84

18 See Bein, "Orpheus als Sodomit," pp 50–52

19 See Díaz y Díaz, *De Isidoro al siglo XI*, pp 31, 81, and generally 59–86

kidnapped the Phrygian boy to be his cupbearer, the Muslim king wants to abduct Pelagius from Christianity for service in his hall. The change of condition from the hillsides near Troy to Olympus is no greater than the change from the dark prison to the resplendent court. But Pelagius is in fact called for service at the table of a higher king. His beauty is the visible sign of his having been chosen for the service of Christ, to whom he will be both *sponsus* and *famulus*, both spouse and household intimate. Christ already intends that he should stand beside the heavenly throne in the chorus of virgins.[20] Pelagius, spurning the crown of the Muslim tyrant, receives the long-promised crown from the hands of Jesus.[21] And his spirit "migrates" to heaven—as if carried by eagle's wings.[22] Of course, and to interrupt the series of echoes, it is always difficult to judge how far these literary associations can be assigned to Raguel. I want to assign them only in the most specific case. Raguel does mean to call up Ovid on Orpheus, though he may not have any clear notion of how he will manage the Ovidian allusions once they are called to mind.

Even if the relation to Ovid were denied, it could not be denied that Raguel suggests complications in the story that he cannot quite control. There is, for example, Pelagius's familiarity with practices of same-sex desire. However the king wished to touch him, no single touch could communicate all that is contained in Pelagius's contemptuous question, "Do you think me like one of yours, an effeminate?" Pelagius already knows that there are "effeminates" and that they serve for certain kinds of sexual uses. He not only recognizes the king's gesture as sexual, he recognizes the sexual script from which it comes. How does he know this? From the clichés of anti-Islamic polemic preached in Christian communities? He does call the king "dog," one of many animal epithets familiar from anti-Islamic tracts.[23] Or does Pelagius know the king's sexual customs from prison whispers, from the sight of prisoners taken out overnight? Or from the bragging promises of servants? However he knows, Pelagius comes into the presence of the king forewarned that he is a likely object of male sexual desire.

So the martyr's next gesture of rejection is the more striking. Pelagius strips off the costly robes with which he has been decorated. He thus repudiates "effeminacy." He also exposes the body that is the object of desire.

20 Raguel *Passio S Pelagu* (Rodríguez Fernáncez lines 66–67)

21 Raguel *Passio S. Pelagu* (Rodríguez Fernández line 120)

22. Raguel *Passio S Pelagu*, "Interea namque spiritus migravit ad deum" (Rodríguez Fernández lines 120–121)

23. See Millet-Gérard, *Chrétiens moʒarabes et culture islamique*, pp. 101–103 (sexual epithets), 104–108 (animal epithets) For the epithet "canis impurus," see p 147

Instead of concealing what the king wants, he presents it aggressively. Raguel assimilates this to the tradition of Christian martyrology by likening Pelagius to an athlete, naked in the palaestra.[24] In context the gesture taunts the king. Pelagius the martyr is quite plainly Pelagius the ephebe, the type of young male beauty. He rips off his own clothes, as an eager lover might, just to show the king what he cannot have. The sight of that body may be one reason the king is slow to anger, preferring persuasion instead. Only when persuasion fails does the royal desire, excited by Pelagius's display, turn ferocious. Even then, the king hopes that the pain of the iron forceps may bring Pelagius to denounce Christ and so recover his body from pain for pleasure.[25]

Pelagius knows the customs of same-sex desire, and he plays with that desire itself when he strips before the king in order to spurn him. He spurns the king as well in what he says. When Pelagius proclaims that he "cherishes Christ," when he chooses to die or to suffer "for Christ," when he invokes no one other than "the Lord Jesus Christ," he is speaking the name of his true love in the face of a rival.[26] For the king, the choice facing Pelagius seems to be between pleasure and pain, between his own gracious self and a fictive god. For Pelagius, the choice seems to lie between ephemeral and permanent pleasure, between an earthly and a heavenly king, between an imperfect lover and a perfect one. The story of the martyrdom is, through Pelagius's eyes, the story of a passionate triangle in which all the parties are male. He does not deny same-sex love so much as he vindicates it by choosing Christ as his lover.

Pelagius vindicates it tacitly. It is remarkable that Raguel nowhere gives a special name to the sin that the king wishes to practice on the body of the young martyr. He does not even describe the king's motives except to note that what he heard of Pelagius "pleased" him.[27] The ensuing events are placed under other, more general categories of sin. The Moors want to "cover over his form with the torrents of vices."[28] Certainly there is no detailed description of the acts the king might have wanted to perform with

24 Raguel *Passio S Pelagu*, "Et ilico uestimenta ibi que indutus erat scidit et fortem in palestra se alletam constituit" (Rodríguez Fernández lines 93–94), with "alleta fortissimus" repeated (119)

25 It would be tempting to take the mention of *forcipes* here as making an allusion to obstetrics, but in fact the medical uses of the term in classical Latin are mainly dental The allusion Raguel intends, perhaps through *Metamorphoses* 12 277, is to the tongs of a metalsmith

26 Raguel *Passio S Pelagu*, "Christus quem ego colo" (Rodríguez Fernández line 89), "pro Christo" (95, 105), "dominum nostrum Iesum Christum" (113)

27 Raguel *Passio S Pelagu*, "ei obtime sed non recte placuit" (Rodríguez Fernández lines 69–70)

28 Raguel *Passio S Pelagu*, "formam gurgitibus vitiorum putabant obruere" (Rodríguez Fernández line 66)

the boy, much less any sense that the king is peculiar in wanting them. If the vices are meant to disgust Raguel's readers, they are also presumed to be familiar to them.

They are familiar not only or principally as acts, but as a cluster of habits. Extravagance, pride in power, and sexual perversion go together for Raguel as they do in late Roman notions of *luxuria*, in patristic commentary on the story of Sodom, and in early medieval categorizations of sin. To say this again: Erotic disorder is caught up in a system of causes with opulence, which is itself viewed as feminizing, and with arrogance, which is the root of all spiritual disorder. Raguel knows this from many sources. He also knows that the vice of same-sex copulation has been implicated in darker causalities—that it has been linked to bestial cruelty, to the loss of humanity. In Prudentius, for example, Luxury is characterized more by violent rage than by softness.[29] Raguel's polemical use of Pelagius's suffering against Islam, his appropriation of Pelagius for the cause of Christian Iberia, is perfectly compatible with a simultaneous use of the story to reinforce the nascent theological project of moral categorization. Within this categorization, sexual sins will come to have a more and more prominent place. Indeed, the sins of same-sex copulation will soon become a favored synecdoche for sin itself.

But not without introducing various instabilities. Raguel's apparently ingenuous testimony to the sufferings of the young boy is polemical and ideological. It is also unstable, so far as it must presume that same-sex desire is familiar, domestic, imaginable. After all, God shows favor to Pelagius by making him desirable, not repulsive. Pelagius is beautiful, not ugly. The boy's body is the body of the ancient ephebe, and the telling of his triumph necessarily calls to mind a string of earlier tales in which ephebes have been loved by gods—and onlooking poets. The passion of Pelagius as retold by Raguel passes down a number of difficult problems alongside its obvious lessons.

The explicit lessons are, on Raguel's telling, eminently scriptural. The *Passion* echoes scriptural language throughout, as it recalls the oldest lives of the Christian martyrs. Beneath these obvious lessons lie others, especially the lessons of Christian struggles against the Muslim regimes. The final request that Raguel makes of the boy-saint is a request for patronage. The martyr who rejected earthly allurements in favor of Christ's promises should accept the offerings of the local church, the church that struggles against his murderers. There is now no mention of his beauty, only a

29 Prudentius *Psychomachia* 40–52

reference to his refusal of "pleasures" (*deliciae*) and "enticements" (*blanditiae*).[30] The details of the caliph's proposal are now subsumed in a crusading spirit, reduced only to an outrage that must be avenged. What is to be retained from the story is a sense of Pelagius's patronage in the coming battle to avenge him. Of the problems posed by Ovid or the customs of the Moors or the descriptions of Pelagius's own desire, the listener is to retain only the motive of pious warfare.

HROTSWITHA'S ARTIFICE

The story of Pelagius did not remain confined within Iberia. It traveled, quickly and far, by unknown means. If the means are unknown, the genres for recording and disseminating the story were anciently familiar to Christians. The story could spread so quickly because it fit—or was made to fit—into one of the oldest of Christian literary forms. The events of Cordoba were not only news, they were confirmation that the God of the ancient martyrs continued to work miracles down to the present day. The passion of Pelagius is incorporated into the writings of the canoness Hrotswitha of Ganderheim in Saxony with just these motives. Much has been written about Hrotswitha, much of it admiring. Rightly so, since her works show eloquence and erudition. Certainly she stands, as an author, above the level reached by Raguel. But my aim here is not to praise Hrotswitha's authorship. It is to notice what changes she makes in rewriting the desires that Pelagius provoked.

Hrotswitha writes her verse passion of Pelagius, as she writes her plays, according to elaborate symmetries. Some of these are thematic, others are formal or ornamental.[31] Her versification of the martyrdom of Pelagius stands out within these patterns for its newness. It is the only hagiographical text to record recent events. The second nearest story is no more recent than the eighth century.[32] Moreover, Hrotswitha's title underscores the story's newness: "The Passion of St. Pelagius, Most Precious Martyr, Who Was Crowned with Martyrdom in Cordoba in Our Own Day (*nostris temporibus*)."[33] Pelagius is particularly present to Hrotswitha because he is so

30. Raguel *Passio S Pelagii* (Rodríguez Fernández lines 133–134) "delicias   blanditiis"

31 On the larger patterns, see Dronke, *Women Writers of the Middle Ages*, pp. 60–64 On the place of the passion of Pelagius, see Petroff, *Body and Soul,* pp 83–84

32. The legend is that of Gongolf, who lived during the rein of Pippin

33 Hrotswitha *Pelagius* titulus, in *Hrotsvithae Opera,* ed Homeyer, p 130, outside system of line numbers Subsequent references will be made to the page and line numbers of this edition Several other Latin editions are available, including that of de Winterfeld in the *Monumenta Germaniae Historica*

recent. Indeed, her knowledge of him comes not from antecedent texts, but from hearing stories.[34] One of her tasks is to bring these tales under the control of the established textual patterns.

Hrotswitha begins to do so in the very first lines. She deploys a literary formula to call on the young saint. Raguel had invoked Pelagius at the end of his narrative as patron of local churches. The invocation was public and corporate. Hrotswitha begins her verse legend with a personal call to the boy-saint. This noble knight of the King who reigns through the ages is to look down on her, his handmaid, who attends to him in mind and heart. He is to grant her the ability to write of his marvels and his triumph.[35] What Pelagius grants is a poem in several parts, much more suited for non-Iberian audiences than Raguel's terse recital.[36] The poem's first part sets the stage by describing the long-standing idolatry and luxury of the Muslims in Cordoba, a city "inclined to delicacies."[37] The next section narrates the reign of "Abdrahemen," a man "stained by the excess (*luxus*) of the flesh," and his successful war against the Christian armies. It ends with the capture of Christian leaders and the Muslim ruler's treacherous dickering over the terms of their release. The poem's third part introduces Pelagius, who is distinguished at once by his bodily beauty. Indeed, Hrotswitha mentions his beauty before going on to talk of his prudence and goodness, and she ends the introductory description by noting the he had attained "the first flowers of the age of adolescence."[38]

Differences from Raguel's account have already appeared, and not merely in the richness of the artifices employed. In Hrotswitha's telling, for example, Pelagius volunteers for imprisonment in place of his father, a Christian nobleman. There is a direct speech in which the boy pleads with his father to be sent as a substitute, using the argument that his body can better withstand the sufferings to be inflicted. The reader notes both Pelagius's filial piety and his physical attributes. What is more, the reader gets to hear the boy's extraordinary eloquence. Both eloquence and beauty bring Pelagius to the attention of some courtiers once he has been imprisoned. For Hrotswitha, the courtiers are mostly blameless in their dealings with the boy. They wish to free him from the harshness of the prison. Unfortu-

---

34 As Hrotswitha herself remarks in the epilogue to the book of legends (Homeyer, p 227).

35 Hrotswitha *Pelagius* (Homeyer 130 1–11)

36 The structure of the poem is capable of several divisions No single one need be chosen for the present reading to be persuasive. For some other divisions, see the notes to Homeyer's edition; Kirsch, "Hrotsvit von Gandersheim als Epikerin," pp. 219–220, and Petroff, *Body and Soul*, p 88

37 Hrotswitha *Pelagius* (Homeyer 130 12–133 68)

38 Hrotswitha *Pelagius* (Homeyer 136.144–148).

nately they decide to appeal to their king's taste for special pleasures. The courtiers know that he has been "corrupted by Sodomitic vices."[39] He wants "to love" beautiful youths "ardently" and join with them in "particular friendship." Surely the king would want to see the outstanding form (*praenitida forma*) of Pelagius—to enjoy his honeyed speech, to have his shining body (*corpus candidulus*) for service in the great hall.[40]

Where Raguel allowed the motive vice to remain nameless and to hang over the whole court as a general condemnation, Hrotswitha names it with the requisite Christian term and confines it to a single, sinning soul. It is the king, and only the king, who has been corrupted by "Sodomitic vices." If Cordoba as a whole was rather too prone to sins of the flesh, 'Abd al-Rahmân was egregiously corrupt, "worse than his parents, smirched with the excess of the flesh."[41] By appealing to his allegedly exceptional vice, the Cordoban courtiers do succeed in persuading the king. He orders Pelagius bathed, swathed in purple, and adorned with a gem-encrusted necklace. The ornamented youth is brought before him. Overcome by the beauty, the king begins to burn. He puts his arm around Pelagius's neck and kisses him. Pelagius responds bitingly to this "pagan king" who is, Hrotswitha says again, "marred by the excess of the flesh." No Christian knight who has been washed by baptism will submit himself to barbarian embraces, much less allow his lips to be touched by the filth of demonic kisses.[42] Pelagius urges the king to turn instead to the "stupid men" who will serve him because of a desire for riches. As in Raguel's story, the king is not angered by this first rebuff. He tries to persuade "the ephebe" gently. "O lascivious boy," he begins, and then goes on to make his offer of riches, power, ease. The king then puts his hand firmly against Pelagius's face, lays another arm around his neck, and draws him near for at least one kiss. Pelagius strikes him hard enough to draw blood. It runs down the king's beard and onto his robes. His sorrow turns to rage and he orders Pelagius's torture.

We need not guess at metaphors to know from Hrotswitha what 'Abd al-Rahmân did to Pelagius. Hrotswitha does also employ metaphors of the game or the joke to describe the king's actions.[43] But she tells the reader quite explicitly how the king touched Pelagius and what he tried to do to him. What she assumes, along with Raguel, is that Pelagius can immedi-

---

39 Hrotswitha *Pelagius* (Homeyer 138 205), "Corruptum vitiis cognoscebant Sodomitis"

40 Hrotswitha *Pelagius* (Homeyer 139 213–217)

41 Hrotswitha *Pelagius* (Homeyer 133 72)

42 Hrotswitha *Pelagius* (Homeyer 140.243–246), especially "Daemonis oscillum spurci captare famelli"

43 Hrotswitha *Pelagius* (Homeyer 141.271), "Callida   ludicra regis"

ately interpret that kiss as a sexual overture. The kiss is not fatherly or brotherly; it does not bear compassion or pardon. It is felt immediately by the youth as the overture to a sexual exchange. Indeed, Pelagius retorts to the king that he ought to save his kisses for his fellow Muslims, with whom he shares the stupidity of idolatry.[44] If Hrotswitha's Pelagius is not so scathing as Raguel's, he is no less well informed about the sexual customs of the Muslim court. So must Hrotswitha's readers be. The "Sodomitic vices" are here condensed into a single kiss, which must be understood as prelude to all of them. The project of moral codification that is suggested in Raguel seems already presupposed in Hrotswitha.

The clarity of the moral code makes it imperative that Hrotswitha be equally clear about her own position as narrator, her own relation to Pelagius. The poem begins as a prayer for the saint's help; it ends with mention of his patronage. The prologue may be considered formulaic and the end is not spoken in Hrotswitha's voice. But it is her voice that describes throughout the beauties of Pelagius's body. How does it keep them at a proper distance? By always juxtaposing them with equally sensual descriptions of his eloquence. Indeed, every character in the poem except one subsumes appreciation for Pelagius's beauty in appreciation for his beautiful speech. Physical beauty is thus etherealized into verbal beauty. The only exception is the caliph himself, who burns with passion on first seeing Pelagius's face. The caliph wants to love the boy's form before ever hearing him speak.[45] This is a mark of the caliph's depravity. The danger of a woman speaking about the body of an adolescent boy is deflected by making mere reaction to a body something ignoble. Hrotswitha can praise his body safely because she praises his divine eloquence more enthusiastically. We see here a recurrent substitution in Christian writing. Christian language takes the full charge of a beauty that it pretends to reject. The beauties of body are condemned in prose of extraordinary beauty.

The poem ends with a longish section on the dispersion and recovery of Pelagius's body. The narrative is considerably more detailed than in Raguel. The recovery of the body is followed by the beginning of a cult of Pelagius. Many persons "of either sex" are moved to sing hymns and offer prayers. After three days, they prepare a fire in which to offer up the body.

44. Hrotswitha *Pelagius* (Homeyer 140.246–249) Boswell misreads this passage as authorizing same-sex relations among Muslims; see his *Christianity, Social Tolerance, and Homosexuality*, pp 198–200. The suggestion cannot stand. Pelagius means to say that demonic kisses between men are caught up in the larger perdition of demon worship. It should also be noted that Boswell, ignoring Raguel's account, tries to read Hrotswitha's poem as a bit of evidence for social history.

45 Hrotswitha *Pelagius* (Homeyer 139.231–232). Contrast this with the description of the bystanders immediately above, who are moved both by his appearance and by his words

The fire is to be a proof of Pelagius's sanctity. Those standing by ask God to show his power in preserving the youth's severed head. After more than an hour in the waves of flame, the head remains intact, the eyes still lustrous. The faithful break forth in final hymns to God.

At least two things are striking in this section. The first is that God's power is shown in the miracle of preserving Pelagius's physical beauty. Hrotswitha typically abridges or omits the details of the mutilations of martyrdom. She does so here, with a twist. Where Raguel stresses the mutilation of the boy's body, Hrotswitha exalts its intact beauty. The unburned head of Pelagius is much like a female martyr's hymen. It is the physical evidence of his virginity, his innocence of Sodomitic kisses. At the same time, second, the Christian faithful show themselves more avid fetishists of the physical body even than the lecherous 'Abd al-Rahmân. He did not think to collect the pieces of the body he had so much desired. The Christians do, and they begin to enact a reverence much stronger and more persistent than the king's burning desire. The name for that reverence is cult.

PELAGIUS'S CULT

The cult of Pelagius—the cultivation of Pelagius as a saint—was obviously more than a dispassionate claim that Pelagius lived a holy life and died a holy death. Saints are made popular because they answer any number of public needs. Pelagius certainly answered them. His death was powerful evidence in anti-Muslim polemic. It was an incitement to vengeance against the Muslim states. It was, in short, the exercise of patriotism by the Christian kingdoms of northern Iberia. The Christian kings of the north were not slow to realize this.

Medieval traffic with saints is very often traffic in saints: the discovery, veneration, exchange, or theft of relics. So it is with Pelagius. Raguel has told of the faithful coming to collect the remains of the battered boy's body and to give it an honorable burial.[46] Hrotswitha describes acts of worship towards his body and a miraculous confirmation of his sanctity. What is more interesting, she stresses that the worshippers were of both sexes.[47] It was two powerful women who are said to have pushed for the recovery of the saint's body from the very ruler who had martyred him. Sancho I of León was urged by his wife, Teresa, and by his sister, Elvira, to sue for peace with 'Abd al-Rahmân and to bring the relics back to León, where

---

46 Raguel *Passio S Pelagii* (Rodríguez Fernández lines 122–123)
47 Hrotswitha *Pelagius* (Homeyer 145 377)

they would be installed in a new monastery.[48] A delegation was sent in 960. The body was recovered only in 967, after both Sancho and the caliph had died. Pelagius was then buried in the monastery with ceremony, next to the body of "many other bishops."[49] Thereafter the relics became potent political symbols for the Christian rulers. In 985, under the threat of Almansor's attacks, they were removed from León to Oviedo along with the bodies of the Christian kings.[50] The symbolic power would last long in the Iberian imagination. In the *Poema de Fernán González*, the hero is urged into battle against Almansor by a double dream-vision of SS. Pelagius and Millán.[51] The symbolic power is not only literary. As late as May of 1483, according to the testimony of witnesses under oath, the bones of Pelagius were heard to rattle in premonition of the Christian conquest of Granada.[52]

The political function of the cult of Pelagius is not the only or even the principal motive behind its continuation. The cult spread quickly during the eleventh century and not only in Galicia and León.[53] From early on, the saint was taken up by communities of religious women.[54] Hrotswitha provides striking evidence for this, but so does the record of church foundings in northern Iberia. The popularity of Pelagius is often explained by pointing out that he is a child saint who embodied in eminent fashion the virtue of virginity. Pelagius could be adopted as a child to a women's community without damage to their purity. Some confirmation of this is found in the popular religion of León. One modern folk song is reported in which Pelagius is invoked as protector of families. The hymn is clearly written in the voice of a woman, wife and mother, and its petitions are for domestic blessings.[55] The folk song brings forward what is hidden in any quick narrative of the spread of devotion to the saint. In it, Pelagius is lauded with

48. *Primera crónica general de España*, ed. Menéndez Pidal, 2:422b.31–42.

49. *Primera crónica general de España* (Menéndez Pidal 2:424a.50–b.4).

50. *Primera crónica general de España* (Menéndez Pidal 2:445b.47–446b.3).

51. *Historia del Conde Fernán González*, ed. Geary fol. 32v line 14 to 33r line 14 in the transcription. This figure is, I think, "san Pelayo" and not a resurrection of the monk Pelagius who appears earlier in the poem as a prophet of Christian victory

52. Vaquero, "La *Devotio moderna* y la poesía del siglo XV," p 116, paraphrasing the *Crónica de Fernán González*.

53. For the spread of the cult in Spain, see Vives, "Las 'Vitas sanctorum' del Cerratense," p. 176; Vives and Fábrega Grau, "Calendarios hispánicos anteriores al siglo XII," p. 143; Fábrega Grau, *Pasionario hispánico*, 1:227, 1:297; Colbert, *The Martyrs of Córdoba*, p. 382; and Janini, *Manuscritos litúrgicos de las bibliotecas de España*, 1:51, 55, 138, 149, 320; 2:357. See also the remarks on church names in Rodríguez Fernández, pp. 16–17, note 13.

54 See Díaz y Díaz, "Passionaires, légendiers, et compilations hagiographiques," pp. 51, 56 The best study of the cult's role in a single community is Colombás, *San Pelayo de León y Santa María de Carbajal*.

55. Some verses of the hymn are quoted by García Abad in his *Leyendas Leonesas*, pp. 148 and 157.

images of fresh blossoming: "dew-flower," "flower of laurel," "holy rose-bud of spring," "red petal." The images want to transmute his body into something less threatening and less sexual than the body of a young adolescent male. If the images are still almost too obviously open for erotic readings, they serve nonetheless to turn some attention away from the actual occasion of Pelagius's martyrdom—his beauty and the caliph's desire. It is essential that attention be turned. Otherwise the cult of Pelagius as saint will reenact the sinful history of the worship of his ephebic beauty.

The danger has already been addressed, of course, in the narratives of Raguel and Hrotswitha. Each of them had to describe Pelagius's physical beauty to an audience of men and women without placing too much emphasis on the beauty of this young man's body. Raguel's narrative defuses the physical attraction of Pelagius by making Christ its cause and dismemberment its result. The risk may seem less for Hrotswitha, so far as she speaks in the voice of a woman. But her vows make her another one to whom it is not permitted to extol young men's beauty. So she too must attempt to cancel out any purely physical attraction by subordinating the beauty of Pelagius's body to the beauty of his eloquence.

The danger of reenacting illicit desire is greatest for the liturgy. The situation of a Western, Latin liturgy (including the Mozarabic) places the words of the liturgy normatively in the mouths of men. Canonical hours are of course celebrated within women's communities in the absence of a priest, but this is an often unacknowledged exception so far as the authors of liturgy are concerned. The normative voice of the Latin liturgies is male. In the liturgies for Pelagius, this male voice is asked to recall for worshipful memory the story of a man's desire for a boy. The telling of the narrative will require the male voice to admit, if not admire, the youth's physical beauties. Antiphons or hymns about Pelagius's beauty will place his beauty in the mouths of men. More pointedly, the prayers of any liturgy actualize the retold history by applying it to the present situation of the worshipers. To actualize a relation to St. Pelagius is to place the male voice of the cleric in the position of soliciting Pelagius even while flattering him. That rhetorical position is just the position of the wicked 'Abd al-Rahmân. How can the liturgies for St. Pelagius escape this rhetorical trap? How can they metabolize same-sex desire into something else?

The best-preserved liturgy for the saint is a Mozarabic text for Vespers, Matins, and Mass.[56] It seems to have been written in the 930s or 940s by a

---

56 It is printed in *Acta Sanctorum, Junii* 7·191B–197C Another version can be found in Migne *PL*

distant disciple of the bishop Hermoygius. Perhaps it was a way of repaying the debt owed to the boy who went as substitute for the bishop. A full reading of the text would have to take account of the context created by all of its parts, including those common to all liturgies for martyrs. Here I will look only to the prayers that are proper to the feast. Some of these are spoken in the saint's own voice. Others refer to his actions. None of them is specific about the homoerotic motive behind the martyrdom. One verse of the evening hymn, for example, says that neither the "blandishments of this age" (*seculi blanditiae*) nor the sword could force Pelagius to deny God. The next verse recalls that he cast off the golden necklace given him by the tyrant in order to flee inflated delights (*pomposasque delicias*).[57] A prayer from the Mass uses similarly vague language,[58] though slightly more specific hints are contained in it. While Pelagius's contemporaries were living voluptuously (*cum eius consodales voluptuose viverent*), he kept his body intact.[59] The lesson is applied with the plea that those present might be freed from wicked customs and protected from devilish persuasion. Nothing more than this is said about the circumstances of the martyrdom. References to Pelagius's beauty are equally rare and slight. One antiphon for Matins begins, "His appearance was beautiful (*candidus*), his face angelic."[60] The prayer following asks rather for the gift of divine strength.

The vagueness of the prayers might seem to be corrected by the short versions of the martyrdom that appear in the preface (*illatio*) to the Mass or in liturgical collections of martyrs' lives. The version preserved in one Mozarabic Mass says that the king desired the beauty of Pelagius and thought that the boy might be open to certain vices.[61] That is a brief mention indeed. The liturgical texts are clearly turning attention away from the particular cause of his martyrdom. They do so by generalizing Pelagius's example. He becomes only a figure for resistance to worldly desires rather than to a quite specific and troubling form of desire. His beauty, moreover, is equally dissipated. It becomes the beauty of a distant and ethereal object.

The clearest objectification occurs, of course, in the religious art produced by the cult. Unfortunately very little of the early art survives; what does is not always revealing. A chest adorned with ivory carvings was given by the royal couple in 1053 to receive the relics of Pelagius alongside

57. *Acta Sanctorum Junii* 7·192D.
58. *Acta Sanctorum Junii* 7:195D, "non adhaesit seculi blanditus. . Perierat autem appetitus ab eo seculi, cesserat amor mundi"
59. *Acta Sanctorum Junii* 7.195E.
60. *Acta Sanctorum Junii* 7 193E.
61 *Acta Sanctorum Junii* 7:196E, "Aude, fili, et vide, quia concupivit Rex speciem tuam; hunc impudice tyrannus foris audebat deamare, putans eum suis aptum vitiis fore"

those of John the Baptist. The carvings show nothing that is particular to the cult of Pelagius. They depict the Lamb of God, the evangelists and apostles, archangels and angels.[62] Again, the drawing of the martyrdom of Pelagius in the Pamplona Bibles is a stereotyped rendering distinguished only by the manner of execution.[63] Pelagius is there represented as the same bearded, mature man who appears in many of the adjacent depictions of male martyrs.

The most striking early image of Pelagius is a facade sculpture from the former cathedral of León. The piece dates to the eleventh or twelfth century.[64] The boy-saint is shown holding a Gospel book as if he were a deacon, his hand covered by a dalmatic. His head is haloed. He looks away into the distance, the expression serene. What is striking is what he wears under his robe. Around his neck there is something like a necklace—the necklace given him by the caliph. On closer inspection, it seems the collar of an ornamental breastplate, one very similar to an ornamented Roman *thorax*. Pelagius may be wearing the armor of the soldier of Christ or the armor of an Iberian Christian knight. The soldier of Christ has become simply a noble knight. But he seems also to have gotten the gifts that the caliph promised, the gifts of a jeweled collar and luxurious clothing. Pelagius has become for the eyes of the faithful the beautiful young man dressed for the service of a king. In this way, the iconography seeks to make visible what the passion of Pelagius left invisible—namely, the saint's glorification in heaven. But the iconography can do this only by replicating, in curious ways, the offers made by the despised caliph.

Pelagius has been transformed from a naked ephebe into a triumphant military saint. The transformation might be read as an accident of Iberian politics. It might seem to enact a dialectic by which the cause of a military struggle becomes a military patron of the struggle. Pelagius's execution is a cause for which to fight; hence, Pelagius must be depicted as a leader in the fight, as a warrior himself. But the transformation from ephebe to glorious captain is also a curious sublimation of homoerotic desire.[65] It would be too obvious for celibate men to revere Pelagius as a naked "athlete" or spouse of Christ. It is much easier for them to revere Pelagius as a recogniz-

62. See the description and photograph in Lasko, *Ars Sacra, 800–1200*, pp. 153–154.

63. Bucher, *The Pamplona Bibles*, vol. 2, plate 505 = Amiens MS Lat. 108, folio 228r Note that the words of the king's command inscribed around the illumination are an abridgment of the corresponding text in Raguel's *Passio* (Rodríguez Fernández lines 101–102)

64 Preserved in the Museo arqueológico in León, the figure is published in Gaillard, *La sculpture romane espagnole*, plate 34.

65 Here and in what follows, I use "sublimation" in its older and more common sense, without meaning to endorse one psychoanalytic theory or another

able adult hero, a comrade in arms, a soldier. No hint of effeminacy remains, nothing of the attraction of youthful bodies. Pelagius is still to be desired, but now as a model of military power. His body has been changed from that of a defenseless boy to that of an armored man. Pelagius is no longer at risk of being raped.

PELAGIUS AND THE SUBLIMATION OF DESIRE

The tellings and retellings of the passion of Pelagius, his invocation and representation, are a kind of emblem of medieval theological relations to same-sex desire. The story explicitly invites the strongest possible condemnations of that desire. These are forthcoming in Raguel and Hrotswitha. For them, the desire characterizes the most visible enemies of Christianity, either as a whole or in their rulers. The desire is depicted not as something present within the Christian world, but as alien, repulsive, imposed from without. For Raguel, same-sex desire is what unites those who enjoy the unbelieving king's favor, the benefits of his opulent power. This fact is known to all, to the courtiers as much as to Pelagius. For Hrotswitha, Cordoba is the very city of luxury, its ruler a man stained with the vices of flesh. All Christians, again, should know these things.

The condemnations are clear enough. So are certain hesitations. Raguel is compelled to elide details in his narrative, to push aside the context of same-sex love in silence. He does not say exactly what the king does to Pelagius. He does not explain how the pure Pelagius knew what the king wanted. If Hrotswitha is more explicit about the caliph's advances, she must begin and end her poem by circumscribing Pelagius's desirable beauty—in the beginning, through prayer; in the end, through purifying fire. Pelagius's physical beauty survives the test of fire, but it is only the beauty of his head. It would be too dangerous to imagine the faithful watching for an hour as the naked body of a beautiful young man withstood the flames. Same-sex desire has to be evoked and then contained, made possible but implausible.

The same is true, more strikingly, in the Iberian cult of St. Pelagius. The Mozarabic liturgy can barely bring itself to mention the cause of his martyrdom. It much prefers to treat Pelagius as a type of the general rejection of worldly desire. His beauty is sometimes mentioned, but never in such detail as to make it troublesome. He is a pure boy, an idealized patron, remote and incorporeal as the heavens. Still, the fact of same-sex desire reasserts itself around the edges. It cannot but appear in the flattery of his beauty that is sung by male choirs. It appears again in some items of iconography. As it begins to act out its own worship of the boy-saint, the Christian community seems as much bothered by his beauty as was the caliph.

At the center of these instabilities, in the text of Hrotswitha's life, there appears a word that means to settle matters. It will circumscribe the sin in question by placing it within a precise theological context. It will specify what exactly was guilty in the caliph's act and why it was so outrageous, so grievous a sin. The word in Hrotswitha is "Sodomitic." Raguel spoke of unclean or illicit tastes; the liturgy, of worldly pleasures and temptations. Hrotswitha speaks precisely, with the technical vocabulary of Christian theology: the caliph was disfigured by "Sodomitic vices." With that word, the passions of St. Pelagius enter into the genealogy of the category of "Sodomy"—a term unknown to Hrotswitha, because it had not yet been invented. The Christian attitudes oscillating around the figure of Pelagius will be condensed in that invention.

TWO

The Discovery of Sodomy

The credit—or rather, the blame—for inventing the word *sodomia*, "Sodomy," must go, I think, to the eleventh-century theologian Peter Damian. He coined it quite deliberately on analogy to *blasphemia*, "blasphemy," which is to say, on analogy to the most explicit sin of denying God. Indeed, and from its origin, Sodomy is as much a theological category as trinity, incarnation, sacrament, or papal infallibility. As a category, it is richly invested with specific notions of sin and retribution, responsibility and guilt. The category was never meant to be neutrally descriptive, and it is doubtful whether any operation can purify it of its theological origins. There is no way to make "Sodomy" objective.

Peter's coining of the term is the result of long processes of thinning and condensing. These processes made it almost inevitable that there would be an abstract term for this specific kind of sin, so specifically stigmatized. One process thinned the reading of the Old Testament story of the punishment of Sodom. That complicated and disturbing story was simplified until it became the story of the punishment of a single sin, a sin that could be called eponymously the sin of the Sodomites. Another process, more diffuse but no less important, had to do with grouping together a number of sins under the old Roman category of *luxuria*. *Luxuria* came to be seen as the source of sinfulness in diverse acts, many of them having to do with the genitals. Peter Damian's coinage can only be understood against these processes.

I said that they were processes of thinning and condensing. The essential thing to notice in the processes by which "Sodomy" was produced is that they first abolish details, qualifications, restrictions in order to enable an excessive simplification in thought. Then they condense a number of these simplifications into a category that looks concrete but that has in fact nothing more concrete about it than the grammatical form of a general noun. The rather dry business of tracking words has in this case a very specific reward. It allows one to see, in the microcosm of grammatical form, the tyranny of generalization that results in there being a category like the category "Sodomy." The history of the word "Sodomy" is a history of the abuse of grammar, which is a reduction of thought.

MISREADING SODOM

Many contemporary exegetes agree that the Old Testament story about the destruction of Sodom cannot be read as a lesson about divine punishment of same-sex copulation.[1] If any lesson is wanted from the story, the lesson would seem to be about hospitality. After all, the story in Genesis 19 is akin to the story of the Levite's concubine in Judges 19. A Levite and his party, on their way home from a trip to the concubine's father, are offered lodging by an old man in the town of Gibeah. The house is surrounded by some townsmen who demand that the Levite be brought out to them (19:22). As he recounts the events later, the Levite understood that they intended to kill him (20:5). The Levite instead pushes out his concubine, who is gang raped throughout the night. She dies on the doorstep in the morning. On returning home, the Levite dismembers her body in order to send its pieces to the tribes of Israel as a bloody call for revenge. The Israelites assemble an army that finally succeeds in killing the inhabitants of Gibeah and nearby towns.

Both of the stories, the one about Sodom and the one about Gibeah, narrate a terrible violation of the obligations of host to traveler. In the case of Sodom, the violation is punished by divine destruction. In the case of the Levite's concubine, the violation becomes an occasion for concerted military revenge. But the story of Judges 19 does not issue in a long tradition of moral reflection, much less in the naming of a special sin. Christian theology did not become preoccupied with a "sin of the Benjamites" (as the inhabitants of Gibeah were called), nor did European countries adopt penal statutes against "Benjamy." This is the more striking because the incidents at Gibeah are more horrible than the events surrounding Lot's hospitality to the angelic messengers in Sodom. The citizens of Sodom do nothing in the end. They are blinded by the angels, who then instruct Lot to hurry his family out of the city in view of its impending destruction. At Gibeah, there are no angels to rescue the sacrificed woman during the dark

---

1. I will not here repeat the detailed arguments made by Bailey, *Homosexuality and the Western Christian Tradition*, and recapped by Boswell, *Christianity, Social Tolerance and Homosexuality*, pp 93–97

night of her torture. She has to suffer and then to die of her wounds. Nor does God punish Gibeah with fiery storm. The Israelite armies must do it themselves, after sustaining heavy casualties. Why is it then that the story of Sodom had such a long afterlife? How does it come to be misread so systematically and for so many centuries? The beginning of an answer lies precisely in the dramatic and total divine judgment executed on the city and its neighbors.

Sodom is already used by several books of the Old Testament as an image. It is not always the same image. Most often Sodom is an image of utter destruction, of desolation.² It is thus a name for sudden divine judgment.³ Sometimes Sodom is an image of a poisonous land, a land producing bitter fruit.⁴ At other times it is an image for brazen or general sin.⁵ When the sin is specified by Old Testament authors, it is a sin of arrogant self-indulgence or self-satisfaction. Thus, the text of Ezekiel says, "This was the iniquity of your sister Sodom: she and her daughters had pride, over-abundance of bread, abundance, and leisure, but they did not extend their hand to the poor. They were raised up and they committed abominations before me" (16:49–50).⁶ The two sentences are constructed in the familiar pattern of parallel repetition. The abomination is not a new sin; it is the sin of the previous sentence recapitulated.⁷

Sodom continues to be used as an image for divine judgment or barren-ness in the few New Testament texts that mention it.⁸ Indeed, there are only two passages in the New Testament that associate Sodom with sexual sins. After invoking Sodom and Gomorrah as examples of divine judgment, 2 Peter adds: "Above all [God] will punish those who walk according to the flesh in the desire of uncleanness (*immunditia*) and who contemn authority" (1:10). The "desire of uncleanness" might be construed as same-sex desire, except that a few verses later the text continues: "They have eyes full of adultery and [are] unceasingly sinful" (2:14).

The other New Testament text is no less problematic. Jude 7–8 reads:

2. Deut 29.23; Isa 13.19; Jer 49:18, 50:40; Zeph 2:9.

3 Lam 4:6; Amos 4.11.

4 Deut 32·32.

5 Isa 3:9; Jer 23.14.

6. Here and in what follows I translate into English from the Latin Bible known to the Middle Ages. My point in doing so is that I am principally interested in the scriptural texts as they were known to Latin theology. It was the Vulgate, and not the Hebrew or the Greek texts, that proved decisive for the construction of the category of Sodomy.

7. A similar interpretation is given in modern versions of Ecclus 16:8· "There was no reprieve for Lot's adopted home, abhorrent in its arrogance." This does not occur in the Vulgate.

8 Matt 10:15, Luke 17 29, Rom 9:29.

"Just as Sodom and Gomorrah and the nearby cities, fornicating and going after other flesh in the same way [as the aforementioned angels], were made an example, suffering the punishment of eternal fire, so too it will be with those who stain the flesh and spurn authority and blaspheme against majesties." The angels here are, of course, not the good angels who came to stay with Lot in Sodom. They are the evil angels who abandoned heaven and are now imprisoned in hell. The author of Jude understands their sin as sexual, as analogous to fornication and seeking after other flesh. The last, mysterious phrase may be a reference to the sort of legend that appears in Genesis 6:1 about the "sons of God" copulating with "the daughters of men."[9] It seems certainly to reflect nonscriptural traditions that identified the sin of Sodom with sexual irregularity. In neither case does it refer necessarily to same-sex copulation. Moreover, in Jude these same sinners are guilty of taking bribes—a sin that exercises the author at greater length.

What is clear, I think, is that Sodom figures in the Christian Scriptures as the unsurpassed example of divine retribution. The challenge would seem to be that of figuring out what provoked it. The answer, as it appears in these lesser texts of the New Testament, is sexual. But within the Gospels, that is, in the mouth of Jesus, Sodom is not a reminder of a specific sin. It is a trope for divine wrath generally. Indeed, as Jesus is made to say several times, the sin of rejecting the Gospel merits greater punishment than the sin of Sodom and Gomorrah—whatever exactly it was. So Sodom is at this point not yet a geographical name for a particular kind of sin. It is a memorial site that records God's power to judge. It refers not to specific human actions, but to a story that is to be remembered for its present pertinence. What happened at Sodom is not an exotic, foreign vice that cannot be mentioned. It is, on the contrary, a most articulate reminder of the consequences of rebelling against God. We remember the story of Sodom because we need to learn obedience from it.

With these considerations, if not from the simple inspection of passages, it should be clear that there is no text of the Christian Bible that determines the reading of Sodom as a story about same-sex copulation. On the contrary, there is explicit scriptural evidence that the sin of the Sodomites was some combination of arrogance and ingratitude. This evidence was not ignored by patristic exegetes writing in Latin. Indeed, many Latin theologians continue to speak of the inhospitality of Sodom, of its pride and arrogance, even as they speak of its association with forbidden sex. I will not here try to prove that remark by a statistical survey of patristic scriptural

9 See Bailey, *Homosexuality and the Western Christian Tradition*, pp 10–23

commentary. Views about the sense of a group of texts become convincing not through numbers so much as by self-directed reading. I will instead offer a few highly visible passages from the theologians that would be most authoritative for the Latin Middle Ages. Traditionally, the four "doctors" of the Western church were Jerome, Ambrose, Augustine, and Gregory the Great. Each wrote on the story of Sodom many times in different contexts. I select the most extended or instructive treatments as examples.

Jerome, master of the scriptural text and its renowned translator, not surprisingly preserves the widest range of readings. In his commentary on the passage from Ezekiel, for example, he paraphrases the prophetic teaching quoted above quite succinctly. The first of the crimes of Sodom and her daughters is pride.[10] Its primacy is supported by abundant quotation from the New Testament. The seedbed of this pride is abundance with leisure, or, in words that Jerome takes from the Septuagint, "the opulence of delicacies and of luxury." The lesson is summed emphatically: "The Sodomitic sin is pride, bloatedness (*saturitas*), the abundance of all things, leisure and delicacies."[11] In another passage, from his commentary on Isaiah, Jerome adds to this list the feature of brazenness. Princes are said to be Sodomites when they publish their sins abroad, not taking any trouble to conceal them. The princes "publicly proclaim" their sin "without having any shame in blaspheming."[12] On Jerome's reading of these texts, the sin of Sodom is brazen arrogance bred of opulence.

Elsewhere Jerome acknowledges that Sodom has taken on a variety of allegorical or spiritual meanings. So, for example, he reports a reading according to which Samaria and Sodom mean respectively "heretics and Gentiles."[13] He contests the heretical interpretation according to which Jerusalem, Samaria, and Sodom signify spiritual, animal, and earthly. Again, in defending the literal sense of Jude 7–8, he refuses to let Sodom mean this visible world.[14] But Jerome's most striking reference to Sodom comes in a letter on a practical matter. Can a woman whose husband is an adulterer and "a Sodomite" count her marriage to him as dissolved?[15] Jerome's answer is a strong no. His phrasing of the question and his answer to it both make clear that to be an adulterer is different from being a Sodomite. They do not make clear what a Sodomite is. It clearly involves some form

10. Jerome *Commentaria in Hiezechielem* 5.16.48–51 (Glorie 75 205.663–664)
11. Jerome *Commentaria in Hiezechielem* 5.16.48–51 (Glorie 75.206.683–685).
12. Jerome *Commentaria in Esaiam* 2 3.8–9 (Adriaen 73:51.19–21).
13. Jerome *Commentaria in Hiezechielem* 5.16 (Glorie 75:204 597).
14. Jerome *Epistulae* 46 7 (Hilberg 336–338).
15. Jerome *Epistulae* 55 4(3) (Hilberg 492–493)

of sexual irregularity, but it might well be irregularity in the mode of copulation with the man's wife or with his mistress. With Jerome, then, we run the full range from the prophetic use of Sodom's arrogance through scriptural allegorizations of it to its use to refer to a specific but unstated sexual act.

In Ambrose the moral sense of Sodom begins to narrow around sexual or at least bodily sin. He does recognize that the threat against the angels was a violation of hospitality.[16] Elsewhere, though, and especially in his treatise *On Abraham,* he identifies Sodom straightforwardly with fleshly indulgence and lasciviousness.[17] The Sodomites were, he says, fierce and sinful, given to crimes beyond the mean of human wickedness. Their special province seems to be that of luxury (*luxuria*) and disordered desire (*libido*).[18] When Lot's wife turns back to look at the burning city, she is turning back to the impure region of lust.[19]

The evidence from Augustine is, as always, complicated. On the one hand, there are passages in which Sodom is understood as a sign of human depravity generally—of "the pernicious society of humankind."[20] The Sodomites were unclean and proud; they were blasphemers.[21] On the other hand, Augustine is quite clear that the citizens of Sodom wanted to rape the male angels. In his narrative of Old Testament history within the *City of God,* Augustine gives as reason for the destruction of Sodom that it was a place where "debaucheries in men" (*stupra in masculos*) flourished by custom.[22] That is why Lot tried to offer his daughters instead. Better for men to violate women than to violate other men.[23] Another passage from the *Confessions* is much quoted by medieval theologians as being equally explicit, since Augustine there mentions the Sodomites in a condemnation of iniquities done against nature (*flagitia contra naturam*).[24] In fact, Augustine uses the story of Sodom in the *Confessions* only as an illustration of divine punishment. The crimes being discussed, the exact nature of which is unclear, are always and everywhere to be published as harshly as the Sodomites were punished.

---

16 Ambrose of Milan *Hexaemeron* 5.16.54 (Schenkl 32/1:181.10).
17. Ambrose of Milan *De Abraham* 1.3.14 (Schenkl 32/1:512.9), 1.6.55 (538.25), 2.6 25 (582.4).
18. Ambrose of Milan *De Abraham* 2.8.45 (Schenkl 32/1:599 9).
19. Ambrose of Milan *Explanatio psalmorum XII* ps.43 34.1 (Petschenig 64 286.18), *Epistulae* 4 11 21 (Faller 82/1·90.230)
20 Augustine *Quaestiones XVI in Matthaeum* 3 (Mutzenbecher 44B:120)
21 Augustine *Sermo* 100 (Demeulenaere 83 = Migne *PL* 38·604).
22 Augustine *De ciuitate Dei* 16.30 (Dombart-Kalb 48:535.3–5).
23 Augustine *De mendacio* 7.10 (Zycha 41 429 4).
24 Augustine *Confessiones* 3 8.15 (Skutella-Verheijen 27 35 3–7).

With Augustine, then, we reach an explicit description of the sin of the Sodomites as the desire for same-sex copulation. It was a custom among them, and it was immediately understood by Lot as the reason for the demand that he hand over his guests. But even in Augustine the sin of the Sodomites is not merely same-sex desire. That desire is a symptom of the madness of their fleshly appetites, of the underlying delirium of their passions. The root sin of the Sodomites is not the desire for same-sex copulation. It is rather the violent eruption of disordered desire itself. The distinction is crucial for Augustine but quickly lost in the readings of him.

One piece of evidence for the sexual fixation of the reading of Sodom comes in a poem written by an unknown author in fifth-century Gaul.[25] The poem narrates the whole story of destruction—from the infamy of Sodom's sin and the mission of the angels through the city's conflagration. The poem makes absolutely clear that Sodom was known for sexual irregularities and, indeed, for same-sex copulation. No male visitor could enter the city without fearing damage to his sex from a citizenry known for its "mixed," incestuous marriages, its rebellion against nature.[26] Lot even tries to reason with the crowd, a foretaste of theological reasonings to come, by arguing that no other animal gives way to same-sex desire. "A woman is spouse to every [man]," he pleads, "and never has anyone's mother been other than a woman."[27] For the author of this poem, the men of Sodom not only like to rape strangers, they like to marry each other. In short, the sexual interpretation of Genesis 19 is now assumed. It has begun to fuel more and more vivid imaginations about what happened that night within the doomed city.

The last of the four Latin "doctors," Gregory the Great, treats of Sodom theologically in two prominent passages. Together they show that alternate readings have been pushed out of the way by the sexual ones. Gregory knows the reading that Ezekiel gives to Sodom. He reproduces it as scriptural commentator and applies it in his own voice.[28] But when Gregory thinks of Sodom, his first thought is of sexual sin, not of pride or inhospitality. This is clearest in his *Moral Readings of Job*, a book that would enormously influence medieval moral theology. At one point in explicating Job, Gregory wants to gloss the image of sulfur. He thinks at once of the destruction of Sodom. "That we should understand sulfur as signifying the

25. There is a very "free" and rather precious English rendering by S. Thelwall reprinted in Hallam, *The Book of Sodom*, pp. 191–197.
26. *De Sodoma* (Peiper 23:213.20–23).
27. *De Sodoma* (Peiper 23:215.49–50).
28. For example, *Moralia in Job* 30.18.60 (Adriaen 143B:1532.79).

stench of the flesh, the history of the holy Scriptures itself testifies, when it narrates that God rained down fire and sulfur upon Sodom."[29] Sodom is punished for "crimes of the flesh" (*scelera carnis*), for "perverse desires from the stench of the flesh" (*peruersa desideria ex fetore carnis*), for "what they did from unjust desire" (*ex iniusto desiderio*). In his *Pastoral Rule,* Gregory makes the moral explicit: "To flee from burning Sodom is to refuse the illicit fires of the flesh."[30]

One other passage from Gregory must be mentioned. It is not theological so much as legal or administrative. The passage comes in a letter in which Gregory instructs one of his subordinates how to deal with a case of a priest who is accused of idolatry and of being "stained by the crime of the Sodomite."[31] Here, as in the earlier letter from Jerome, the meaning of the accusation is presumed. In both cases, it is interesting that it accompanies an accusation of idolatry. But I mention the letter now in order to emphasize a terminological point. Gregory writes "the crime of the Sodomite." In two tenth-century copies of the text, there is a telling scribal error. "Of the Sodomite" becomes "of Sodomy."[32] This slip is the reason a number of dictionaries will record Gregory's letter as the first appearance of the abstract term "Sodomy."[33] In fact it is not. The term appears after Gregory, and then as a scribal error. But its absence here is worth noting. If patristic readers of the Christian Bible fixed on a sexual interpretation of the sin of Sodom, they did not yet make up a word to single it out. The entire Latin interpretation proceeds through Gregory and beyond without the help—or hindrance—of that kind of abstraction. You would not know this from the English translations, of course, which tend to become particularly irresponsible when translating terms having to do with same-sex copulation. Some translators disappear into prim vagueness; others apply an overly precise and definitely modern vocabulary. Either tactic will obscure important features in the history of moral theology, such as the entire absence of an abstract category "Sodomy" for some ten centuries of Christian theology.

29 Gregory the Great *Moralia in Job* 14 19.23 (Adriaen 143A 711 8)

30. Gregory the Great *Regula pastoralis* 3 27 (Rommel 382 452 80)

31. Gregory the Great *Registrum epistolarum* 10 2 (Norberg 140A:827 7–9)

32 The manuscripts called *e1* (Milan, Bibl Ambrosiana MS C 238 inferior, tenth century, from Bobbio) and *e2* (Paris, Bibl. Nationale MS Nouvelles acquis lat 1452, tenth or eleventh century, from Cluny) See the apparatus for 10 2 (Norberg 140A:827.9)

33 Most authoritatively, Blaise, *Dictionnaire latin-français des auteurs chrétiens,* s.v "Sodomia." The article "Sodomy" in the *Encyclopedia of Homosexuality* confidently asserts that *sodomia* appeared "around 1180 as a designation for the 'crime against nature'" As will be seen, it appeared a century and a half earlier and preceded the preference for the term "crime against nature"

We need to move forward in order to witness the birth of the term. But before we can do so responsibly, we have to notice one other process that has run parallel to the misreading of Sodom. The passages from Gregory make two things clear. The first is that Latin exegesis had by the end of the patristic period fixed on a sexual interpretation of Sodomitic sin, even if it kept repeating the other interpretations offered by the Scriptures. In some passages, though not in all, the sin is specified as that of same-sex copulation. In most passages, it is stigmatized as a sin of corrupted, luxurious flesh. The second point, the one yet to be investigated, is that the interpretation of Genesis 19 has been taken up into a much larger system of moral teaching about a sin called *luxuria*. The scope of the teaching can be seen especially in Gregory. When Gregory speaks of Sodom and *luxuria*, he says something quite specific. For Gregory, *luxuria* is one of seven principal or capital sins. It has a certain rank among sins, as it has certain properties or consequences. The misreading of Sodom has intersected with the formation of Christian moral categorizations in the Latin-speaking West.

BAPTIZING LUXURY

When Jerome chose the Latin *luxuria* to translate several different terms in the Old and New Testaments, he imported into Christian theology a moral category with an ancient Roman pedigree. That pedigree is more important than the sense of the Hebrew or Greek terms that *luxuria* displaced. *Luxuria* recurs in Latin moral texts as the opposite of the stern virtues of the Republic.[34] It is often coupled with *licentia*, with the threat of a general social dissolution, the loosening of bonds necessary to keep the city and then its empire intact. Whatever may have been the original Christian teaching on the dangers of the flesh, it arrived in the Latin-speaking portions of the empire both reinforced and distorted by the teaching of Rome itself.

The results of Jerome's choices appear in a number of passages. In the Latin Old Testament, *luxuria* is associated with drunkenness or gluttony and with sexual excess.[35] In the Gospels, it appears only once—in the description of the life of the prodigal son when he has run away from home to dissipate his wealth.[36] But the most important uses for later writers occur

34 For some Roman texts on *luxuria* and a reading of them, see Edwards, *The Politics of Immorality in Ancient Rome*, pp. 176–206.

35 For example, Deut 21·20, gluttony and drunkenness; Prov 20·1, drunkenness, 2 Macc 6:4, gluttony; Jer 5·7, prostitution.

36. Luke 15:13

in the New Testament letters. *Luxuria* appears as one term in Paul's lists of sins in Galatians. It follows immediately after fornication and uncleanness, just before idolatry.[37] In the letters ascribed to Peter, *luxuria* gets connected with blasphemy and the desires of the flesh.[38] And in Jude, just before the text that links the sin of Sodomy with lusting for alien flesh, *luxuria* is named as the sin of certain false teachers who have corrupted the word of God.[39] Already in Jerome's Latin Bible, then, *luxuria* covers an enormous range even as it begins to condense around the flesh as the site of opposition to God.

I jump forward from Latin Scripture to Gregory the Great's *Moral Readings of Job*. That text will fix for medieval moral theology a certain view of *luxuria* and its place among the principal and most lethal sins. Gregory's schemes of classification are fairly straightforward. Seven chief sins spring from the malignant root of pride: vainglory, envy, wrath, sadness, avarice, gluttony of the stomach, and *luxuria*.[40] *Luxuria* comes last, not because it is least important, but because Gregory means to emphasize it. With malice and pride, it forms a trio of sins that particularly attack the human race.[41] It leads to idolatry and to one or another of its sibling sins along various causal chains.[42] The "daughters" or consequences of *luxuria* are identified by Gregory as mental blindness, inconsiderateness, inconstancy, haste, self-love, hatred of God, passionate attachment to the present, and horror or despair over the future.[43]

These schemes and causal connections hardly suggest the flexibility of *luxuria* in Gregory's thought. It agitates the soul in countless ways—burns it, beats it, stimulates it, rushes through it.[44] *Luxuria* seems in such passages to mean self-indulgence, self-gratification. It is both of the flesh and of the heart, of the deed and of thought.[45] Many fall because they rid themselves

37 Gal 5:19

38 1 Pet 4:4, 2 Pet 2·18.

39. Jude 4

40 Gregory the Great *Moralia in Job* 31 45.87 (Adriaen 143B:1610.15). There is a complicated history before this list and a more complicated posterity after it. For the briefest introduction, see Newhauser, *The Treatise on Vices and Virtues*, especially pp 180–202.

41 Gregory the Great *Moralia in Job* 33.15.30 (Adriaen 143B:1700.22).

42. Gregory the Great *Moralia in Job* 33.38 67 (Adriaen 143B.1730 13), compare 25 9.24 (143B:1249.79)

43. Gregory the Great *Moralia in Job* 31.45 88 (Adriaen 143B.1610 34).

44. Gregory the Great *Moralia in Job* 3 31.60 (Adriaen 143·153.32), "inflammat", 9.65.98 (143·526 54), "ignis", 26 32.58 (143B.1311.6), "pulsat", 30 10.38 (143B·1518.87), "stimulis", 30.3 9 (143B:1497.20), "fluxa" Compare 32.14.20 (143B:1645.14–15) and 32.14.21 (143B:1645.40)

45. Gregory the Great *Moralia in Job* 21.2.5 (Adriaen 143A:1067.65)

of fleshly *luxuria* only to lapse into the inward *luxuria* of pride. So long as *luxuria* agitates the soul, salvation is impossible.[46]

At the same time, in adjacent texts, Gregory teaches that *luxuria* is what we would call a sexual sin. It is linked to the genitals.[47] More symbolically, Gregory says that it is tied to the "loins" in men, to the "umbilical," that is, the center in women.[48] The devil holds these members in subjection and from them produces the salacious images and the physiological pulses that lead to acts of *luxuria*, outward or inward.[49] The sin is connected with effeminacy and animality.[50] It is symbolized by the ass, the pig, and the worm. Considered as fleshly sin, *luxuria* is described as staining, polluting, stinking.

Gregory's teaching on *luxuria* doubles the sin. On the one hand, it is a sin subject to indefinite modulation through the chambers of the body and the soul. It appears in one guise, then in another. Beaten down in the flesh, it returns through images projected from memory. If the memory of one kind of pleasure is successfully controlled, control itself may become an occasion for *luxuria*. On the other hand, the sin is housed in the genitals as in a part of the body that has been given over to demonic control. It flames out of those organs through specific channels of desire. It reaches out to fornication, adultery, to every perverse ordering of the flesh.

One way to ease this duality is to believe that Gregory means to elevate sexual sins to a unique prominence as cause of sin. The "loins" would become the source of the whole of *luxuria*. There is something to this belief, but it ignores the different logic implicit in the two views of *luxuria*. The logic of generalized *luxuria* is the logic of mutation, infiltration, reactivation; the logic of genital *luxuria* is the logic of disruption, direct assault. This dual logic is not accidental. It is important to Gregory's argumentative strategy. To have a category that bridges the two logics, the two models of causality, is to have a category that can be used to prevent troublesome sins from being subjected to corrective analysis. *Luxuria* has two logics built into it by Gregory. If one is attacked, it can be retired and the other brought into play.

There is more. The two logics are not deployed symmetrically. It is rather the case that the generalized *luxuria* is used to defend the genital

46. Gregory the Great *Moralia in Job* 21 12 19 (Adriaen 143A:1079.19–24).

47 Gregory the Great *Moralia in Job* 7 28.36 (Adriaen 143·361.131); 31.45.89 (143B·1611 57)

48. Gregory the Great *Moralia in Job* 32 14.20–21 (Adriaen 143B:1645.10– 37).

49. Gregory the Great *Moralia in Job* 21.2.5 (Adriaen 143A:1067.87–96)

50 Gregory the Great *Moralia in Job* 26.17.29 (Adriaen 143B:1287.86); 26.35.63 (143B.1314.7)

one from criticism. To the charge that Gregory's teaching gives too much weight to genital sins, it can be replied that *luxuria* is much broader than that. It is more like Augustine's notion of disordered desire, a fundamental inversion in the will that shows itself in dozens of secondary disorders. But as soon as this expansive doctrine is advanced, Gregory will bring all of its weight to bear on genital sins, as if they just were the fundamental inversion. Certain sins of the flesh are brought into the system of moral teaching at one level, then linked by the term *luxuria* to much graver dysfunction. It is easy enough then to transfer the sense of gravity out, down to the sins of the flesh.

Whatever the doublings of Gregory's notion of *luxuria*, it is a relatively less potent device for moral reorganization—for moral condemnation—than the term "Sodomy." "Sodomy" represents a level of abstraction beyond the slippage encoded within *luxuria*. Indeed, "Sodomy" will have the advantage of carrying within it all the polemical resources of *luxuria* and more besides.

FIGHTING WORDS

We have followed so far two textual processes. The first is a thinning down of the reading of the story of Sodom. The other is a condensation of the ancient category of *luxuria* around what we would call sexual sins. The two processes intersect and then reinforce each other. The story of Sodom becomes a story about one particular form of *luxuria*. Still, the abstraction of the sin from the story and the moral explanation has not yet taken place. There has so far been no mention of the term *sodomia*, "Sodomy."

The exact form of the name is important, both for what it says and for what is suggests. Abstract nouns based on proper names are rarer in classical Latin than a speaker of modern English might think. We routinely speak of "Platonism" and "Aristotelianism," thinking that we are using terms that would be recognized at once within ancient Latin philosophy. But neither *Platonismus* nor *Aristotelismus* is found in Latin before the modern period. The nearest Latin comes is *Platonicus* and *Aristotelicus*—adjectival forms, like our "Platonic" and "Aristotelian." The difference might seem negligible. It is not. An adjectival form always applies to some kind of thing, expressed or implied. There can be Platonic philosophy or Platonic customs or Platonic books, but not just the abstract, untethered essence "Platonism." It is the same with the word "Sodomitic." It has to be affixed to something, has to qualify some underlying thing. Most often in

Christian theology it qualifies a sin or a crime, which is then blamed and analyzed, depicted and condemned. The discourse proceeds not by studying a free-floating essence, but by looking to particular things in the world.

The immediate ground for abstracting the essence of Sodomy was provided by attempts to classify particular acts for the sake of punishing them. The attempts are recorded in the early medieval books of penances. These penitentials seem to have been first compiled in Irish and Anglo-Saxon monasteries for the use of confessors.[51] They typically group together certain sins, which are carefully described, in order to assign appropriately graded penances for each kind. The books were popular from the seventh century onward, and they spread widely. They certainly spread into the church schools and administrative circles of Italy, where they seemed important enough to Peter Damian to require an extended refutation. If their influence was much diminished by the twelfth century, it was in part because their project of moral classification had been entirely appropriated by the common theological traditions.

It is no easy thing to draw inferences from the penitentials about sexual attitudes or practices, much less about theological reasoning on sexual matters. As Peter Damian will delight in pointing out, the penances assigned are hardly consistent indications of the gravity of the sin committed. More generally, penitentials were written for use in a comprehensive system of spiritual practices, monastic and nonmonastic. They had important relations to liturgy, and they need to be read with an eye to ritual functions as much as to juridical or descriptive ones. So I mention the penitentials here not as social records or even as pieces of coherent theology, but rather as samples of theological speech about same-sex acts.

Their speech is pertinent because it shows that by the seventh or eighth century Sodom and its inhabitants were being mentioned as a way of designating a particular kind of sexual intercourse.[52] Some sections of the penitentials refer simply to "Sodomites" as a class meriting a certain punishment.[53] Others speak more precisely of fornication "in the Sodomitic manner" (*sodomitico more*), where the immediate context suggests a contrast with simple fornication.[54] Yet other passages speak more cryptically

51. For a convenient survey of different studies of the genre, see Driscoll, "Penance in Transition Popular Piety and Practice."

52. For a survey of the teaching of many of the penitentials on sexual matters, see Payer, *Sex and the Penitentials*, which contains a very useful list of passages on same-sex relations at pp. 135–139.

53. To cite only a few examples, Wasserschleben, *Die Bußordnung der abendländischen Kirche*, pp 222 (Bede), 234 (Egbert), 599 (ps-Theodore); and Bieler, *Irish Penitentials*, p. 68 (Grove of Victory), 100 (Columbanus), 114 (Cummean).

54. Wasserschleben, *Die Bußordnung der abendländischen Kirche*, p 532 (Vigilia)

of the "Sodomitic sin."[55] There are a few lines in which descriptions of
this sin are attempted, but they are not particularly helpful. The so-called
Penitential of Columbanus describes fornication "according to the Sodomitic custom [or style]" (*sodomitico ritu*) as sinning by having "female intercourse" with a man.[56] This would seem to be an allusion to the Latin of
Leviticus 18:21. Other passages do speak frankly of fornication "in the
rear" or "between the legs," but passages in which these frank descriptions
are equated with the Sodomitic manner of fornication are not easy to find.
Even in the penitentials, which are noted for their blunt speaking about
sexual matters, references to Sodom or Sodomites are used both to conceal
and to reveal. They reveal to those who already know what the geograph-
ico-biblical reference means. Otherwise they conceal.

There is a more important point about the speech of the penitentials.
The prescriptions against Sodomitic intercourse are not the same as the
construction of the category *sodomia*, for which the appearance of the abstract noun serves as an important index. What are the implications of abstracting an essence from a proper name? Again, what are the implications
of abstracting from a historical name? To abstract an essence from a proper
name is to reduce the person named to a single quality. All that you need
to know about the Sodomites is that they practiced Sodomy. In this way,
abstraction from a proper name is deeply connected with the project of
essentializing persons. A term like Sodomy suggests, by its very grammatical form, that it is possible to reduce persons to a single essence, which can
then be found in other persons, remote from them in time or place. This
kind of essentialism is necessarily antihistorical. The isolated essence is to
recur across time, like an Aristotelian species, never subject to evolution.
As a recurring essence, it would seem to justify recourse to the same means
of control in every case—to a punishment as near as one can get to the
divine fires that poured down on Sodom. If such dramatic punishments are
not available, then at least the sin should be subjected to relentless denunci-
ation.

A polemical character is suggested in a curious way by the form of the
word *sodomia*. Its ending is not a native Latin ending; it is borrowed from
the Greek. Now *sodomia* is unattested in theological Greek, but the habit
of coining abstract nouns from names was a habit the Latins learned from
Greek theological polemics. Most of the name abstractions that appear before the Middle Ages are specifically Christian and specifically polemical.

55 Bieler, *Irish Penitentials*, p 96 (Columbanus)
56 Bieler, *Irish Penitentials*, p 102

"Christian" itself is a nominalized proper name, and one that was originally applied as a term of derision. Christian authors picked up the naming habit, it seems, and began to speak of such heresies as "Arianism" or "Sabellianism." The abstractions serve an obvious polemical purpose. They allow a writer to reduce an opponent to a schematic caricature. Arian authors could protest that they did not recognize themselves in the caricatures of their views given by pro-Nicean polemicists. But the damage was done. The nuances and dialectical complexities of a teaching, the circumstances and motivations of particular teachers could be swept away in an attack upon a malignant essence, everywhere the same and everywhere to be combated.

I say "malignant" deliberately, because the kind of transhistorical essentializing that goes into a name like "Arianism" is much like bad medical reasoning. Ancient medicine in the Hippocratic and Galenic traditions, whether empirical or dogmatic, was marvelously attentive to variations of individual body, custom, season, situation. The diagnosis of a disease was not an excuse to import a reductive explanation or to employ a prefabricated therapy. But the Hippocratic and Galenic traditions were for that very reason difficult to learn. The reaction against them, most famously expressed in the methodist or methodical school, wanted to make things easy by reducing complexities or particularities to a small scheme of invariant causes of disease. A disease, once identified, could be treated by the same treatment every time—and the treatments themselves would be few in number. The same logic of willed simplification is at work in coining terms like "Arianism." Such words are in effect slogans. They reduce an opposing position to an easy caricature, one that can be ridiculed or refuted memorably because briefly.

It is hard to say how many of these considerations were in Peter Damian's mind when he coined the term. Certainly he was thinking of analogies to Greek names for sins, because the sentence in which *sodomia* first appears is built around that kind of analogy: "If blasphemy is the worst sin, I do not know in what way Sodomy is any better."[57] *Blasphemia, sodomia.* Linked grammatically, linked by the seriousness of the sin, linked by being terms most useful in polemic. *Sodomia* does not make its appearance as a neutral description of acts. It is a brand that burns condemnation into certain acts. It burns into them as well the presumption of a stable essence, a sameness found wherever the acts are performed. The sameness links those who perform them back to the criminals who suffered the most severe divine punishment.

57. Peter Damian *Liber Gomorrhianus* (Reindel 328.2–3)

That transition from acts to persons is perhaps what an essence does best. By coining an abstract term to group together a series of acts, Peter Damian has made the inference from acts to agent almost automatic. The acts display an essence, the essence of Sodomy. Where is that essence? Derivatively in the acts, fundamentally in the actor—the Sodomite who expresses his essence, his identity, by acting. The unity of the abstract essence, Sodomy, points back to the unity of the identity in Sodomites. They are no longer persons who perform a few similar acts from a myriad of motives and in incalculably different circumstances. They are Sodomites doing Sodomy. The abstractive power of the word abolishes motives and circumstances.

Of course, it is one thing to coin a word, to project an essence in discrete acts, to assert a unitary identity that binds together persons across time. It is another thing to keep the essence and the identity from generating equivocations, paradoxes. "Sodomy" was no sooner coined than it began to be bent. Indeed, it was coined in the middle of a text ripped apart by the pressures of its dialectic. In order to see this, we must go to Peter Damian's little book.

THREE

Peter Damian

Books in Gomorrah

"Outstanding warrior" his first biographer would call him.[1] The battles were church controversies and the weapons most often letters, tracts, and treatises. In these, Peter Damian shows himself a superb polemicist—not to say a constant one. From first to last, he displays a talent and a taste for attack.

One early battle is waged against a "vice" and a "hot disgrace" (*flagitium*) that Peter Damian calls "most wicked" and "most shameful." The attack comes in a booklet titled by some of its first manuscript witnesses *Book of Gomorrah* or, more literally, *Gomorran Book*.[2] This booklet risks excesses not only of polemic, but of obscenity. Peter Damian claims to be worried that the frankness of his remarks will offend readers. It certainly offended later editors, who bowdlerized the text.[3] While there is no convincing case that its first readers were scandalized, it is true that the text was not embraced by its immediate recipient or his successors.[4]

The booklet as we have it is addressed to Pope Leo IX, who reigned from 1048 to 1054. Peter Damian was then in his forties.[5] He continued in office as prior of the community of hermits at Fonte Avellana, a community

---

1 John of Lodi *Vita Petri Damiani* 16 (Migne *PL* 144:133A): "egregius bellator."

2. I follow the edition by Reindel, who prints the *Liber* as *Epistola* 31 in *Die Briefe des Petrus Damiani* 1. I will cite this edition by volume, page, and line numbers. For testimonies to the title, see p. 286, note *k*. An English translation of this edition is available in Peter Damian *Letters* 2, pp. 3–53.

3. See the edition reprinted in Migne *PL* 154, columns 159–190. An earlier English translation by Pierre Payer was based on this censored version. Modern scholars have also been reluctant to discuss the booklet. Jean Leclercq, for example, says that it discusses "a delicate subject . . . with precision and clarity, without any vulgarity. . . It introduces with tact all of the required nuances" (*Saint Pierre Damien*, p. 70). Whatever the *Liber Gomorrhianus* might be, it is neither tactful nor nuanced

4. I do not think that Alexander II stole the book from Peter Damian to prevent its circulation Compare Boswell, *Christianity, Social Tolerance, and Homosexuality*, pp. 212–213, especially note 17

5. The dates and ages are to be treated with the kind of cautions spoken by Little, "The Personal Development of Peter Damian," pp. 319–322.

that he had joined when twenty-eight (around 1035) and governed from
the age of thirty-six (since about 1043). The booklet was neither his first
work nor his first intervention in church controversies. Peter Damian had
already adopted the polemical tone for his inaugural public utterance, an
admonition in the form of a life of Fonte Avellana's founder, Romuald. He
had written public letters against the selling of church offices since 1043.
His principal doctrinal work, *Gratissimus,* was also written for Leo IX, if
against the pope's opinions. But it is the polemic of the *Book of Gomorrah*
that enters into the genealogy of Sodomy.

PERSUASIVE ADDRESS

Peter knew himself to be a writer of persuasions rather than of histories, of
arguments and not of records. In the prologue to the life of Romuald, he
explicitly sets aside the task of a history (*historia*) for that of an admonition
(*commonitorium*).[6] The *Book of Gomorrah* itself opens with a blunt statement
of a rhetorical end. The booklet is meant to persuade the pope to eradicate
a widespread sin and all of its consequences. So it offers different kinds of
arguments directed against a sin that it calls most often the "Sodomitic
vice," sometimes the "Sodomitic manner" of copulation, and once, fate-
fully, "Sodomy."[7] The arguments are presented to the pope for his use in
convincing other bishops to stop the spread of this vice.

The booklet begins by identifying the vice's four species: self-pollution,
mutual grasping or rubbing of "manly parts" (*virilia*), pollution "between
the thighs" (*inter femora*), and fornication "in the rear" (*in terga*).[8] The
order of these four is an order of increasing offense, but each belongs to
Sodom and each merits suspension from ecclesiastical office and deposition
from priestly orders. To establish the point, Peter provides first a basic
demonstration from Scripture, expounding especially the Pauline exhortations to purity. In a second section, Peter criticizes allegedly authoritative
texts adduced by his opponents to support claims that such sins are not
serious. Finally, in a third part of the body, Peter describes the spiritual
condition of the Sodomitic soul and appeals in various ways for it to repent.

Both the criticism and the appeal rest on the argument of the first part,
an argument that is at once legal and theological. According to Peter, good

6 Peter Damian *Vita Romualdi* praefatio (Tabacco p. 10 = Migne *PL* 144.954a)
7 This is the passage discussed in chapter 2 when I consider the coining of *sodomia* on analogy to
blasphemia and similar theological terms.
8 Peter Damian *Liber Gomorrhianus* (Reindel 1:287.19–21). Further citations will be to the *Liber*
unless otherwise specified

theology and coherent jurisprudence both require that persons guilty of
Sodomitic vice be deposed from church office. Peter is clear that he means
to include all four species of the vice in his judgment. He mocks the claim
that only those guilty of "fornication in the rear" should be deposed. Clerics engaged in masturbation or femoral intercourse are just as much to be
deprived of church income and removed from the clergy.[9] Peter is not so
clear on the question of frequency. At one point he speaks of practicing
the vice "customarily" (*consuetudinaliter*): persons who have the custom of
Sodomitic vice are not to seek ordination, much less to remain in priestly
office. The scriptural example is that of Onan, who repeatedly or always
ejaculated on the soil rather than obey divine law by impregnating his
brother's widow.[10] But then Peter argues that a single violation of the scriptural prohibition against "sleeping with a man" is sufficient to prevent ordination.[11] At a minimum, he teaches that customary masturbation or a single
act of intrafemoral fornication is sufficient to debar one from the church
service. This judgment cannot be waived on a plea of urgent need. It is
better for a community to be without a priest—or the church without a
pope—than to be served by a Sodomite. This basic argument carries an
appendix on those who practice the Sodomitic vice with persons entrusted
to their pastoral care and, what is worse, who then hear the confessions of
their sinful partners. Sexual relations with someone in your care is incest,
and confessions made to a partner in Sodomitic acts are invalid.[12]

The second and third parts of the booklet must also seem supplements
or appendices to the first. The second part carries the argument into a textual dispute. There are some who want to use the authority of rule books
for assigning penances, the penitentials, to hold that Sodomitic vice is not
so serious after all. Peter replies that the specific rules in question are falsi-
fications and interpolations. He opposes to them condemnations from an
undisputed church council. The third part fills in the principal argument by
supplying what looks to be an anthology of exhortations, rebukes, and appeals. The anthology is apparently to be used in reinforcing the lesson that
Sodomitic vice is a great crime against God.

This outline, however, describes only the evident structure of the *Book
of Gomorrah*. It seems a loosely arranged series of arguments meant to exco-

9. Reindel 1.288.6–28.
10. Reindel 1.289 1–3 / 13–15.
11. Reindel 1:289 16–19
12. Reindel 1 297 16–24 The unequivocal claim that confessions heard in these circumstances are invalid has scandalized later readers. See Cavigioli, "De sententia s. Petri Damiani circa absolutionem," pp 35–39.

riate the vice and its defenders by all available means. The booklet's emphasis would seem to fall on characterizing types of the vice and their consequences in other sins, on refuting specific passages in the penitentials, and on showing how to make effective exhortations or condemnations. This reading of the structure is not implausible, but also not fully helpful in seeing how the treatise works. It is more helpful to reconstruct the booklet as a therapeutic address to the concealed Sodomite, who must be persuaded without being identified, since he must be persuaded to identify himself. The booklet aims to produce self-judgment.

The *Book* is framed by direct speech to the pope, who is addressed not only in the work's salutation, but in opening and closing passages.[13] The frame is closed quite explicitly: "Now let us return to you, most blessed pope, at the end of this little work." Peter wants to persuade the pope to suppress the vice by punishing those who practice it with penances and, what is more important, with deposition from clerical status and ecclesiastical office. The persuasion employs a number of styles of argument, some of them obtrusive. In the opening, for example, Peter warns that delay in papal action will bring about divine intervention—or, at least, will allow the vice to grow so much that it will be unstoppable by human agency.[14] At the end, Peter offers the pope the reward of historical fame.[15] In both passages, he flatters the pope's discernment and erudition.[16] Between these direct addresses and their transparent stratagems the rhetorical gaze of the booklet is refracted.

Near the beginning, as if with a slight turn of the head, Peter begins to speak past the pope to bishops who have been less than rigorous in pursuing the vice. These "more humane" church leaders have refused to depose from clerical office those guilty of the lesser forms of the Sodomitic vice.[17] Peter's stated aim is to show that this ill-conceived leniency is contradicted both by reason and by the canonical sanctions of the church Fathers, by which he means both the approved theological writers and legally binding papal or conciliar actions. The arguments laid out for the pope serve simul-

---

13 Reindel 1 287 4–5, "sacris auribus", 287.18, "vobis"; 289.4–5, "in maiestatis vestrae praesentia", 329.6, "papa beatissime"; 329.9, "clementia vestra", 329 10, "vobis notissima"; 329 14, "solam profunditatis vestre peritiam", 329 21, "beatitudo vestra"; 329.28, "auctoritatis vestre lucerna"; 330.1–2, "reverentissime pater" and "tempore apostolatus vestri."

14 Reindel 1·287 3–4, "quod divini furoris gladius in multorum perniciem immaniter crassaturus impendet", 287 16–17, "effrenata nequitia cum restringi voluerit, a cursus sui impetu desistere nequeat"

15. Reindel 1 330 1–3

16. Reindel 1:286.24–29, 329 8–17

17 Reindel 1 233 9–13

taneously to convince other bishops who will inevitably read his very public letter. But Peter does not continue long to address just the pope and his brother bishops. After presenting arguments by way of amplifying exegesis of passages from the Old Testament and Paul, and after having cited a passage from Gregory the Great, Peter breaks out into exclamations on the horrors of this vice.[18] Engaging in *luxuria* with another man is worse, he concludes, than sinning with a beast. Bestiality brings damnation only to oneself, not to another.

Why does Peter allow his authorial voice to break with passion here? It is just here that Peter begins to speak to his true addressee, the practitioner of Sodomitic vice. The address is perfectly clear a few lines later: "Now I come face to face with you, Sodomite, whoever you are."[19] This encounter occurs at the rhetorical center of the treatise. The principal addressee of the *Book of Gomorrah* is not the pope, not overly lenient hierarchs, but an inhabitant of Sodom. Addresses to him punctuate the rest of the booklet. He is sometimes cursed, sometimes caressed.[20] Indeed, Peter will switch from compassion to imprecation in the course of a few lines.[21] If he lays out a number of arguments that treat the Sodomite in the third person, as an object rather than an addressee, he will often enough pause in them to invite the Sodomite's attention or to forestall his likely counter arguments.[22]

Peter must address the pope on the rhetorical presupposition that the pope is opposed to the sin being discussed and lacks only arguments or precedents for treating it with the required rigor. He can suppose otherwise about bishops. They appear in the third person, as intended but unspecified recipients of the booklet. If their eavesdropping is not problematic, their moral character is. Peter begins by supposing them lenient; he goes on to charge that they are idle and worse.[23] They must fear that they will have a share in the Sodomites' guilt.[24] Moreover, at least some of the bishops are themselves Sodomites. They engage in unnatural, incestuous acts with their spiritual children, with men they have brought over from the world into the monastery or men they have ordained to the clergy. What is more troubling for the construction of Peter's booklet, these Sodomitic hierarchs are unidentifiable. The booklet addresses a higher clergy on the correction

18. Reindel 1:294 22–297.3
19 Reindel 1·298 8.
20. Reindel 1 316 6, "dampnabiles sodomitae"; 311 20 and 312.22, "infelix anima."
21. As from "miser" (Reindel 1·313.3) to "homo effeminate" (313.14) and then back to "infelix anima" (313.33).
22. For example, Reindel 1:308.12, "Hic sodomita studiose perpendat"
23. Reindel 1·294 16: "desides clericorum sacerdotumque rectores"
24. Reindel 1 294 17.

and punishment of a vice that is practiced secretly by an unknown number of its members.

Peter Damian fears a church of Sodom within the church of God. He suspects or infers the operation of a shadow hierarchy with its own means of governance and of recruitment. Sodomitic bishops protect Sodomitic priests. The priests in turn corrupt those whom they have baptized or heard in confession. The threatening images of Peter's prologue are now specified. The threat posed by Sodomy to the church is a lethal one. Sodomy attacks the church by attacking the clergy, who seem particularly susceptible to it. Once in the clergy, the vice conceals itself behind the bland face of piety or the hypocritical face of condemnation.

Peter's first address to the Sodomite shows the extent of the danger: "Sodomite, whoever you are." The qualification is repeated twice in the following chapters; once it is just by itself the form of address.[25] "Whoever you are" names the Sodomite in some special way. It means not just "whatever your rank or office," but also "wherever it is you hide." Peter acknowledges in the phrase that he cannot know who among his official readers will be guilty of the very sin he enjoins them to punish. He must deploy a range of arguments in the effort to catch out as many of his hidden opponents as he can. So Peter must rely not only on the authority of Scriptures or church law, but on the general appeal to reason. Since the individual Sodomite hides, Peter brings out the most universal traps, the traps of rudimentary logic.

There is as well the universal threat of shame. The Sodomite comes forward to be addressed in Peter's booklet only after all of his sins have been catalogued. The reader has learned not only that there are four types of Sodomitic activity, but also that such activity sometimes occurs between religious superiors and their subjects, between confessors and their penitents. The reader is meant to be shocked—and if a Sodomite, ashamed. The Sodomite appears in the middle of the discussion of confessional abuses because the Sodomite needs to be shamed into becoming an authentic penitent. How to bring this about? By combining sweetness and sternness, by mixing third-person refutation with direct personal address that is alternately aggressive and gentle. The "Sodomite" is only ironically styled a "good man"; he is, literally, "damnable." But he is also an "unhappy" or "miserable" soul, a fellow "human being" (*homo*), and, at the end, a "beloved brother."[26] The cycle of address attempts to turn the Sodomite round

25. Reindel 1:303.22, "quicumque es"; 325.16, "karissime frater, quisquis es."

26 Reindel 1:301.20, "o bone vir sodomita", 316.6, "o dampnabiles sodomitae", 314.1, "o miserabilis anima", 322 1, "o homo", 325 16, "karissime frater, quisquis es."

towards repentance, even when repentance requires him to surrender his office or his orders.

Peter's more colorful calls for repentance depict the horrors of Sodomy and the blessings of chastity. The tyranny of the "most pestilent queen of the Sodomites" is drawn in a row of antitheses. "She humiliates in the church, condemns in court; she dirties in secret, dishonors in public; she chews the conscience like worms, consumes flesh like fire; [the Sodomite] wants to fulfill his pleasure, but fears to be among others, to go out in public, to be known by men." [27] This "queen" is in reality a poisonous snake that destroys the soul's powers, a deadly disease (*pestis*) that ends by undoing each of the virtues, both theological and cardinal. In contrast, the reward for chastity is not only to join the household of God, but to have first place in it. [28] The prospect of this exalted prize should be held always in front of one's eyes, should be turned over in the mind. [29] It should always be contrasted with the hellish life of concealment--of what the modern reader must call "the closet." Peter knows well that the vice requires, especially in clerical circles, a lifetime of deception and disguise. He hopes by magnifying the pains of secrecy, the ever-gnawing fears of exposure, to force the Sodomite out.

These are a few of the rhetorical colors in Peter's address to the Sodomite. The address depends still, and to an important extent, on the disputative exegesis of texts. Peter spends much energy quoting texts, then expounding them in detail. He guides his readers through difficult passages, explains context and legal force, links one locus to another for more clarity. His principal address to the Sodomite is an address through and about books.

DISPUTING BOOKS

The *Book of Gomorrah* presents itself as a seamless fabric woven from its author's learning. The presentation is deceiving. If Peter is careful in citing his remote authorities, he is completely silent about immediate sources. But his booklet is in many ways just a collection of well-known texts on sexual matters. It is a text written out of other texts, caught up in their network, supported and made complicated by them.

Peter's relation to textual traditions appears at once in the booklet's body. The fourfold classification of the "criminal wickedness" (*nequitia*

27. Reindel 1:310 14–17.
28. Reindel 1:324.9–325.15.
29. Reindel 1:324 9–10, "promissa castitati praemia incessanter aspicias", 325.10–11, "in mente nostra omnia studio revolvendum."

scelera) issues from a long line of previous texts. The nearest antecedent seems to be the *Decretum* attributed to Burchard of Worms, originally composed in or shortly after the year of Peter's birth.[30] The nineteenth book of the *Decretum*, called the *Corrector* or *Physician*, is a guide for confessors. It contains, among many other directives, a list of questions supposedly to be used in jogging the penitent's memory. The questions are in fact a lengthy interrogation of the penitent's way of life. After questions on homicide, perjury, false oaths, and theft, the interrogation turns to what we would consider sexual matters. The first is adultery, the second fornication, that is, sexual relations outside of marriage and with protected classes of women.[31] There then comes a section on "abuse of conjugal union" (*conjugium*). The questions concern copulation in prohibited postures ("from behind, in the canine manner") or during prohibited times (menstruation, late pregnancy, visible pregnancy, on Sunday, during Lent).[32] After other questions about bearing false witness, practicing magic, sacrilege, contempt for fasting, and failure to practice religion, Burchard returns to the earlier topics for more careful probing.

These supplemental sections contain two further sets of questions on fornication. The second set asks, "Did you commit fornication as the Sodomites did, so that you put your penis (*virgam*) in the back of a man and in the rear parts (*in masculi terga et in post[e]riora*), so that you copulate with him in the Sodomitic manner?"[33] Three different penances are assigned, depending on whether the penitent has a wife, does this habitually, or does it with his blood brother. Then come the next three questions:

> Whether you made fornication with a man between the hips (*coxas*), as some are accustomed to do, I mean, that you put your male member between the hips of another, and by agitating it pour out seed? . . .
>
> Did you make fornication, as some are accustomed to do, I mean that you take the shameful part (*veretrum*) of another in your hand, and he yours in his, and thus alternately moving the shameful parts with your hands, so that by that pleasure you eject seed from yourself? . . .
>
> Did you make fornication with yourself alone, as some are accustomed to do, I mean that you yourself took your manly member in your hand, and so slide your foreskin (*praeputium*), and move [it] with your own hand so as by delight to eject seed from yourself?[34]

30 See the summary of evidence in Ryan, *Saint Peter Damiani and His Canonical Sources,* pp 28–31, nos (15)–(25) The redactional history of the *Decretum* is complicated, but it need not be mastered in order to read Peter Damian I will speak of it here as if it were written entirely by Burchard
31 Burchard of Worms *Decretum* 19.5 (Migne *PL* 140 957–959)
32. Burchard of Worms *Decretum* 19.5 (Migne *PL* 140 959–960)
33 Burchard of Worms *Decretum* 19.5 (Migne *PL* 140 967–968)
34 Burchard of Worms *Decretum* 19 5 (Migne *PL* 140 968)

These four questions treat, in reverse order, Peter Damian's four species of Sodomitic vice. Note at once some differences. First, Burchard invokes Sodom only in the first question, with regard to anal intercourse. Moreover, Burchard is more specific about the motions involved, as he uses a less refined vocabulary.[35] Third, Burchard twice mentions pleasure as the cause of ejaculation; Peter omits any mention of pleasure altogether in this listing. Fourth, finally, Burchard's interrogatory has necessarily the immediacy of the singular second person; Peter speaks of third parties in the plural. These differences suggest that Peter is distancing himself from the sins and even from ordinary pastoral involvement with particular cases.

Of course, Burchard's *Decretum* is not the only antecedent, and so differences from it cannot be seen as direct revisions. There are several families of northern Italian penitentials, written a century before Burchard, that recognize at least these many kinds of genital sin. Those penitentials depend in turn on older compilations. To take one example, the so-called first Vallicella penitential, composed in northern Italy at the end of the ninth century or in the first half of the tenth, depends directly on another penitential called "Merseburg a."[36] The latter distinguishes "fornicating as do the Sodomites" or "doing the Sodomite thing" (*facere sodomitam*), men fornicating "between the thighs" (*inter femora*), and boys or men fornicating "between the legs" (*inter crura*), as well as ejaculations into the mouth or in various circumstances of self-pollution.[37] But each of these regulations comes in turn from earlier sources.[38] The canons on intracrural or intrafemoral copulation, for example, descend from the so-called *Excarpsus Cummeani*, a digest of a famous Irish penitential attributed to Cummean.[39] The canons are also echoed in other works of Italian origin. Himself the product of northern Italian schools, Peter need not have gone far to find a dozen texts.

Peter learns from them not just distinctions among types of sins, but which authorities are to be used in condemning. Many pertinent passages of Scripture would have been known by any learned cleric from patristic and earlier medieval exegesis, but the authoritative nonscriptural sources

35 Consider the following pairs, with Burchard's phrase first, Peter's second: *intra coxas, inter femora, virile membrum* or *veretrum, virilia, veretrum commoveritis, virilia contrectantes, duceres praeputium commoveres, polluunt*

36. Hagele, *Das Paenitentiale Vallicellianum I*, pp. 93, 99.

37. See, respectively, canons 4 and 145, 154 (compare 56), 155, 56 and 153, 57/59 and 142 of the Merseburg penitential, in Schmitz, *Die Bußbucher und das kanonische Bußverfahren*, 2:359–368.

38. See the table of sources in Hagele, *Das Paenitentiale Vallicellianum I*, pp. 65–68.

39. *Excarpsus Cummeani* 4.2–7, in Schmitz, *Die Bußbucher und das kanonische Bußverfahren*, pp. 608–609

could just as easily have been garnered from earlier texts. For example, the texts that Peter quotes from the Council of Ancyra are found in a number of earlier collections, including Burchard.[40] Peter's quotation of "Basil" derives from Burchard, at the least; of Syricius, from Burchard and an earlier collection.[41] Peter draws his authorities not so much from a fresh reading of the original sources as from generations of predecessor texts.

This dependence is not easy for Peter. The Sodomites have their books as well, their precedents among the penitentials. Indeed, the most closely argued section of Peter's booklet is the refutation of the penitential canons on which the Sodomites rely. He has multiple arguments against these texts. Their authors are unknown or uncertain, whereas Peter can provide contrary texts of clear authorship and authority.[42] What is more important, the penitentials cited by the Sodomites are self-contradictory and irrational. They are convicted not only by contrary authorities, but by "reason," by the "things themselves," by the "clear reasoning of arguments."[43] The unbiased reader will reject their specious canons as unnatural monsters: "like some chimerical monster it roars terribly in the guise of a menacing lion, then *baahs* humbly like a wretched little she-goat."[44] They are as unnatural, as unconvincing, as the crimes they condone. They must be rejected as interpolations, as the fabrications of sinful ingenuity.

Peter's labor in these passages can be seen in one way as the attempt to establish his reading of the penitentials against a competing reading. He does this by systematizing the canonical sources and using principles of consistency to rule out discordant canons. Such exegetical activity characterizes the study of canon law that preceded Peter in the Italian schools and would go on beyond him to more famous triumphs, the masterpieces of Irnerius and Gratian. If this labor of systematization always tacitly admits that the received texts are more discordant than one would like, it quickly drowns out the admission in a striking concord. When the Sodomites try to argue from the very discord of the penitentials, they set themselves against rudimentary rules of reason, against reason itself.

Yet Peter's appeal to reason is something more than the application of new techniques for legal codification. It is, I think, a claim on the Sodomite—a curious claim, and one not fully concordant with others of Peter's

40 See the source apparatus at Reindel 1:305, note 33, and 307, note 34, to which compare Kottje, *Die Bußbucher Halitgars von Cambrai und des Hrabanus Maurus*, p 262

41. Reindel 1, p. 308, note 36, and p 309, note 39.

42. Reindel 1 304.14–305 5

43. Reindel 1·289 3, "rationi contrarium"; 301.4, "rebus"; 305 3–4, "perspicua argumentorum ratione"

44 Reindel 1 302 30–303 1

rhetorical effects. On the one hand, Peter seems to proceed against the Sodomites by appealing to their sense of what is rational in exegesis and moral regulation. On the other hand, Peter has already likened their blindness to a divinely inflicted inward clouding.[45] He has interpreted Paul as teaching that God abandons those guilty of same-sex copulation to a "reprobate sense" by which they entirely mistake the seriousness of their actions.[46] Peter will go on to place the Sodomites among demoniacs. Those who "hand over their flesh to demons by such a fetid exchange, against the law of nature, against the order of human reason" are indeed rightly likened to the possessed.[47] How can those of "reprobate sense" be convinced by appeals to consistency in exegesis or to an intuition of proper ranking in the punishment of sins? What can Peter hope to accomplish by arguing with demoniacs?

An obvious answer would be that Peter is primarily interested not in the interpretation of canons, but in the interpretation of the Christian Scriptures. He addresses the Sodomites with the full force of scriptural condemnation: the horror of divine fire at Sodom, the executions prescribed by Leviticus, the trumpet call of Paul's excoriation in Romans.[48] Indeed, Peter strengthens the scriptural passages by taking them most literally. While the penitential tradition reads the death penalty metaphorically, Peter gives no hint of any other than a literal reading.[49] But his booklet rests on more than an appeal to the letter of Scripture. It spends too many lines of arguments against the Sodomite. Beyond the arguments about how to read the penitential canons, there are arguments from animal behavior and challenges to same-sex desire. The "miserable" Sodomite is so blinded by the fury of self-indulgence (*luxuriae rabies*) that he does what no buck, ram, stallion, bull, or even ass would do.[50] And what kind of desire can this be? Every natural desire seeks to find outside what it does not find within. Every natural desire is desire for difference. What can one man find in another that he cannot find in himself? "If then you have a craving for the feel of male flesh, turn your hand to yourself and know that whatever you do not find in yourself, you will seek for vainly in another [man's] body."[51] Peter

45. Reindel 1:293.12, "in tenebras interiores."
46. Reindel 1:293.20–22
47. Reindel 1·307.10–12
48. Reindel 1:289.10–12 / 16–17, 292.8.
49. Reindel 1:290 7–8 / 16–17 / 19 / 21, "per vetustae legis sententiam morte mulatur" and "quem dignum morte crimen abiecerat," "in mortalis culpae baratrum," "quod sine dubio mortale crimen est."
50. Reindel 1:313.5–13.
51. Reindel 1:313.20–22.

says all of this in a plea to the Sodomite, a plea that is much more than
proof texting from Scripture. Then he ends the plea, again, by announcing
that the Sodomite's sin has made him the "prey of demons."[52]

Peter argues from reason in a booklet that draws from a number of other
books, from the Christian Scriptures down to the latest redactions of the
penitentials. He argues for the rational reading of these books, and he supplements their lessons with lessons drawn by reason from the natures of
things—of animals, of bodies, of desire. Peter's reasonableness is not in
the end his last hope of appeal to the Sodomite. Reason is not for him, as
it will be for Thomas Aquinas, the last resort in arguments with interlocu-
tors who do not accept the authority of any common text.[53] It is, rather, the
only safe vantage from which Peter can encounter the Sodomite, encounter
the distortion of texts, the rupturing of animal nature, and the reversal of
desire. An erudite reason safeguards Peter's authorial position. He means
to emphasize the agreement of reason and Scripture by making bookishness
into reasonableness.

The dangers to his position are several. First, there is the question of
how Peter knows what he must describe. Burchard in *Decretum* 19 can
claim to know the practices of sinners both from the experience of the
confessional and from the teaching of his predecessors. Peter is not writing
a confessor's questionnaire, and he is not forthcoming about his penitential
sources. He must then present himself as a well-informed reasoner, as
someone who can speak about the kinds of Sodomitic vice from the distance of learned deduction. He must at all costs forestall the suspicion that
he has been himself an invisible Sodomite. Second, there is the danger to
Peter's authorship presented by any attempt to naturalize or universalize
the Sodomite's desire. Nothing can be permitted to make Sodomitic vice
seem possible as a desire, much less to make it seem permissible. Hence,
Peter must invoke the most evident principles of reason, as well as the easy
observation of animal life, to argue the irrationality and irregularity of
same-sex desire. Every compassionate plea must be balanced by disgusted
rejection. Of course the use of reason does not resolve these difficulties,
because in speaking reasonably to the Sodomite Peter humanizes him, ac-
credits him as a reasonable interlocutor. Reasoning is integral to human
nature. What is Sodomitic vice in relation to reason? If it corrupts reason, it
too would seem to function at the depth of nature. More important, Peter's
oscillation in addressing the Sodomite, his viewing the Sodomite alter-

52 Reindel 1 313 23
53 Thomas Aquinas *Summa "contra Gentiles"* 1 2

PETER DAMIAN / 57

nately as reasoner and as demoniac, as miserable brother and more-than-bestial madman, must raise questions about the kind of identity asserted in naming someone a "Sodomite."

The Sodomitic identity is not principally medical or legal, though medical and legal considerations attach to it.[54] Being a Sodomite is also not an identity in ways that might occur to a modern reader. For Peter Damian, it does not seem to go along with certain styles of dress or deportment. It is associated with effeminacy, though chiefly in the sense that the Sodomite is unmanned, is womanish, in seeking for completion in men.[55] Being a Sodomite does entail a taste for soft satisfactions, but so does every form of *luxuria*. Matters are most complicated in Peter Damian with regard to whether the identity can be changed. Clearly, the hortatory structure of the *Book of Gomorrah* supposes that the Sodomite can be reformed by exhortation. At the same time, its pessimistic analogies between the Sodomite and the demoniac suggest that reformation would be miraculous. Moreover, the urgent recommendation that all persons guilty of Sodomy be deposed from office and defrocked implies that there is something ineradicable in the condition or its effects. What is more, Peter Damian insists that it is a crime meriting punishment by death. It is, in that way, a sin from which there is no return in this life. The Sodomite is deaf in the way the dead are, and he dwells already in the house of the dead.[56] For Peter Damian, then, it is too simple to argue that a Sodomite is not a fixed sort of human being because he can always change himself by reforming his ways.

Any exhortation or therapy that will succeed against Sodomy must be

54. Medical images occur throughout. Sodomy is likened to the cause of plagues (Reindel 1:287.5, "virus plagarum"; 307.17, "invasi pectoris tartarum virus") or simply a plague (312 10 / 13, glossing Jer 14:17), to a tumorous growth (287.7, "cancer"), to a wound or wounded member (288.19, 294.13, "vulnus"), a raging contagion (288 2, 289.2, 321.22, "contagio," and at 309.8 in the quotation from Syricius), an aggressive contagious disease (294.15, "peremptoria pestes," to which compare 314.14, 318.7, 320.8, 325.17, 328 15), and leprosy (297.16, 315 2 / 7 / 17). What is more striking, Peter Damian explicitly recalls "the teaching of doctors" (*dicta physicorum*) in arguing that semen is generated from blood. As the wind changes seawater into foam, so the handling of the genitals excites blood into the basic physiological component, the *humor*, of semen (318.2–6). The physical causality justifies a reversal in scriptural exegesis some mentions of blood can be construed as references to semen.

55 Consider the following allusions to gender expectations: Reindel 1·294 28, "Quis de clerico fecit pelicem, de masculo mulierem?"; 313.13–15, "vir evirate . homo effeminate"; 315 3–4, "virilis vite fortia facta relinquere et femineae conversationis illecebrosam mollitiem exhibere" There are also several calls to act "like a man": 320 8–9, "lenocinantem libidinis lasciviam viriliter edomare"; 322.16 / 24, "viriliter extrahat in vires collige, viriliter execute." Following Leviticus, Peter routinely characterizes intrafemoral copulation as "fornication in the feminine manner," but I take him to mean "as one would with a woman" He is certainly not suggesting that intrafemoral copulation is a permissible form of heterosexual intercourse.

56 Reindel 1:294.10, 311 10–11 / 19, glossing Lam 1 20.

more tenacious and more radical than the sin itself. It must be a school somehow beyond this life, a cure (the image is Peter's) conducted on the other side of capital punishment. In many other contexts, Peter Damian describes the monastery and especially the hermitage as that kind of school. A cluster of hermit's cells is an otherworldly place of repentance and reeducation. One goes there to suffer for past sins and to prepare for life with the angels. Is the Sodomite permitted to enroll in these desert schools? Does the prohibition against seeking church office or ordination apply as well to entry into eremitical life? The questions can be reversed: Where are monks and hermits in the argument of the *Liber Gomorrhianus*?

DANGEROUS SOLITUDE

Monks are mentioned in the *Liber* very few times.[57] The first mention comes just after the appearance of the Sodomite himself.[58] Monks are introduced in an argument by analogy: The Sodomite would not deny that a male monk who "was experienced" (*periclitatus fuerit*) with a consecrated woman should be removed from his holy order. Hence the Sodomite cannot consistently deny that Sodomites should be deposed from ecclesiastical office. But when Peter rehearses this conclusion a few lines later, male monks appear both as violators of female monks and as the victims of sexual domination by other men, by certain "prostitutors of monks."[59]

The angelic monk as victim of sexual violence must call to mind the angels in the scriptural story of Sodom. There are several connections. Peter Damian insists in many places that monks and especially hermits lead already an anticipation of angelic life.[60] Angels and hermits are easily exchanged in spiritual exegesis. Second, the two angels sent to Lot are likened by Peter Damian to the two persons of the Trinity most essentially described by masculine relation—I mean the Father and the Son. The superior of an eremitical community is father to his spiritual sons. So too is the confessor to his penitent or the professed monk to the novice apprenticed under him.[61] Hermits are bound together in multiple relations of paternity and filiation, just as were the angels in Sodom. Finally, the violence that

---

57. Peter Damian does speak of monks some eight times when paraphrasing the inconsistent penitentials; see Reindel 1:300.5 / 9 / 11, 301 6 / 17 (twice) / 28 / 31. But these are not mentions made in his own voice

58. Reindel 1·298.8–29

59. Reindel 1.298 28.

60. See Leclercq, *Otia monastica*

61. Compare Reindel 1:299.15–16.

contemporary Sodomites want to work on their spiritual children and the body of the church is exactly the violence that the scriptural Sodomites wanted to work on the angels.[62] Peter Damian feigns reticence at first about what happened within the walls of Sodom.[63] But he begins soon enough to speak of the threats to the angels. He then emphasizes quite graphically the ways in which Sodomitic ambition is like trying to penetrate a wall not meant to be breached.[64] The likeness to anal rape is not far to seek. If male monks can figure in the penitentials as violators of women, they inhabit Peter Damian's Sodom only as objects of violation. They are angels surrounded by demons intent on penetration.

Such is Peter Damian's explicit description of the border between Sodom and the cells of hermits. The description omits much. Peter Damian knows clearly that the cell is the site of extraordinary trials for the flesh. He appropriates elsewhere Cassian's teaching on the dangers in solitude for chastity.[65] What is more striking, and perhaps more calculated, Peter Damian elsewhere describes his own solitary obsession with fantasies of a clerk's concubine watched long ago during his days in Parma.[66] The description is strategic so far as it diverts attention from the exclusively masculine setting of eremitical life. The absence of women is not hard to understand if one remembers the eremitical context. The cell is also the site of extraordinary intimacy between men. After all, Peter Damian's community trains its new members by placing each of them in the cell of another monk. These two men must not only live together in a small space, in conditions that are likened to nudity; they must discuss the most private details of life in the body and share the practice of physical disciplines that appall most modern readers by what seems their violent masochism.[67] The dangers of this kind of intimacy had not been ignored in the authoritative writings of the monastic traditions. There are numerous discussions of sexual activity pro-

---

62. Reindel 1:293.10

63 Reindel 1:289.10–12.

64 Reindel 1:293.37–294.8.

65 For example, *Epist.* 50 (Reindel 2:84.11–15, 111.19–113 5, 116.13–117.5).

66. Peter Damian *Epist.* 70 (Reindel 2:320 7–321.8). The passage has figured prominently in attempts to fix the chronology of Peter Damian's life; see Little, "The Personal Development of Peter Damian," pp. 319–320. Elsewhere Peter Damian describes in parallel his experiences of anger and *luxuria*, but without specifying the object of the latter. See *Epist* 80 (Reindel 2:415.24–416 20).

67. On two monks living in the same cell, see *Epist* 18 (Reindel 1 173 23–24) = *Epist* 50 (2·95 1–2), to which add the rule about one being superior to the other (2:108 10–14); on allowing novices and their cell-mate teachers (*institutores*) to speak, 1:174 8–9 = 2:97.2–3, on the conditions of undress in the cell, 1:174.12–13 = 2.97.19–20 For a survey of Peter Damian's teaching on physical "discipline," see Leclercq, *Témoins de la spiritualité occidentale*, pp. 112–125

voked by the conditions of the cell, in authors explicitly approved by Peter Damian.[68] Peter Damian writes elsewhere of the special difficulties of chastity for the young.[69] More important, related discussions appear in the very penitentials that Peter Damian approves. He reads there cases of crimes in shared quarters, long-term prescriptions against solitary journeying for those who have committed these crimes, and so on.[70]

Peter Damian reads these texts, but he omits them from the arguments and exhortations of the *Book of Gomorrah*. The single remnant of them comes at the booklet's second significant mention of monks. The mention is a moral tale, an *exemplum*—and a very curious one. There was a hermit, Peter Damian tells, who was tricked by the devil into thinking that semen was no different from any other bodily superfluity.[71] Just as he blew his nose when congested, so the monk masturbated whenever he felt the tickle of desire. On his death, the hermit was seized by demons in full view of his companion (*socius*). The companion, knowing the man's practice of the virtues but not his sexual crime, despaired that anyone could attain salvation. An angel stood by to explain that the departed hermit had befouled all of his good deeds by the unrepented sin of uncleanness. The example of this wretched hermit is meant to teach the superlative seriousness of masturbation. It carries other lessons as well. First, it establishes that some hermits are Sodomites, if only by misapprehension. It reveals, second, that the conditions of eremitical life permit the concealment of Sodomy: His companion did not so much as suspect his crime, and so was cast into despair. Third, most surprisingly, the story suggests that a long life of ascesis is inadequate to forestall rudimentary deceptions about Sodomy.

The borders of Sodom and of the hermitages overlap. Some hermits are

---

68 For a collection of Latin passages from authoritative authors, see Espejo Muriel, *El deseo negado*, pp. 217–234 The passages from the lives of the desert fathers and John Cassian are particularly important, since Peter Damian incorporates both by reference into one of his "rules" for eremitical life, *Epist* 50 (2 111 10), "quicquid in vita patrum, quicquid in institutis sive collationibus [scil Cassiani] dictum, huic competere disciplinae perpendimus."

69 For example, *Epist* 123 (Reindel 3·400 14–402 20).

70 For example, the penitentials on Sodomitic vice have as one refrain the need to separate the two parties and to prevent them from ever sleeping with someone else. See *Penitential of Columban* B 3 (Bieler, p 100, line 3), *Penitential of ps-Theodore* 13 2 (Wasserschleben, p 598), *Capitula iudiciorum* 7 1 (Schmitz, *Die Bußbucher und das kanonische Bußverfahren*, p. 222), *Burgundian Penitential* 4 (Schmitz, p 320), *Bobbio Penitential* 3 (Schmitz, p. 323), *Paris Penitential* 37 (Schmitz, p 329), *St Hubert Penitential* 4 (Schmitz, p 333), *Fleury Penitential* 4 (Schmitz, p 341), *St Gall Penitential* 14 (Schmitz, p 347), *Vienna Penitential* 4 (Schmitz, p 351), *Merseburg Penitential* 4 and 145 (Schmitz, pp 359, 367), and *Excarpsus of Cummean* 4 2 (Schmitz, p 608)

71 Reindel 1 319 3–12

Sodomites, at least to the first degree of Sodomy. They share with Sodomites in the larger church a disturbing hiddenness, a gift for concealment. And they do lie concealed in several passages of the booklet, most obviously in the penultimate section of Peter Damian's self-justification. He imagines an objector to his sharp tone. The objector is characterized as someone with an overly sensitive conscience who counts Peter a traitor to his brothers, an informer (delator) against them.[72] The brothers might be Christians or clerics generally, and Peter must intend to be read as referring to them in general. But at the time of the writing, he had been at Fonte Avellana for at least fifteen years and his travels away from it had consisted mainly of stays in other monastic or eremitical communities. Moreover, whatever his actual itineraries, he speaks as one who dwells far from the curia in the remoteness of the hermitage.[73] On whose sins might he be reporting? On whom could he be spying, on whom informing as delator? The language of his exculpation suggests that Peter has indeed been watching the progress of this sin. He is called upon to correct just because he has seen his brother sinning.[74] He is called to write invectives against Sodomites because they are now so bold in their freedom. If they had been as evident in patristic times, the church Fathers would have filled codices with their condemnation.[75] This excuse itself contains a curious concession. The sins of Sodom have grown with the church itself. God's punishment of the city seems to have been notably ineffective in stopping them. So too have the sacraments and preachings of the church. The long Christianization of Italy has only allowed Sodomy to become more visible within the church. It must be expected, if not admitted, that Sodomy has spread to every corner of the church, including its monasteries.

These remarks remind the reader of a striking moment earlier on. Just after a praise of those who make themselves eunuchs by the practice of chastity, Peter speaks to the Sodomite: "beloved brother, whoever you are."[76] Context restricts the address. The "beloved brother" stands near or in the household of hermit-eunuchs, alongside or amid the white-robed choirs of virgins. The Sodomite is Peter Damian's brother both in a general

72. Reindel 1 325 30, "cui conscientia minime suffragante"; 326 1, "proditorem delatoremque fraterni criminis"

73. For example, Reindel 1 329 6–18, with its description as if from outside of a circle of advisors around the pope.

74 Reindel 1 326 7, "Si videris fratrem tuum inique agentem et non corripueris eum"

75. Reindel 1:328 14–16.

76. Reindel 1 325 16, "karissime frater, quisquis est" The eunuchs appear earlier in the chapter, in a gloss on Isa 56·4–5 (see 324 15–19)

and in a quite specific sense: he is not just a Christian, he is sometimes or often a fellow monk. The fraternal compassion that makes Peter weep is also a domestic one; the fraternal good that he seeks in polemic is the good of his own house.[77]

The coextension of parts of Sodom and Fonte Avellana disrupts the imaginary topography of Peter Damian's booklet in various ways.[78] Most literally it confuses a set of topographical images that have been built up through the exhortation. The burnt cities of the plain have been contrasted again and again with happier cities. First, with the city of one's home: the vice of the Sodomites tears down the walls of the *patria* in order to rebuild Sodom itself.[79] It is entirely appropriate then that the modern Sodomite be exiled from home.[80] The sin imported from Sodom brings destruction as surely as barbarians let into the city, as unbelievers in the earthly Jerusalem.[81] Next, obviously, Sodom is contrasted with the heavenly city. The Sodomite will never cross the threshold of that blessed place: he is exiled from it to the house of death.[82] His homecoming from the one to the other is possible only by repentance and ascetical practices.[83] Third, there is the microcosmic city of the Sodomite's soul. This city is much nobler than any fortified tower, any temple made by hands, any public treasures.[84] The inward city is ruined by the sin of the Sodomites. It is ruined in some sense along with Sodom itself. Peter regularly threatens the vicious with details of their divine punishment.[85] The superb intensity of the punishment makes one think that the sin was worse even than blasphemy.[86] But the firestorm is not only a past destruction or a future judgment. It is enacted in the present over the inward city.[87] The sulfurous cinders rain down already within the Sodomite, in part as warning, in part as ineluctable consequence of his vice. If he cannot stay out of the accursed city altogether, as Abraham

77 Respectively, Reindel 1.314.8–9, "eo amarioribus fraternae compassionis est fletibus deploranda", and 328 18, "non obprobium sed provectum potius fraternae salutis inquiro"
78 For other examples of Peter Damian's ingenuity with spiritual topography, see Phipps, "Romuald—Model Hermit," pp 75–77.
79. Reindel 1·309 4–310 2.
80 Reindel 1 311 8.
81. Reindel 1 310.31–311 1, for the barbarians; 311.1–4, for the earthly Jerusalem, glossing Lam 1.10
82. Respectively, Reindel 1 324 6–8 and 311.10–11, 19, glossing Lam 1:10
83 Reindel 1 324 6–8
84 Reindel 1 311 25–312 5 ff Note that Peter Damian here condescends in some way to Jeremiah, placing his own lamentation higher in virtue of its object
85 Contrast the assumed reticence of Reindel 1 289 10 ff with such passages as 317 20–23 or 321 6–11
86. Reindel 1 328 8–10
87 Reindel 1 312 13–14.

did, he should flee from it with Lot as quickly as possible.[88] But this is where the geographical images become incoherent. There is no strict separation between Sodom and the hermitage, hence no linear path from one to the other. What is it to flee from a city that one is? And how can one even begin to learn how to flee if therapeutic practices are taught only much nearer the heavenly city, by someone who has already escaped from the charnel house? And don't both the Sodomite and the hermit find themselves in exile from the earthly *patria*, and only ambiguously en route to the heavenly one?

Here everything depends on the exact diagnosis of the condition and causality of the Sodomite's vice. It is, according both to Peter and the growing moral tradition of the Latin church, a form of *luxuria*. *Luxuria* is best described for Peter by metaphors of furious, irrational force. *Luxuria* is a flame, a flammable mixture, as well as a raving madness.[89] Its effect is willful denial of realities by onrushing desire.[90] Augustine's name for disordered desire, *libido*, is in fact Peter Damian's second term of precise description. *Libido* too is a raging fire, as it is madness, poison, and infection.[91] But it is more exactly motive force, *impetus*, that deceives its subject by a pimping wantonness.[92] *Libido* is like a physical force endowed with a rhetorical capacity. It presents the physical pleasure of a single organ, the moment's pleasure of ejaculation, as sufficiently attractive to set aside all the rest.[93] The mad pull of unsubordinated desire has become somehow articulate.

One can imagine that this view of Sodomitic desire as pimping propulsion, as a pander with the cunning of madness, would justify Peter Damian's choice of rhetorical counterstrategies. He will meet the sophistry of fevered desire with the true rhetoric of restored reason. He will contest the sales pitch of Sodom with a frank representation of contrary and much more substantial goods. He will attack the pimp directly by showing that what he wants to sell is not worth buying—is ugly, diseased. Peter Damian certainly does employ such counterstrategies. But they cannot, on his own account, be sufficient to turn the Sodomite away from his purchase. Indeed, so far as they offer a counterpurchase, they risk reinforcing the condition of desire that is the Sodomite's disease. An alternate offer can only be prelude to what is really needed, namely, a long therapy of *libido*. That therapy

88. Reindel 1:325.22–23.
89. Reindel 1:323.19, "flamma"; 309.19, "incentorem luxuriae", 313.5, "rabies."
90. Reindel 1:313 8–9, "insensibilitas luxuriae."
91. Respectively, Reindel 1·310.23 and 321 10; 323.18–19; 312.13, and 325.17
92 Reindel 1:320 3 / 8–9
93 Reindel 1:323 30–31, 324 1–2.

requires divine grace, of course, but it must apply the grace precisely and persistently, under the conditions of a *conversio morum*, a turning of the economy of desire back towards lawful subordination.

To overcome the disorder of desire in the Sodomite means recognizing that his vice is allied with other sins, other forms of *luxuria* of course, but also other classes of sin not immediately recognizable as its siblings. It may seem easy enough to link the sin of the Sodomites to the larger problem of clerical unchastity.[94] It is perhaps less immediately obvious that it ought to be coupled with the selling of church offices. Yet Peter Damian often puts clerical unchastity and avarice together; indeed, he insists that they should go together.[95] They do go together not only as deformations of church life, as threats to church order, but as sins with scriptural names, with specific scriptural antecedents. As Peter explains, Nicolaitism is so called after a deacon consecrated by the apostle Peter.[96] Simony is named after Simon the Magician, who tries to buy the imposition of hands from the apostle.[97] Nicolaitism and Simony are sins named after figures in the early history of the church. Sodomy is named after a Gentile city of the Old Testament. The distinction is not without a difference. Nicolaitism and Simony can occur only after the foundation of the church, since they are sins against the right order of its divine institution. Sodomy is an older and a deeper sin, a sin not against an institution, however divine, but against the order of creation itself. There is also a difference of persistence. Simony is a newer sin, and one punished in Scripture only by way of promised pain. Peter predicts of Simon that he will suffer for his wickedness; Simon asks for Peter's prayers. Nicolaitism might seem to simple readers to be sanctioned by certain passages in the New Testament, so that it is undeserving of punishment. But Sodomy was punished long before and in terrible fact. If God's punishment at Sodom was insufficient to stop the vice there, if apostolic judgment on Simon Magus could not halt traffic in ecclesiastical office, what hope for Peter Damian's writing?

He is not unaware of this difficulty. He tries to meet it in the case of Sodomitic vice both by arguing that the sin has seen a resurgence and by

---

94. This association is in fact deceiving. Peter regards Sodomy and Nicolaitism as different problems, and he rarely mentions the former when discussing the latter Moreover, Sodom and Gomorrah are recalled elsewhere in his writings with a range of spiritual meanings, none of which have explicitly to do with the matters discussed in the *Liber Gomorrhianus*. Some readers, perhaps a little embarrassed themselves, have found Peter Damian less graphic when discussing clerical concubinage than the Sodomitic vice, see, for example, Palazzini, "S Pier Damiani e la polemica anticelibataria," pp 127–133

95 As in the letter to Hildebrand, *Epist* 65 (Reindel 2:230.4–5 and throughout)

96 Peter Damian *Epist* 61 (Reindel 2 216 19–217 2), with reference to Acts 6 5

97 Acts 8 18–23

noting that the church Fathers did not exercise themselves against it. Peter Damian has excused his polemic by suggesting that he was completing the work of the Fathers in combating a sin that they would have combated had it been so prevalent. The sin is spreading again from those black ruins on the plain. How to stop it? Not by writing simple books of appeal to Sodomites, nor even by writing books in hopes of persuading the pope to repress the spread by severe sanctions. An invisible, ancient vice rooted in deep disorder of desire, armed with its own books and a pandering rhetoric, linked with the ancient disorder of avaricious ambition—such a vice can be countered only by a book that insists urgently on the confession of hidden sins, the rejection of corrupting books, the stripping away of remunerated offices, and a permanent penance. But a book that advocates such measures would seem to abandon the hope of therapy for the certainty of punishment and confinement. The question, Can the Sodomite enter the hermitage? becomes the question, What is the hermitage for the Sodomite? Is it a school or a prison, a place of healing or of execution? Peter Damian's central address to the Sodomite is in fact and rather clearly an exhortation to someone to step forward for execution. If the clerical Sodomite confesses to a non-Sodomite, as he must, he will on Peter Damian's own prescription be punished by permanent exclusions. The author's voice in the *Book of Gomorrah* is at once the voice of the brother and the father, the diagnostician and the surgeon, the advocate and the sentencing judge. Whatever consolations he offers are offered on the way to an inevitable punishment.

It is easy, with this end of a reading, to view the *Book of Gomorrah* as a ruse, as a way of entrapping the Sodomite into confession with sweet images of healing. Peter Damian is in fact unclear about the possibilities for healing, as about the communities in which it might be undertaken. He is equivocal about the future of the self-confessed Sodomitic hermit, as he is about the chances for overcoming the vice even by long ascesis. Peter Damian is not equivocal about punishment. This difference is not so much a sign of bad faith as a sign of despair, which is another defect of faith. The *Book of Gomorrah* is unsettled by its own inability to make good on its offer of persuasion. In this way its rhetoric is less effective than the confusion of the illicit penitentials or the pandering promises of desire. *Libido* does provide the momentary pleasure it promises. Peter Damian is uncertain whether or how to provide the conversion to which he invites. His booklet ends by being less powerful an exhortation than is the fallacious reasoning of the books of Gomorrah.

Peter Damian has also built into his coinage of the category "Sodomy" one of the fundamental paradoxes that will trouble its theological history. He seems to conceive Sodomy as a sin that cannot be repented. This conception violates the fundamental Christian teaching about sins of the flesh, namely, that they are always repentable. To conceive of a fleshly sin that cannot be repented is to set in motion an interminable dialectic. The dialectic can be stopped only by admitting that what has been categorized as an unrepentable fleshly sin is either not a sin or not fleshly. To think otherwise, to insist on the paradoxical categorization, would be to deny that Christian life can serve as an ongoing conversion, as a turning of the soul back to God. There would then be no need for schools of repentance, for monasteries. The category of unrepentable Sodomy threatens in this way the institutions of moral reformation to which Peter Damian has committed his public life.

FOUR

Alan of Lille

Natural Artifices

Peter Damian wrote theology as polemic. He used as well the devices of courtroom indictment and, if we trust him, of therapeutic exhortation. There is a lesson here about theological style. On many medieval understandings, the theologian is not confined to academic forms. Theology is to be written in every genre, didactic, rhetorical, and literary. The theologian should speak with every human tongue just because he speaks a truth that regards the rest of human speaking as a preparation or instrument. So the theologian uses every genre. He should define, explain, inquire, and demonstrate, of course, but he should also beseech, reprimand, praise, describe, and lament.

Alan of Lille writes theology superbly and in all these ways. A student and teacher in the Parisian schools of the liberal arts in the decades around the middle of the twelfth century, Alan was immersed in a remarkably literate culture. His first writings show the influence of Bernard Silvestris, the cosmologist-poet associated with Chartres, as well as of the patriarch of polymaths, Thierry of Chartres.[1] He shows himself an expert in the rules of prosody and of rhetoric. What is more, Alan was acquainted with newly available texts in physics and astronomy, as with the philosophical readings of them. Alan went on from Paris to various ecclesiastical duties, including the contest with heretics. He may have been given a modest church appointment. Toward the end of his life, he retired into monastic solitude, perhaps for a time among the Cluniacs, certainly at last with the Cistercians.

Alan's writings traverse the genres. They begin, it seems, with two allegories of interleaved poetry and prose. They go on through treatises, expo-

---

1. There is very little evidence for reconstructing Alan's life. For a survey of what there is, see d'Alverny, *Alain de Lille*, p. 11–29

sitions, and homilies to a summa of the whole of theology. Alan composed a dictionary of allegorical interpretations for Scripture and a geometrically inspired list of rules for theological speech. Of these works, the one that figures so prominently in the genealogy of Sodomy is also one of the most elaborate. It is the involuted poetic artifice called *The Plaint of Nature*.

Alan's *Plaint* looks to be a refracting mirror of moral persuasions—an allegory that depicts and that is moral rhetoric. Surely the work wants to change its readers by showing them images of themselves as they are and as they ought to be. It will shame them to abandon sin. It will encourage them to hold fast in virtue. After all, both the narrator and Nature herself deploy the full range of rhetorical colors, the devices of forensic dispute and epideictic display, to picture the natural prescription for human lives. So it seems. But the *Plaint of Nature* is not a mirror. Its sheen, its colors are semblances woven into what is explicitly conceived as a cloth. The cloth is a covering. Alan has read the didactic fictions of Bernard Silvestris, in whom, as in several others, he has encountered a well-developed theory of the literary "covering" (*integumentum*), of the use of an attractive surface to hide a deeper, different truth.[2] Nature will tell us in the poem that she typically conceals herself.[3] She will set forth the beginning of a doctrine of esoteric writing in poetry.[4] We have no mirror, then, but rather a *trompe l'oeil* tapestry, behind which there is something or someone hidden.

Modern readers have certainly found any number of things concealed there. The *Plaint* has been read as personal satire, as religious allegory, as an extended claim for the spiritual importance of the verbal arts rightly practiced.[5] I do not mean to settle these disputes. I mean only to investigate some of the gaps in the covering that is supposed to be the main moral teaching of the text—the condemnation of same-sex copulation. No one disputes that there is this teaching in the text, although most modern readers seem a little reluctant to test its categories or examine its arguments. Whatever they take it to be representing, they assume that the moral argument has a coherence of its own. After all, an *integumentum*, an allegorical covering, needs shape and texture. These may conceal another teaching,

---

2 For Alan's own use of the term here, see *De planctu* prose 4 (Haring 838 170), "Hoc ergo integumentum"; prose 4 (841 253), "sub integumentali inuolucro." There is an English translation by Sheridan, *Alain of Lille The Plaint of Nature* I will consider below the question of a prose prologue to the *Plaint*, a text included neither by Haring nor by Sheridan

3 *De planctu* prose 3 (Haring 828 121–829.127).

4 *De planctu* prose 4 (Haring 837 133–136).

5 Respectively, Bernhard Bischoff, as reported in d'Alverny, *Alain de Lille, Textes inédits,* p 43, note 53, and Hudry, "'Prologus Alani *De planctu Naturae*,'" pp 176–179; Sheridan, *The Plaint of Nature,* pp 49–54, and Ziolkowski, *Alan of Lille's Grammar of Sex,* pp 141–144

but they must hold together at least long enough for the concealment to work. Investigation will show that surface shape and texture do not hold in Alan's *Plaint*. They are not intended to hold. Alan's purpose in the *Plaint* is to criticize the uselessness for certain Christian moral teachings of the rhetoric of pagan myth.

Before turning to the gaps in the *Plaint*'s representations, in its *integumentum*, let me rehearse its outermost story. The voice of the narrator—whom I will continue to distinguish from Alan—speaks first in a lament over the perversion of nature (meter 1). Men have made themselves into women, have turned active into passive. The dreadful conversion is glossed by analogies taken from the *trivium* and illustrated by a string of classical references—a first indication that the poem means to engage the moral teaching of the Roman poets. There then appears to the narrator a woman who is identified only later as Nature herself. The woman's appearance is meticulously described: her crown and clothing represent the cosmic order (prose 1 and meter 2). The arrival of the person of Nature provokes in the natural world a universal rejoicing (prose 2 and meter 3). Nature confronts the narrator and then explains the marriage of body to soul, together with analogous harmonies (prose 3). But the narrator notices and asks about Nature's tears (meter 4). She replies with the story of man's sexual disorder and its origin (prose 4). The narrator interrupts to request a discussion of desire, which Nature supplies under protest (meter 5). She then returns to her story of how Venus introduced disorder into natural reproduction, how she brought about the onslaught of lust and the other vices (prose 5). Nature describes the other principal vices as they follow upon or incite lust—we see gluttony, avarice, arrogance, and envy (meter 6 through prose 7). We are told how to resist these incitements (meter 8).

There then arrive, unexpectedly and without prelude, the guests for the celebration of a marriage—or of marriage itself: Hymen, the cuckolded husband of Venus, whose garments show scenes of happily wedded life; then Chastity, Temperance, Generosity, and Humility (prose 8). But they are mournful. They have come in fact to ask for Nature's judgment on the sorrowful perversion of humankind. Nature sends for Genius, her fellow judge and priest. A symphony of instruments resounds (meter 9). Nature adds a final representation and a final teaching—that the virtues are unified (prose 9). Genius arrives to speak the terrible excommunication: Those who fall to lust or any of the other sins are to be afflicted by an absolute infertility of fulfillment, an eternal, unsatisfied desire. After this judgment, in the last lines, we are informed by the narrator that the whole of the representation has been a dream.

That describes only the outermost story of the *Plaint*. Something else lies hidden behind it. We can look for what is missing by looking for gaps in the story's representations. From these we will eventually learn why Alan means to complain against the very representation of "natural" arguments in morals.

NATURE AND HER ANOMALIES

There is no better place to begin than with Nature's extraordinary garments. We are assured in retrospect that the marriage of fibers in them is "divorced" only where it comes to represent humankind.[6] The rest of the tapestry must be presumed to represent things in their intended courses. But there are a number of peculiarities in its details, especially in the invocation of classical precedents. So, for example, in rejuvenation the eagle changes back from Nestor to Adonis, whom the poem elsewhere takes as a figure of disordered love.[7] The dove is drunk with the "sweet evil" of Venus's mother and so wrestles as in a Greek gymnasium.[8] The bat, "hermaphrodite bird," stands as a zero among the other birds; it stands in the infertile position from which no number can be produced.[9] The ram betrays marriage by taking many wives.[10] The beaver castrates himself in the hopes of avoiding capture.[11] It is true that other animals typically associated with irregular copulation are moralized here in positive ways. The hare, for example, dreams in terror of hounds; it is not accused of being hermaphroditic.[12] Still the anomalies of surface remain: Nature's plan seems to include the drunkenness of desire, hermaphroditism, polygamy, and sexual self-mutilation.

The depiction of plants is equally peculiar. The narrator hesitates to describe these images at all, because they appear on Nature's underclothing (*camisia*).[13] They are closest to her body and to her own genital organs, which, we have been assured, have never been unlocked by Venus.[14] The

6. *De planctu* prose 1 (Haring 817 234–235), prose 4 (838.161–163)
7. *De planctu* prose 1 (Haring 814.149), compare 835.72–74, where Adonis's mother is consumed by incestuous love, and 843 30, where desire turns Adonis into a slave.
8. *De planctu* prose 1 (Haring 815.172–174)
9 *De planctu* prose 1 (Haring 816.192–193).
10. *De planctu* prose 1 (Haring 818.266–819 267)
11 *De planctu* prose 1 (Haring 819.274–275).
12. *De planctu* prose 1 (Haring 819.268–270); compare Pliny *Historia naturalis* 8 81, and Boswell, *Christianity, Social Tolerance, and Homosexuality*, pp. 137–141.
13. *De planctu* prose 1 (Haring 819 281–282)
14 *De planctu* prose 1 (Haring 809 34–35).

narrator stresses that he could not see these garments. Whatever he guesses about them will serve in aid only of a "fragile probability." [15] The probability is that the undergarments show the cycles of reproduction in trees and herbs. What is closest to the skin of Nature is the reproduction of trees and herbs. But it was notorious in medieval science, both before and after the translation of Aristotle's physical books, that the distinction between male and female could not be understood in trees or herbs as it was in animals. [16] So the form of reproduction closest to Nature is one in which the sexes are improperly distinguished.

What is more peculiar, Nature herself seems to be a hermaphrodite. She is called and calls herself a mother, and the descriptions of her often include images of maternal care. [17] But the reader knows that she is a virgin. Moreover, Nature describes her own begetting in terms that she elsewhere specifically reserves for male copulation. God's original delegation to Nature gives her the task of hammering out the coinage of creatures on the appropriate anvils. Nature is also handed a stylus with which to write the exemplar in its images. [18] When Nature in turn delegates her work to Venus, she passes along both hammers and stylus. [19] Hammers and stylus are among the very first images used by the narrator to describe the approved male role in copulation. A misuse of the hammer or the stylus is the original image for the deviation of human sex. How can the female Nature wield hammers and write with a stylus? Nature is a virgin "mother" who begets by means of the instruments of masculinity.

There is worse. Truth was begotten by "generative" (*genialis*), incestuous kisses between Nature and her son, Genius—kisses repeated as they greet each other in the poem. [20] These kisses are associated with others: the kiss of female Idea and female Hyle that is mediated by Icon, the kiss of Being and Nous that produces Generation, and the healing kisses, the

---

15. *De planctu* prose 1 (Haring 819.282–283).

16. For accounts of the doctrine in sources familiar to Alan, see, for example, Pliny's *Historia naturalis* 17.10–13, 25 1–6. For the teaching of the Aristotelian tradition see ps-Aristotle (Nicholas of Damascus?) *De plantis* 1.2, trans. Alfred of Sareshel (Drossaart Lulofs and Poortman 521–525); and Albert the Great *De vegetabilibus* 1.1.7 / 12 (Meyer 5, 8).

17. For example, *De planctu* prose 3 (Haring 825.16), "nutricis", meter 4 (831.1), "genitrixque rerum"; prose 4 (838.15), "mater"; prose 5 (850.179–180), "ut mecum maternis excitatus uisceribus."

18. *De planctu* prose 4 (Haring 840.224–232)

19. *De planctu* prose 5 (Haring 845.25).

20. *De planctu* prose 9 (Haring 877.94–95, 114–116). Some readers seem to miss or mistake the "natique" in this passage, and so they overlook the complexity of the relations between Nature and Genius. See, for example, Economou, *The Goddess Natura in Medieval Literature*, pp. 90–94, where the word is not remarked; and Nitzsche, *The Genius Figure in Antiquity and the Middle Ages*, p. 96, where "natique" is taken as "and the natured."

"chaste kisses," that Nature first bestows on the narrator.[21] The relation between Nature and Genius seems odd in other ways. Nature describes him as a mirror reflecting the sameness of herself. They are twin halves of a circle of reciprocal love.[22] Together they preside, mother and son, over a church from which irregular generation is to be expelled.[23] Yet the appearance of Genius is by context the appearance of the bridegroom for the incomplete wedding feast. We have the guests, the music, and now the partner. It is a wedding of mother and son consummated once already in the spiration of Truth, consummated anew in an excommunication of those who pervert natural fertility. Even on its surface, then, the *Plaint* is hardly a seamless representation of orderly fertility.

If there are holes in the narration of the *integumentum*, as there plainly are, our first suspicions must fall on the narrator. Who is he? Where does he stand with respect to these unstitched patches?[24]

THE NARRATOR'S (MIS-)EDUCATION

The *Plaint of Nature* announces itself as an imitation of Boethius's *Consolation of Philosophy*. Its beginning is a quotation from the *Consolation*'s beginning, and its form is a simpler version of the *Consolation*'s elaborate sequence of poetical meters.[25] What then of analogies of plot? The plot of the *Consolation* is the reeducation of its narrator. The blows of misfortune have made him so forget his philosophical education that he cannot recognize Philosophy when she first appears. He has fallen from her tutelage to the company of the theatrical whores of lyric poetry. Slowly, by the alternation of poetic and dialectical persuasions, Philosophy brings Boethius's narrator back to his intellectual homeland.

On analogy, the *Plaint of Nature* would need to describe its narrator's reeducation in Nature's original purposes.[26] This would imply that the narrator begins in a condition at least of forgetfulness, perhaps of perversion.

---

21. Respectively, *De planctu* prose 9 (Haring 877.95–97, 874.19–20) and prose 3 (825 9)

22 *De planctu* prose 8 (Haring 871 190–194)

23 *De planctu* prose 8 (Haring 872 212), "a sacramentali ecclesie nostre communione"

24 I assume that narrator is male, though the evidence for this in the poem is curiously slight In the absence of gendered self-description, we learn the narrator's gender only through such grammatical features as the gender of terms of office applied to the narrator, as in *De planctu* prose 4 (Haring 836.104)

25 *De planctu* prose 1 (Haring 808.1) = Boethius *Philosophiae consolatio* prose 1.

26. I here agree with Lynch that the narrator's education is central to the structure and purpose of the *Plaint* It will shortly become clear that I draw opposite conclusions about the "success" of that education See Lynch, *The High Medieval Dream Vision*, pp. 79–103

It is true that Alan's narrator, like Boethius's, does not recognize his teacher on her first appearance. She is simply a woman or, at most, an unrecognized if virginal relative (*cognata*).[27] The lengthy description of Nature's appearance and clothing passes without further identification. Even the world's rejoicing at her arrival is not declaration enough. After the narrator faints away, the woman begins a rebuke of his forgetfulness. The rebuke recalls her past favors to the narrator, her role in the world, her subservience to God, the course of human errancy. Then, only then, does Nature name herself: "I, Nature, am ignorant of this second birth," that is, of the regeneration accomplished by grace.[28] Again, "I am Nature," who gives the narrator the gift of her instruction.[29] After the second naming, the narrator recognizes her, falling down to kiss her feet.

What exactly caused the narrator's forgetfulness? His opening speech bewails Nature's absence. He is aware at least of her having gone. Moreover, the speech is full of invective against the rejection of natural ways in same-sex copulation. It seems that the narrator has forgotten nothing. But there are difficulties. The same speech also assures the reader that the (male) narrator eagerly desires the kisses lying fallow on the lips of young women. The assurance is scrambled. Kissing takes two, and the kisses lying on virgins' lips are the kisses of their otherwise preoccupied male lovers. Whose kisses does our narrator mean to harvest? Moreover, the effect of harvesting the kisses is to impregnate not the maidens, but the narrator himself.[30] In him they grow into honeycomb. Then there are the narrator's classical illustrations of the robust, male-female love that has now disappeared. Unfortunately, the allusions are to everything but married love.[31] The first allusion is to Paris, who is explicitly called "the Phrygian adulterer."[32] The second is to Pyramus and Thisbe, whose love is never consummated because of the wall between them, and this despite the vulgar pun that the narrator makes on the image of the wall's cleft.[33] The third allusion, the last, is to Achilles hiding in drag—Achilles who, no matter

27. *De planctu* prose 1 (Haring 808.1), "mulier"; prose 3 (824 2, 825 1), "virgo" and (824.4) "cognata."
28. *De planctu* prose 3 (Haring 829.146), "ego Natura."
29. *De planctu* prose 3 (Haring 830.167), "ego sum Natura."
30. *De planctu* meter 1 (Haring 807.45–808.46)
31. Since Alan comes out of a long tradition of reading Ovid allegorically, it cannot be assumed that the literal surface of the Ovidian text serves as its main teaching for him Even so, Alan cannot entirely disregard that surface when he is using the actions of Ovid's characters to specify certain types of act I will return to Alan's relation to Ovid below.
32. *De planctu* meter 1 (Haring 808 51), "Frigius . adulter"
33 *De planctu* meter 1 (Haring 808 53–54)

how many children he fathered or women he subdued, remains for the literate reader the companion of Patroclus.[34] Perhaps we are to understand that the narrator, though a harsh critic of deviant love, has somehow forgotten the fullness of Nature's plan, the fullness of marriage. Too much taken with the fables of poetry and with crude jokes that betray ill-constrained desire, he has forgotten that rightly ordered desire is about the reality of being a husband and a father—a father of children, not of poetic honeycombs.

Nature does rebuke a misapprehension in the narrator something very much like this. He is confused about the truthfulness of poetry. After her first catalogue of sins, the narrator is troubled by a question. Why does she condemn human beings alone when the poets tell that the gods have run in the same eccentric orbits? After all, he continues, Jupiter took Ganymede, Bacchus and Apollo their young men. Nature is irked by the question. Rightly so. The narrator seems to have forgotten the first lesson of Greek philosophy: poets tell lies. But their lies, it turns out, are of very different kinds.[35] Some lies are naked falsity, paraded before hearers to bewitch them. Some lies are falsity palliated by the "hypocrisy of probability," in which the representations of *exempla* gain credibility for what is proposed. What is both more important and more confusing, some poets conceal truth within the covering of a lie, so that it may be discovered with pleasure. Again poets sometimes connect historical happenings to pleasant fables in an elegant "suture" (*sutura*)—or, indeed, satire. In none of these is truth to be found on the surface. The reader is required to judge whether this particular representation, this particular patch of cloth, is or is not a lie.

If our narrator has forgotten how to tell fiction from fact in the poets, then his cure will require reeducation in discernment. We do not see this in the *Plaint*. What we see instead is an unstitching of all the fictions, of every representation of moral matters. The explicit course of the narrator's therapy is this. Nature's first speech acts as a purgative that causes him to vomit forth all the fantastic remains of misconception.[36] His mind is brought back from wandering to the full recognition of Nature. So he tells us. His self-diagnosis must be much too optimistic. Only after this purgation does he begin to question Nature, and some of his questions, as we have seen, show that he is still trapped by fantasies. Where then is the real moment of cure? The narrator asks five questions: about the motive for

34   *De planctu* meter 1 (Haring 808.55–56).
35.   *De planctu* prose 4 (Haring 837.128 ff).
36.   *De planctu* prose 4 (Haring 830.174–175), "Et per hanc ammonitionem velut quodam potionis remedio omnes fantasie reliquias quasi nauseans stomachus mentis euomuit"

Nature's visit, about her failure to indict the gods for lustful misconduct, about the rent in her garment, about the cause of human deviation, and about the nature of Desire.[37] The first four are clearly put in the form of questions.[38] The last, which is explicitly an interruption of Nature's discourse, is expressed as a desire to understand.[39] The shift is not coincidental. After the description of Desire and the conclusion of Nature's interrupted narrative about the cause of its generation, the narrator asks no more questions. He confesses no more doubts. He speaks rather as Nature's collaborator in the completion of his own treatment.[40] What has brought about the end of questioning and the beginning of therapeutic collaboration? The explicit answer is the narrator's brief acquiescence in Nature's depiction of Desire and her history of its deviation. To say this more precisely: The therapy has culminated in the corrections to the narrator that Nature inserts into these central speeches. The narrator says, at their conclusion, that he accepts these corrections and is eager to hear more.[41]

We should go over this part of the cloth again. The narrator's question about Desire interrupts Nature. He begins with an ambiguous exclamation that may be read as joy or laughter. His language is appropriately submissive, but also titillatingly specific. The narrator asks for a picture of the nature of Desire (*cupido*).[42] Nature does not take the question as a humble petition. She takes it as an act of derision. She accuses the narrator of being a mercenary in the army of Desire, of having a familial bond to Desire as close as that between twin brothers.[43] His question comes from darkest ignorance.[44] Somewhat later, between the answer to the interrupting, fifth question and the end of the answer to the fourth, Nature justifies her "theatrical speech" against Desire as the only kind suited to the narrator's childishness.[45] She concludes with the sad but presumably untheatrical history

37. *De planctu* meter 4 (Haring 832.41–48); prose 4 (836 115–837.122, 838.161–163, 839.174–178, 841.247–254).

38. First question, "Cur . . . Cur . . . cur . . . quid," meter 4 (Haring 832.42–46); second question, "Miror cur," prose 4 (836 115); third question, "Miror cur," prose 4 (838.161); fourth question, "que . . . que," prose 4 (839.175–176).

39 *De planctu* prose 4 (Haring 841 251–252), "uellem . . . agnoscere."

40 *De planctu* prose 6 (Haring 852 1–4), especially "uellem ut . explicares"; prose 6 (857.149–150), "Vellem ut . . . impugnares", prose 7 (864 141–143), "Vellem . ut roborares."

41. *De planctu* prose 5 (Haring 850.184–185)

42 *De planctu* prose 4 (Haring 841 252), "pictura tue descriptionis."

43. *De planctu* prose 4 (Haring 841.261–262), "in Cupidinis castris stipendiarie militantem quadam interne familiaritatis germanitate eidem esse connexum."

44. *De planctu* prose 4 (Haring 841.263), "affectanter inuestigare conaris" and (842.267) "ignorantie tenebras."

45. *De planctu* prose 5 (Haring 845.17–18), "theatralis oratio," "tue puerilitati," "ad pueriles tue infatie fescenninas"

of Venus's fall and the consequent deviations of sexual practice. It is then that the narrator speaks his perfunctory acquiescence to her therapy.

I cannot read this acquiescence as marking a conversion. Indeed, it is hard to know what happens to the narrator in that answer or after it. He speaks briefly and rarely in the rest of the work. His last words are the request that Nature strengthen him further against the vices she has depicted.[46] After them, the narrator stands as mute observer to the arrival of the other figures and their conversations with Nature, mute too during the rites of Genius. The last silence is particularly striking. Nature had first told the narrator that she had come to earth to solicit his cooperation in pronouncing judgment on the erring. She wanted him to serve as familiar assistant and secretary in the proceedings.[47] But the narrator is never asked what punishment is to be meted out to the violators. Nature herself prescribes the excommunication in her summons, and Genius performs it without comment. Either the narrator has done all that Nature wanted in acquiescing and then standing mute, or else he is held back from judgment on deviant love—by Nature or by himself.

The separation of the narrator from the concluding judgment is made more interesting by his final words to the reader. There he tells us that it has all been a dream (*insompnium*), a vision of the imagination, an ecstasy (*exstasis*).[48] There are many different uses of dreams in the Latin literature that Alan could be citing or reworking. In a poem about sexual couplings, any mention of a dream must be at least partly ambiguous. The sex of dreams is necessarily solitary, unfruitful, even polluting.[49] A dream of Nature's representations of sexual reproduction is then a curious thing. Moreover, dreams have already been associated in the poem with the errors of the most voluptuous and mendacious philosophy—"the dreams of Epicurus."[50] Those philosophic dreams have been linked in turn to the pandering lies of the poets. The figures on Nature's clothing are also "dreams of the picture," at least near that point where the garment is ripped by human miscopulation.[51] Dreams are akin at once both to philosophic or poetic fic-

---

46 *De planctu* prose 7 (Haring 864 141–143)

47 *De planctu* prose 4 (Haring 836 103–107).

48 *De planctu* prose 9 (Haring 879 164–165)

49 This is truer if the narrator means *insomnium* in the technical sense known to twelfth-century readers from Macrobius's commentary on the dream of Scipio. For Macrobius, an *insomnium* is a disturbance of sleep that brings no truth with it To call the whole of the previous text an *insomnium* is to call it a deceit

50. *De planctu* prose 4 (Haring 837 143), "Epicuri   insompnia."

51. *De planctu* prose 4 (Haring 838 163), "picture . insompnia."

tions and to Nature's own representations. Or Nature's representations are themselves like fictions.

If the reader asks, on reaching the end, when the narrator's dream began, the obvious answer is that it began before the beginning of the poem—that the poem starts up in the middle of a dream.[52] But a verbal parallel suggests a more interesting answer. The narrator speaks precisely of falling into an "ecstasy" when he first gazes into Nature's face, before she has even identified herself to him.[53] It is tempting to think of all that occurs from that moment to the end of the poem as an ecstasy from which the narrator revives just at the end. Nature's teaching and Genius's excommunication would be episodes in this ecstasy—episodes within the mind of the narrator when he is lost within himself, before he hears the real teaching of Nature, if there is any. On either demarcation of the dream, the *Plaint*'s didactic sections would be figures of our narrator's fantasy.

Whether or not one takes this reading of the ecstasy, it remains true that the narrator cannot be taken as Nature's servant. His perfunctory acquiescence, his formulaic encouragements, his hints about her prolixity, his increasing silence all suggest withdrawal rather than conversion. This is appropriate to the poem's action. The only "reproduction" the reader sees in the *Plaint* is the production of poetry. We see everything but animal reproduction on Nature's garments; we are only told of Venus's miscopulations with Antigamus; we are deprived of the wedding for which the guests have assembled. But we do see Genius at work. He is represented right before our eyes. This reminds us, if reminding is needed, that we have from the first been watching the products of Alan's making.

ALAN'S STERILITY

Of Alan himself, the reader sees just the poem, the offspring of Alan's solitary dreaming, of his artificer's ecstasy. The reader also sees within Alan's poem a representation of poetry making. Writing representations is what Genius does. Genius writes or, rather, draws images brought to life and

---

52 That is the interpretation in Lynch, *The High Medieval Dream Vision*, p. 82. The edition of *De planctu* reprinted in Migne's *PL* gives an alternate ending (62.482c), which has led some readers to conclude that the narrator here first falls into sleep. See Economou, *The Goddess Natura in Medieval Literature*, p 96. But even on Migne's reading, the narrator would be falling into another kind of sleep, as Lynch suggests, p. 219, note 19.

53 *De planctu* prose 3 (Haring 824.5–6), "in exstasis alienatione."

going down to death, ceaselessly replaced by the on-running stylus. The figures are those of pagan epic, mythography, and philosophy. When the right, the proper hand tires, the left takes over to draw their opposites or antitypes: Thersites, the ugly and arrogant coward; Paris, captured by lust; Sinon, who lied the horse's way into Troy. The mention of lying leads "naturally" to the poets themselves, antitypes of the philosophers: here only Ennius and Pacuvius, the former promiscuous in his meter, the latter in the sequence of his plots.

The work of Genius is shown as necessarily doubled, as producing representation and misrepresentation. Genius gives life as a man should, stylus on pliant parchment, to the nobler figures of poetry. But Genius also produces, with the same stylus in a different hand, their inverted, ignoble negatives. This reminds us of that other fruitful miscoupling—the adulterous dalliance of Antigamus ("Anti-Marriage") with Venus that produces Jocus.[54] Nothing is said of the parentage of Antigamus, except that it is "ignoble."[55] This is a curious omission in a work where so many other significant figures are placed geneaologically. One might wonder whether Nature herself has not been guilty of some miscegenation, mothering or fathering Antigamus. Or Nature may stand in a more distant familial relation. Nature admits to being fastened to Desire by a link of kinship: she is his aunt, through Hymen, her brother.[56] Perhaps she is also an aunt to Antigamus, sister to his mother. Nature's sister, Generosity, is moved to tears at the impending judgment on Prodigality, her "foster-child."[57] Perhaps Generosity has been too generous in other ways as well.

Whatever Nature has or has not contributed to his genealogy, the narrator makes clear that Jocus is a friend of poets. Early on, we were told that poets use jocose fables to produce elegance.[58] The narrator himself, who is at least a poet in training, has turned his own jocosity into the poetic tears of a lament.[59] And, of course, Jocus is itself a joke of naming, since its

54. With most recent readers, I prefer the reading "Antigamus" to Haring's "Antigenius" "Antigamus" is attested in some of the manuscripts, while "Anti-Genius," as Sheridan notes, would be without literary precedent Compare De planctu prose 5 (Haring 849 153), with the apparatus of variants, and Sheridan, The Plaint of Nature, p. 163, note 27
55. De planctu prose 5 (Haring 849 153).
56. De planctu prose 5 (Haring 845.4–5), "quadam germane consanguinitatis fibula connectatur" and (849.151) "uterine fraternitatis michi affinis confinio." Fibula means generally a fastening, but it is used in Roman medicine for a device for suturing (e g., Celsus, Ars medicinae 5.26.23, 7.4) Nature may mean to suggest that she and Desire are two sides of a wound. Or she may be punning, as she does elsewhere, on sutura/satura, suture and satire.
57 De planctu prose 9 (Haring 874 12), "suum alumpnum"
58 De planctu prose 4 (Haring 837.137), "ioculationibus fabulosis"
59. De planctu meter 1 (Haring 806 2), "in lacrimosa iocos [verto]"

bearer is just the opposite.[60] What is more striking, Nature herself characterizes the whole of meter 5, her depiction of Desire, as a "theatrical ora-
tion, spread out into lascivious jocosities" and as "Fescennine satires."[61] If
Nature seems somewhat defensive about having spoken so colorfully, she
still shows herself as familiar with Jocus and his games as a relative might
be. Indeed, meter 5 is studded with allusions to classical poetry. The
strongest condemnation of Desire's perversions—and perhaps the central
moment of Nature's teaching—is also the moment of greatest poetic jocu-
larity.

The prominence of linguistic artifice brings into view the most obvious
and most puzzling feature of Alan's work—I mean his choice of grammatical metaphors for describing deviations of human copulation. Now it is
true that grammar does not mean for Alan what it typically means for his
modern readers. It has in him and in medieval traditions he knows a greater
didactic weight and moral gravity than is now usual.[62] Still, he also knows
that grammar is classically opposed to natural things as convention to nature. This is an elementary logical doctrine reiterated in the logical text-
books of Alan's time.[63] How odd, then, to play out the analogies between
Nature's moral prescriptions and the rules of grammar. These analogies
would ordinarily make one think that moral prescriptions were, like human
languages, subject to local variation, to customary specification, to the en-
richments of artifice.

Nature almost concedes something similar. The rending of her garment,
she explains, is the result of violence from her human children. They rip
her clothes apart by their vices and send her naked, like a woman "going
whorishly to prostitute herself" (*meretricaliter lupunare*).[64] The allusion is

60. *De planctu* prose 5 (Haring 849 146–148).

61. *De planctu* prose 5 (Haring 845.17–18), "ioculatoriis euagata lasciuiis," "fescenninas." The Fescennine satires could have been known to Alan through Horace *Epistulae* 2.1, lines 145–146, "Fescen-
nina per hunc inuenta licentia morem / Versibus alternis opprobria rustica fudit." Horace is telling a
story about the genesis of Roman drama. He makes the Fescennine verses degenerate into too mordant
satire. Compare Martianus Capella *De nuptiis* 9 §914.

62. Ziolkowski, *Alan of Lille's Grammar of Sex*, pp 109–139.

63. If Aristotle's *Categories* is willing to use certain grammatical or syntactic features as ways of
mapping the features of substance, his *On Interpretation*, for example, begins by insisting that spoken
words are not naturally given, that they are not the same among all peoples. See Aristotle *On Interpretation* 1 1 16a4–9. For some specimens of twelfth-century reflection on the conventionality of grammar,
see Isaac, *Le Peri hermeneias en Occident*, pp. 52–59; Hunt, *Collected Papers on the History of Grammar
in the Middle Ages*, pp. 1–38 and 39–94; Bursill-Hall, *Speculative Grammars of the Middle Ages*, pp.
26–31; and Pinborg, *Logik und Semantik im Mittelalter*, pp. 13–18, 55–126 These will help correct the
view that grammar is for Alan simply "natural," as in Richard Hamilton Green, "Alan of Lille's *De
planctu Naturae*," p. 661.

64 *De planctu* prose 4 (Haring 838.165–170)

to Boethius's *Consolation*, where the garments of Philosophy are torn apart by rival philosophical schools, each claiming to have possession of the whole.[65] The vices of sex that rip Nature are like philosophical schools. Yet the schools of philosophy are, in patristic literature, notoriously the result of petty differences, of disputes over conventional matters, of personal pique.[66] Are the vices of sex then also conventional schools? Alan's choice of the analogies to grammar and, less strikingly, to philosophical schools must raise a question about the rhetorical strategy of the *Plaint*, about its attempt to deduce moral teaching from the regulations of Nature.

The question can be drawn in this way. Alan's complaint, his condition, is one of bodily sterility. Even his narrator only dreams of kisses and then imagines their sequel as his pregnancy with poems. From Alan himself we have poems, not children. The poems are well made, are regular, obey the regulations. Nature, on the other hand, seems always to produce both type and antitype. Genius writes with the right hand and the left; Nature, his mother, can't keep reproduction on track; Venus is both celestial and perverted.[67] It would seem that regularity is possible in poems, not in things. Hence, Nature's attempts to represent the orderly ideal of reproduction, to argue for it from *natural* rules, must end in incoherence. This is nowhere more apparent than in her attempt to name and then to condemn same-sex copulation—an attempt that Alan means to expose rather than to endorse.

CATEGORIES, PERSUASIONS, PERVERSIONS

The construction of categories is the great beginning of moral teaching. Moral categories almost always contain moral judgments and so are an important anticipation of moral arguments. Now moral categories show marked variation both between rival contemporary accounts and over time in what claims to be the same account. There is no better example of this than the category of Sodomy. Nature has said that she knows little of theology beyond its distant existence and some points of analogy with her own doctrine. She can gesture towards it, not enter into it. But Sodomy is essentially a theological category, as much an artifact of Christian systematization as the categories of grace or sacramental character. Some medieval readers, together with many modern ones, have failed to notice the *absence* from Nature's teaching of the term "Sodomy" and of the pertinent Old

---

65 Boethius *Philosophiae consolatio* 1 prose 3

66 The masterly treatment would be Augustine *De ciuitate Dei* 6

67 The duality of Venus is particularly striking given the precedents for breaking her apart into two separate figures See Economou, *The Goddess Natura in Medieval Literature*, pp 85–87

ALAN OF LILLE / *81*

Testament allusions.[68] The term is absent, and so is its category. The question becomes, What category will Nature put in its place? The short answer is, Nature has no satisfactory substitute.

Nature begins her attempt to educate through myth by producing an extended taxonomy of sins against reproduction.[69] The categories are established by reference to classical myth—the first four, by reference to women in myth: Helen for adultery, Pasiphaë for bestiality, Myrrha for incest, Medea for infanticide. Helen's adulterous copulation is fruitless. Pasiphaë's produces a monstrous birth in the minotaur. Myrrha gives birth to Adonis. Medea undoes birth by murder. Nature then turns to describe what seem to us, on quick reading, to be sins of male homosexuality. But she is in fact describing something else, and even that something else eludes her. Remember that there are no Ovidian precedents for singling out same-sex copulation as a heinous vice. The *Metamorphoses* refers at least eight times to same-sex passion, but never to denigrate it.[70] On the contrary, Ovid recounts moving stories of fidelity between same-sex lovers. Alan's Nature knows this, and she is thus rather selective in her mythographic allusions. Take her mention of Orpheus, which occurs just before the taxonomy of sexual sins.[71] Ovid describes Orpheus as a teacher of the love of young men; Nature mentions only the bewitchment of his music.

In the embarrassment over mythic precedent, Nature seizes on the figure of Narcissus, who has already been linked in the *Plaint* with that Adonis born to the incestuous Myrrha. "Overclouded with shadows," Nature says, Narcissus was deceived by the shadowy image of himself and "by himself incurred the danger of loving himself."[72] From this self-love Nature gener-

68 One medieval reader refers to the *Complaint* as "De planctu Nature contra prelatum sodomitam" See Oxford Digby MS 166, folio 93, as noted in d'Alverny, *Alan de Lille*, p. 43 For other samples of medieval misreadings, see Kohler, "Natur und Mensch," pp. 65–66. Modern readers have made the same or corresponding assumptions. See, for example, Richard Hamilton Green, "Alan of Lille's *De planctu Naturae*," p. 650, note 2, and p. 673, "sodomy"; Economou, *The Goddess Natura in Medieval Literature*, p. 87, "sodomites" and "sodomy"; Ziolkowski, *Alan of Lille's Grammar of Sex*, p. 2, "homosexual acts," p 4, "homosexuality," and so on throughout; and Kohler, "Natur und Mensch," p 65, "Sodomie" and "Homosexualität."

69. *De planctu* prose 4 (Haring 835.68–836.92)

70. Ovid *Metamorphoses* 3.351–510 (Narcissus), 5 47–73 (Athis and Lycabas), 7.371–377 (Cycnus and Phyllius), 9.704–797 (Iphis and Ianthe), 10.82–85 (Orpheus), 10.105–144 (Cyparissus and Apollo), 10. 151–163 (Ganymede and Jupiter), and 10.164–225 (Hyacinth and Apollo) Compare those who change sex, 3.322–327 (Tiresius), 4.280 (Sithon), 9 782–797 (Iphis again), 12.175–207 (Caenis), 15.11–15 (the hyena); those who have both sexes, 4 285–388 (Hermaphroditus and Salmacis); and those who have the beauty of both sexes, 3 607 (Bacchus), 4 17–20 (Bacchus), 10.581–582 (Adonis, as described by Venus within the songs of Orpheus).

71. *De planctu* prose 4 (Haring 834.54–55).

72. *De planctu* prose 4 (Haring 835 78), "de se sibi amoris incurrit periculum"

alizes: "And many other young men, dressed by my grace in the honor of beauty, drunk with the thirst of money, exchanged their hammers of Venus for the roles of anvils" (*in incudum transtulerunt officia*).[73] If Narcissus was deceived by love of an image, these other young men, unnamed and untethered to any classical allusion, seem to be moved by avarice. Nature had mentioned male prostitution just above to embellish her claim that human beings alone violate the natural order: "But from this rule of such universality," she said, "man alone is seduced as an anomalous exception, stripped of the state robe of modesty (*pudor*) and prostituted as an immodest and whorish hustler (*prostibulum*)."[74] Prostitution now recurs in order to give some motive for the generalization of same-sex copulation. Generalization is needed, because these "other young men," a seeming handful, turn out to be "a *multitude* of monstrous men" spread over the earth.[75] Their practices are apparently attractive or contagious, which is to say, self-reproducing.

Nature represents seven kinds of practices by fairly specific analogies to doctrines of the *trivium:* (1) copulation with women only, (2) with men only, or (3) with both men and women, all matters of grammatical genus; then (4) copulation alternately with men and women, likened to heteroclite or irregular declension; then (5) copulation as either active or passive partner, which is linked to sophistical disputation; next (6) copulation as active partner only, which is not knowing how to predicate; and finally (7) copulation as passive partner only, which is like wanting to be a predicate only without ever having one's subject properly subjected. There is an eighth practice described not by a grammatical, but by a topographical metaphor: the lamentable game of those who never enter the realms of Venus, preferring to play in her vestibule. Now this last practice is obviously obscure, but I want to emphasize that a similar obscurity covers the whole list.

If we assume that the taxonomy is written from a male view, from the perspective of "the multitude of monstrous *men*," and if we deploy our own terminology for the moment, then the first practice is exclusive heterosexuality; the third and fourth, types of bisexuality. Only the second practice would be exclusive homosexuality. The last three practices, (5) through (7), refer, eruditely but graphically enough, to one's position in copula-

---

73 *De planctu* prose 4 (Haring 835.78–80).

74 *De planctu* prose 4 (Haring 833 12–15), "Sed ab huius uniuersalitatis regula solus homo anomala exceptione seducitur, qui pudoris trabea denudatus impudicitieque meretricali prostibulo prostitutus."

75 *De planctu* prose 4 (Haring 835.81–82).

tion. It is tempting to take these as kinds of homosexual copulation—what would be called in modern slang "versatile," "top," and "bottom." But Nature states no gender for the sexual partner, and given medieval restrictions on the forms of heterosexual copulation, there is no need to assume that Nature means to speak of two men. The exchange of active roles between man and woman could be just as illicit as homosexual copulation.[76]

What groups these sins together for Alan's Nature? What is the common account of their sinfulness? We are given only two clues: the figure of Narcissus and the reference to greedy prostitution. Recall for an instant Ovid's telling of the myth. At the border between boyhood and full youth, Narcissus is extraordinarily attractive to both sexes.[77] He refuses both with equal vehemence. His fate is called down on him by a young man he has spurned.[78] When Narcissus is lured to the solitary pool and led to gaze into its perfect silver, he does not at first know that he is thirsting after a bodiless image of himself. He sees only a beautiful body, lovingly described by Ovid. Narcissus tries again and again to kiss, to embrace the image. Failing this, he breaks out in lament against the watery surface that separates him, unaccountably, from his beloved—and then he realizes that he has fallen in love with an image of himself. "What should I do? Be pursued, or pursue? But why pursue at all?"[79] Consumed by an inner flame, which also, of course, consumes his beloved, Narcissus passes to the underworld, where he can gaze at himself, ageless, in an ageless pool.

The Ovidian Narcissus suffers at least two vices, pride and credulity.[80] The pride, note well, expresses itself as a refusal to copulate. Alan's Nature is obviously not interested in recalling the story to condemn proud chastity. She means to illustrate the danger of self-love, that is, the danger of the love of a body for another of the same kind. This danger is then grouped with the danger that beauty will sell itself into service as a mirror for like bodies—will sell itself into same-sex prostitution. This somehow brings up the sevenfold series of irregularities in intercourse, irregularities of partner or position. Nature's taxonomy is not only disconnected, it is incoherent. For example, Generosity will tell us that her protégé, Prodigality, was,

76. Of course, Alan may be craftier still, and he may mean to pun in the sixth and seventh categories on *predicare* and *pedicare*, if he knows the latter word through Martial or Catullus.

77. Ovid *Metamorphoses* 3.351–355, "poteratque puer iuvenisque videri / multi illum iuvenes, multae cupiere puellae; . . . nulli illum iuvenes, nullae tetigere puellae."

78. Ovid *Metamorphoses* 3.404–405.

79. Ovid *Metamorphoses* 3.465.

80. Ovid *Metamorphoses* 3.354, "dura superbia"; 3.432, "credule."

like Narcissus, credulously deceived by phantasms into a rebellion against his own nature and the reign of Nature herself.[81] The vices of self-love, the confusion of phantoms, and the greed that lead one to sell oneself are general features of vice as such, and they are elsewhere stigmatized by Nature without any specifically sexual allusion. So what exactly does she mean the narrator to understand about the ground of the sinfulness of same-sex copulation or about its connection with adjacent sins? The taxonomy is not articulate enough to give an answer to the question.

Its stammering is made worse, I think, by another of Alan's central metaphors, the likening of copulation to the minting of coins. The metaphor has run from the narrator's own prologue down to this passage. It justifies the talk of hammers and anvils, not to say the association of same-sex copulation with prostitution. The "monstrous" young men are vicious counterfeiters: they attempt to produce coin by the illicit pounding of bodies. The metaphor inevitably tangles itself. Coinage is an artifice that becomes indispensable, that comes to seem natural. Disruptions in coining are in fact disruptions of convention, though they may seem disruptions of nature. The sin attaching to coin is greed, a sin notoriously omnivorous of objects. Greed will hoard almost anything. It cannot specify a sin that is characterized just by a mistake in object. Or does Nature mean that the only possible explanation for same-sex copulation is greed? No one would do that except for money. But then the weight of accusation is moved from same-sex copulation to greed. Moreover, Nature has been entirely too eloquent about carnal desire to dismiss it now.

No clearer explanation is to be found in Nature's story about the fall of Venus. The story looks simple enough. God entrusted to Nature the regulation of reproduction, the steady stamping out of new copies of animal natures. Nature could not do the work alone, and she preferred, in any case, to stay in the celestial court rather than at the cosmic outskirts where the shops of reproduction had to be located.[82] She thus delegated the task of reproduction to Venus, together with her husband, Hymen, and her son, Desire. Venus had already shown herself a skillful artisan, and Nature gave her elaborate instructions about permissible and impermissible couplings.[83] The official story goes on to claim that the delegated arrangement was working well until Venus grew bored—or, more precisely, until she lost

81 *De planctu* prose 9 (Haring 875.49–54), especially "qui suam naturam abhominationis dampno uenumdans" and "quamuis umbratili credulitatis deceptus imagine"
82 *De planctu* prose 4 (Haring 840 235–841 246)
83 *De planctu* prose 4 (Haring 840 240–241), "Venerem in fabrili scientia conpertam"

her "appetite" and felt her "interest" close up.[84] What Venus suffers is a disorder of desire, a disruption of her desire to continue obeying the now tedious regularity laid down for her. So too the narrator interrupts Nature's story just when Venus is doing her job well. He interrupts with his question about the nature of Desire. The theatrical answer he is given is that Desire is the principle of metamorphosis by which things become their opposites. I say "metamorphosis" deliberately, because Ovid is here again very much on Alan's mind. Nature introduces her selected allusions to Ovid with this rhetorical question, "Doesn't Desire perform many miracles, to speak anti-phrastically, shape-changing [literally, 'Proteizing'] every kind of man?" Desire makes bodies be other than what they are meant to be.

Venus has been infected by Desire, mother overcome by son. She succumbs to the impulse to make things irregularly. The detailed rules of copulation set down by Nature are violated out of the desire for difference. Only this force of variation has the effect, in one salient case, of producing an illicit sameness. In order for there to be reproduction of the same, hammers must be joined to anvils in stamping out the images of natural bodies. Venus takes the hammers from their natural anvils and gives them "adulterine" ones.[85] Nature has already rejected this miscoupling, this literal enactment of same to same. It can never be indulged as a means to conception; it must always be blamed as an inexcusable monstrosity of a solecism,[86] just because it is the demise of reproduction. The sickle of fate now mows down humankind unhindered; no new seeds sprout to replace those fallen. The sins of Venus, in their various categories, are sins of infertility. There seems to be no special sin attaching to same-sex copulation beyond infertility.

But then the story has added nothing to the taxonomy. Nature would have us believe that the abiding moral oppositions are between regular repetition, harmony, and reproduction on the one hand and bored variation, disharmony, and sterility on the other. Her representations have shown us otherwise. The story of Venus's fall, the main point of Nature's story, suggests that irregularity arises naturally within the cycles of reproduction. In the official narrative, Venus's culpable boredom leads her to disarrange hammers and anvils. But Nature herself had conceded earlier that she could carry out the exacting work of writing reproduction only if her hand were constantly guided by God.[87] A moment without divine guidance, and the

84 *De planctu* prose 5 (Haring 848 120–130)
85 *De planctu* prose 5 (Haring 849 135–136).
86 *De planctu* prose 5 (Haring 846.50–57).
87 *De planctu* prose 4 (Haring 840 232–235).

writing would immediately deviate—not into sterility, but into illicit reproduction. How then could she delegate this work to Venus, placing the powerful stylus in her lesser hands?[88] And, a fortiori, how can human beings be blamed if their couplings go astray? Nature says that the only way to combat the ravages of Desire is by fleeing it.[89] Any learned reader will know already from Ovid how useless flight from Desire is. Flight ends in a rape or a metamorphosis, in violence that produces unlike from like. Within such a world, same-sex copulation might even seem like a nostalgia for regularity, a cleaving of like to like.

After all, Nature herself seems to have put a capacity for metamorphosis or transmutation into things. Venus tends naturally to be both orderly and disorderly. Men can by nature change their "offices" in copulation. The possibility for sportive copulation inheres in bodies. Nor is every irregular coupling infertile. On the contrary, Nature's own list alludes to adulterous births (Adonis of Myrrha) and even monstrous births (the minotaur of Pasiphaë). Venus's own adultery produced Jocus, and the young men's greedy prostitution gives birth not just to money, but to the irregular poetry of deviation. Fertility, shape changing, poetry making are not constrained by Nature's rules of propriety, even if she would have us believe otherwise.

In summary, Nature does not and cannot give a coherent argument against same-sex copulation, for the same reason that she cannot repress it. The seeds of irregularity are planted in things. The most Nature can do is to deny ordinary issue to irregular copulations. She does this through Genius's formula of excommunication. Here again there is a difficulty, because just as mythographic adulteries yield births, so the sterility of same-sex coupling seems curiously akin to the sterility of poetic production. The narrator dreams; Alan versifies. Each is sterile in the terms of bodily reproduction. Each is caught up in the curious reproduction of images from out of a relation of self to self, of man to man.[90] Everywhere we turn, Nature's rules seem to spawn their own violations in same-sex fertilities.

The disparity between what Alan requires in moral argument and what Nature can provide is no place clearer than in the contrast between the narrator's opening plaint and Nature's reply to his questions. The narrator began with the metamorphosis of man into "woman," with the abdication of male activity for a false passivity. For the narrator, the sins of adultery

88. *De planctu* prose 5 (Haring 846 32–34)
89. *De planctu* meter 5 (Haring 844.71–72).
90. I owe this insight to Eve Sedgwick's use of it in a very different case, that of Henry James in the prefaces to the New York edition of his works See her "Queer Performativity. Henry James's *The Art of the Novel*," pp 1–16

and the passions of the gods are preferable to this ultimate rejection of Nature's decrees. The narrator ends with the judgment that a man who "sells his sex out of love of money" ought to be thrown out of the temple of Genius.[91] In her central narrative of Venus's fall, Nature loses the specificity of this sin in the troubled taxonomy. Moreover, Genius's excommunication is pronounced not only against all infertile intercourse (those "who block the licit entry to Venus"), but against gluttons and drunkards, the greedy and the proud, the envious and flatterers.[92] One could suggest that the narrator's original fixation on a particular sin has been properly resituated in a larger context. That may be. But it is equally true that the category of sin that the narrator seemed most intent upon has not been recognized by Nature. It has not been recognized, because it cannot be recognized by her.

THE FAILURE OF NATURAL REPRESENTATIONS AND THE ADVENT OF THEOLOGY

Let me step back from this central hole in the *integumentum* of the *Plaint* to draw a conclusion and to frame questions. The conclusion is that Alan intends for these gaps in the cloth of his *integumentum* to show. He intends that they suggest the limits of Nature as a guide in morals. Nature cannot provide a compelling argument against a vice that directly affects what most concerns her, the reproduction of bodies. She is too various and variable to yield or to enact convincing regulations. Her representations tangle themselves or else are unraveled by the very conditions of their own making. In order to make the argument for rules against same-sex copulation, something more is needed. Alan knows that what Nature needs is not Ovid, even Ovid moralized, but Christian Scripture traditionally read. She especially does not need Ovid's favorable depictions of same-sex love, but rather the Pauline condemnations of such couplings. Nature does not have the right word for this sin, much less the right myth. The right word would be "Sodomy," and the myth is the medieval reading of Genesis 19. Alan's title has by now become a pun. The *Plaint of Nature* is not only a complaint against sexual sins, it is a complaint against Nature's failure to speak satisfactorily about those sins.[93]

91. *De planctu* meter 1 (Haring 808 56–60), including "Cum sexum lucri uendit amore suum."
92. *De planctu* prose 9 (Haring 878.145–149), including "legitimum Veneris obliquat incessum"
93. Here I differ markedly from most others who have tried to place the *Plaint* in some story about the development of medieval teachings on same-sex copulation. See, for example, Bailey, *Homosexuality and the Western Christian Tradition*, pp. 118–119, and Boswell, *Christianity, Social Tolerance, and Homosexuality*, pp. 310–311.

Finally, the questions are these: What does Alan gain by representing in the regular sterilities of poetry the final insufficiency of Nature? What is the point of engaging Ovid on his own ground, as it were? It would be condescending to answer this question by dismissing the *Plaint* as a sample of youthful virtuosity, a display piece from a talented young teacher of the liberal arts. It would be somewhat better to regard it as yet another of the long line of medieval attempts to come to terms with pagan moral teaching—not here in Seneca's treatises or Aristotle's *Nicomachean Ethics*, but in the persuasive representations of the Roman poets. I would prefer to advance the question about Alan's purposes by suggesting that the *Plaint* is meant to show the exhaustion of a certain kind of moral representation. The dream from which the dreamer awakes is the dream of mythographic poetry, of civic virtue taught by allegories. Ovid moralized is still not sufficient as a teacher of morals. Although Nature can teach the evils of the seven capital sins, she cannot properly specify the sinfulness of same-sex copulation. Nor can she offer a remedy for it. Alan knows this. His *Plaint* is in no small measure a reply to the Ovidian pedagogy of which he is himself and finely the result. Alan is writing a revisionist gloss on the morals of the *Metamorphoses.*[94]

We can see this quite plainly in a text that I have so far kept out of sight, a short text that may or may not be part of the *Plaint*. The text is a prose prologue to the *Plaint* that circulated apart from the main text early on.[95] Some readers have thought that this prologue is the work of Alan, even though it refers to him in the third person. Others have judged it a later addition to the poem. Whatever the authorship, this text makes clear the Ovidian problem that confronts Alan. The only text quoted in the prose prologue is a line from Ovid's *Fasti:* "But it is proper to join to each his partner (*par*)."[96] What is most striking is that the text does not make clear who the appropriate partner is. Out of its narrative context, the only indication is grammatical gender, which varies in Ovid's use of this phrase.[97] Now the prologue to the *Plaint* explains the Ovidian sentence as prohibiting whorish solecizing. How is the reader to understand that given the rules of gender agreement in Latin? Whorish solecism would seem to be precisely the mixture of male with female.

94. For an introduction to medieval readings of the *Metamorphoses* as moral allegory, see Ghisalberti, "Medieval Biographies of Ovid," perhaps especially the texts on pp. 51–58 For the role of Ovid in moral systematizations of the twelfth and thirteenth centuries, see Viarre, *La survie d'Ovide*, pp 55–62.
95. Edited from the single known manuscript by Hudry, pp 182–185
96. *Prologus Alani De planctu Nature* (Hudry 183) = Ovid *Fasti* 4 98
97 Compare Ovid *Fasti* 3 193, 3.526

The prologue continues by imagining those golden centuries in which a modest chastity was properly fostered. Things have degenerated. No longer does Jove steal Europa on a bull, or Neptune Ceres on a horse; no longer does a cloud image of Juno deceive Ixion. Rather, in these miserable times, Bacchus is supplied by Bacchus in unexampled couplings.[98] The golden age is, in other words, an age of rapes, real and imagined. The present times, alas, are times of pleasure, in which the fields of Mars have been abandoned for the camps of Venus and a pillow is more common as uniform than a cuirass. Virtue has been overcome by pleasure. The cycles of reproduction are undone. In this prologue, I conclude, the Ovidian problem is not so much resolved as strengthened. The prologue recognizes, more explicitly than the poem following, that the cycles of fertility are cycles of war. Reproductive coupling is based on violence. Unreproductive couplings are based on pleasure. Who then is the partner one ought to choose? The question is reiterated here, not resolved.

The answer, if there is one in Alan, would seem to lie outside the *Plaint*. I mean not just in the appeal by Christian faith to a revelation, but in the style of unadorned, direct address cultivated in the Fathers and practiced by Alan himself as a teacher of Christian morals—an address that is popular, affective, and productive, that reproduces itself not in the regularities of poetry, but in conversion. We hear this voice from Alan in some of his sermons, where there is straightforward and general condemnation of the tyranny of the flesh.[99] There the wine of the Sodomites is, as it is in Deuteronomy, the source of the drunkenness of *luxuria*, a sin about which Alan speaks with passion.[100] Indeed, he singles out for particular reprobation gluttony, pride, and avarice.[101] What would seem more important, Alan provides a model sermon against *luxuria*. But it makes odd reading when juxtaposed with the *Plaint*. The two texts share some of the same advice— for example, that the only antidote to temptation is to flee it or that the effect of succumbing is to destroy every good of human living.[102] The texts are distinguished not only in the range of examples, which are entirely scriptural in the sermon, but also in the main motive of argument. For Alan's model sermon, the first argument against *luxuria* is its filthiness. *Luxuria* is a fly born in dung (*sterquilinium*) and dwelling in filth (*in im-*

98 *Prologus Alani De planctu Nature* (Hudry 184), "sed Bachus a Bacho . voluptuoso more insolito suppeditatur."

99 Alan *Sermo de cruce Domini*, in d'Alverny, *Alain de Lille*, pp 279–283, at p. 282.

100. Alan *Sermo ad sacerdotes in synodo*, in d'Alverny, *Alain de Lille*, pp 283–287, at pp 286–287

101 Alan *Sermo de Trinitate*, in d'Alverny, *Alain de Lille*, pp 252–262, at 260–262

102 Alan *Ars praedicandi* 5 (Migne *PL* 210:122a, d), *De planctu* prose 5 (Häring 844 53–72) Compare also Alan *Liber poenitentialis* 2.6 (Longère 48), which matches his *Summa* 5 (Migne *PL* 210 122a)

mundis), infecting whatever it touches.[103] This is an argument that Nature cannot make, of course, since it depends on repulsion for natural things. It is an argument that Alan the preacher likes. He repeats it in the model sermon for clergy, where *luxuria* is likened to decomposition (*putredo*).[104] It is developed in more detail in an actual sermon probably by Alan.[105] After listing ways in which *luxuria* is like dung, the sermon argues that dung at least has this advantage over *luxuria:* when added to the earth it fertilizes. *Luxuria*, by contrast, sickens the earth, the flesh, of our body.

In these sermons, I do not find any supplement to the failed arguments of the *Plaint*. Nor do I find one in Alan's penitential compilation. He says quite plainly that the confessor is not to inquire into the details of illicit coitus, including the sin against nature.[106] To do so is to give occasion for sin. Alan himself obeys this precept. When providing the schema of questions to be used in inquiring after sexual sins, he mentions but does not describe the sin against nature.[107] He does quote, for the confessor's benefit, one of Peter Damian's favorite canons from the Council of Ancyra in which fornication against nature is divided into coitus with men (a male subject is typically presumed) and coitus with animals.[108] Nothing more is said.

A similar lack troubles the systematic treatment of virtues and vices, which may be part of Alan's *Summa "Quoniam homines."*[109] The free-standing text, as it survives, provides nothing like a theological argument against same-sex copulation. We are given only the driest definition of the sin against nature, which is "when semen is deposited outside of the place specified for this."[110] It is taken for granted that the reader knows what that place is—and what the sin is that is being not defined, but circumscribed. Much longer treatments are given of all the sins falling under avarice. Indeed, the treatment of *luxuria* is something less than a fifth of the treatment of avarice. There is no emphasis even in structure on the sins of sex.

No room is left in Alan for a theological analysis of same-sex copulation.

103. Alan *Ars praedicandi* 5 (Migne *PL* 210 122b).

104. Alan *Ars praedicandi* 44 (Migne *PL* 210·191d)

105. Alan *Sermo* "Gloriosa dicta sunt de te / Fratres karissimi, Rex regum qui imperat" (Migne *PL* 210:202d–203a) Compare the entry in d'Alverny's list of sermons, *Alain de Lille,* p 132

106. Alan *Liber poenitentialis* 1.4 (Longère 27)

107. Alan *Liber poenitentialis* 1.32 (Longère 35).

108. Alan *Liber poenitentialis* 2.125 (Longère 110)

109. See Glorieux, "La Somme 'Quoniam homines' d'Alain de Lille," p. 115.

110. Alan *Tractatus de virtutibus, de vitiis, et de donis Spiritus sancti,* as edited by Lottin, p.75. This text replaces Lottin's earlier edition, in "Le traité d'Alain de Lille sur les vertus, les vices et les dons du Saint-Esprit"

The analysis is foreclosed in the move from the unsatisfactory allegories of the *Plaint,* through the excesses of invective in the sermons, to the terse discretion of the moral manuals and the *Summa.* The paradoxes uncovered in Nature's teaching are never made good in a plain-speaking doctrine for Christians. On Alan's understanding of the rhetoric available to various modes of theology, it seems that they cannot be.

Alan succeeds in postponing this disconcerting conclusion beyond the *Plaint of Nature.* He postpones them beyond the end of the dream, into the unfolding of Christian theology, which can remain for the allegory a superlative promise and not an incomplete realization. Postponement may be the sweetest charm of the allegory of the *Plaint.* It may explain why Alan would labor so hard to show the limits of Nature and Nature's arguments. How pleasant to sport with Ovid, to escape for the space of a dream the disquieting and all-too-natural survival of Sodom in the midst of the City of God.

FIVE

The Care of Sodomites

Medieval practices of penance, of confession and reconciliation, lent themselves for use by many motives. So now do their histories. It is easy enough to tell a story about the development of confessional practice as the growth of ecclesiastical control over population, as the construction of new and more manipulable subjects, as the encroachment of persecution into the life of every believer. It is also easy to tell the story as one of pastoral seriousness for populations too long left untended, of the bringing of the Gospel to the people. Whatever the master narrative, it remains true that the writings for and about confessors reveal as few others can the detailed application of moral categories. This is especially true for the category of Sodomy.

Manuals or treatises about confession appear abundantly in the early decades of the thirteenth century. They do not appear out of nothing. Many are applications or simplifications of the moral and legal teaching accomplished in the twelfth century by masters such as Alan of Lille, to name one of dozens. The interest in pastoral care would issue in and be invigorated by the fourth church council held at the Lateran (1215). Innocent III's call for the council listed among its first tasks "to extirpate vices and to plant virtues, to correct abuses and to reform morals."[1] The council passed a number of constitutions encouraging pastoral care, of which the most important was one specifying already customary expectations for annual confession and communion. Every believer, male and female, was now required to confess sins "faithfully" at least once a year to his or her own priest. The priest hearing these confessions was to be "discreet and cautious, so that in the manner of an expert physician he might 'pour wine and

1. Innocent III *Vineam Domini Sabaoth* = Epistle 16.30 (Migne *PL* 216 823d–825c).

oil' on the wounds of the injured."[2] He should conduct a full diagnostic investigation before trying various experiments to heal the sick soul. Above all, he was to take every care not to reveal what the penitent had disclosed in the confessional.

The strictures on confessional secrecy are certainly one reason the good confessor must be "discreet and cautious." Others are acknowledged more or less candidly in writings on confession. One danger is that the confessor's questions will suggest to the penitent sins that the penitent might not otherwise have imagined. This danger is obvious enough, especially in sexual matters. Another danger, equally apparent, is that the very attempt to instruct penitents about sins will raise questions about the reasons for certain prohibitions. Robert of Flamborough's *Penitential Book*, for example, contains any number of exchanges in which the penitent asks the confessor to justify a certain rule or to explain what seems a contradiction between some rule and some authoritative opinion. So far as the renewal of confession was meant to rationalize the moral life of Christians, it risked revealing any inconsistencies in traditional moral teaching.

These risks are evident. A third danger, somewhat more subtle, is that the teaching in the confessional would serve to reinforce a particular sin by tacitly admitting its commonness. To give a penitent a technical name for a forbidden act is to tell the penitent that the act occurs frequently enough to have been named. The penitent's act is not a solitary, unspeakable deed. It is one of a number of such deeds, the ongoing existence of which has been recognized by theology. This is related to a fourth danger, the subtlest and most interesting. It is the danger that the penitent will come to feel a kinship with others guilty of the same sin. To be told, "What you have done is what the Sodomites do," is to be invited to search out the Sodomites, your concealed brethren. The confessional risks becoming one station in a network of sinful communication. The confessor himself might serve as unwitting go-between.

TAKING SODOMY SERIOUSLY

Paul of Hungary's *Summa of Penance* was written shortly after and because of the Fourth Lateran Council. The treatise was meant to summarize and make applicable the council's constitution on regular confession. It may have been suggested by St. Dominic, whom Paul quotes as "Master Domi-

2. Lateran IV *Omnis utriusque sexus* (Alberigo 245); the reference is to Luke 10:34.

nic, our prior."[3] The reference would place the writing of the *Summa* between 1219 and 1221, when Dominic served as prior of St. Nicholas in Bologna up to his death.[4] Whether because of its intrinsic usefulness, its seniority, or its connection with Dominic, Paul's treatise circulated widely. It remained popular enough to attract revisers. Cardinal Berengar Fredoli was producing a third version of the work about a century after its original composition.

As Paul wrote it, the *Summa of Penance* is divided into two parts.[5] The first treats the practice of confession: who is obliged to confess, when, and to whom; what the confessor should say to elicit a full confession; how absolution of sins works and how it is limited. The second part of the *Summa* is a synopsis of the principal vices and virtues. The vices are organized, following Gregory's classification, around the seven capital vices, listed here in the order vainglory, anger, envy, sloth, avarice, gluttony, and luxury. The virtues are the three theological and the four cardinal, but they are intermingled in an odd way: prudence, justice, faith, hope, charity, fortitude, and temperance. Each of the principal vices and virtues is subdivided by Paul into further categories, yet these categories are given no more than a brief definition. Indeed, most of the separately titled sections in the second part of the *Summa* consist of no more than a few lines: "Impatience is not restraining an impetuous motion of the soul" or "Drunkenness is excess in drink."[6] The principal vices are given slightly more attention, and three subvices occupy Paul for more than the usual handful of lines. He deals with contempt and perjury at a length usually reserved for principal vices, and he devotes three separate sections to mendacity. But these are small dilations in the pattern of the text.

There is nothing to prepare the reader for Paul's enormous digression on the sin against nature. The digression makes up ten sections, one of which is the longest section in the entire treatise. Taken together, the sections on the sin against nature make up about 40 percent of the treatise on

3 Paul of Hungary *Summa* (*Bibliotheca Casinensis* 4:197a). For Paul's place among the first Dominican authors of confessors' manuals, see Boyle, "Notes on the Education on the Fratres Communes in the Dominican Order in the Thirteenth Century," pp. 252–253.

4. See Mandonnet, "La *Summa de poenitentia mag. Pauli presb S. Nicolai*," pp. 525–544, Diekstra, "The *Supplementum*," pp. 34–35, and Kaeppeli, *Scriptores Ordinis Praedicatorum medii aevi*, 3 207–209

5. The third section in the printed edition is clearly not part of Paul's original plan. He says early on that he will conclude the treatise with the discussion of vices and virtues: "in fine tamen totius huius tractatus si potero et tempus habuero tractabo de istis vitiis principalibus ponendo descriptiones que ex ipsis procedunt et de virtutibus cardinalibus" (p. 195a–b). In what follows, I will thus not consider the last three columns of the printed edition as part of the *Summa*

6 Paul of Hungary *Summa* (pp. 203b and 206b).

all the vices. To say this differently, Paul gives the sin against nature more attention than the capital sins of vainglory, anger, envy, sloth, and gluttony combined. What ought to be no more than a subcategory of the capital sin of *luxuria* comes to dominate the whole taxonomy of vice and to rival in length the whole discussion of virtue. It is not surprising then that medieval readers excerpted Paul on the sin against nature and counted it a freestanding work.[7] Certainly its detail and its vehemence seem out of place in the plan of his *Summa*.

The careful reader may have noted how seriously Paul regards the sin. It is first mentioned in a section on whether a husband who has sexual intercourse with his wife sins in doing so.[8] The answer depends in part on the motive for intercourse. There is no sin if the motive is begetting children or paying the marriage debt, that is, fulfilling the sexual obligation to one's spouse entailed by marriage. There is venial sin if the motive is avoiding incontinence, that is, preventing oneself from committing a worse sin out of sexual desire. Sexual intercourse within marriage is a mortal sin if the cause is either an excess of desire produced by aphrodisiacs or a habit of copulation when there is little desire. The most lethal sin of all arises when a man "knows his wife against nature."[9]

As is his custom, Paul tethers the remark with a citation from Gratian's *Decretum*, one of several compilations of church law that serve as his constant sources, even for quotations from patristic writers. The reference here is to a passage imputed to Augustine, which had already been noticed by earlier collections of theological authorities.[10] As it appears in Gratian, the passage is attributed to Augustine's *On Adulterous Couplings*, but it is in fact manufactured from fragments of his *On the Conjugal Good*.[11] The conflated passage does suggest, if it does not define, what is meant by "against nature." But Paul turns to it here and repeatedly later on for its startling assertion that unnatural copulation with one's wife is worse than incest with one's mother.

Augustine is made to say this:

The evil of adultery outweighs that of fornication, but is outweighed by the evil of incest. *It is worse to lie with one's mother, than with the wife of another*

7. Diekstra, "The *Supplementum*," pp. 33–34.
8 Paul of Hungary *Summa* (pp. 198b–199a).
9. Paul of Hungary *Summa* (p. 198b): "aut cognoscit uxorem suam contra naturam et tunc mortalissime peccat."
10. Gratian *Decretum* pars 2 causa 32 q.7 cap.11 *Adulterii malum* (Richter-Friedberg 1:1143) Compare Ivo of Chartres *Decretum* 9.10; and Peter Lombard *Sententiae* 4 38.10 (Grottaferrata 2:481–482).
11. The text conflates passages from *De bono coniugali* 8.8 and 11 12, but it cites *De adulterinis coniugiis*. Compare the reference in Peter Lombard's *Sententiae* (Grottaferrata 2:481).

[*On the Conjugal Good*, 8.8 beginning]. But worse than all of these is what is done against nature, as when *a man would want to use a woman's member not given for this* [11.2 middle]. Now the natural use if done beyond measure *is something venial with a wife, something damnable with a prostitute. What is against nature is execrable if done with a prostitute, but more execrable if done with a wife. The ordering of the creator and the order of the creature holds so far, that it is much more tolerable to exceed the mean in things given to be used, than in those things which were not so given* [11.2 from beginning].[12]

I have italicized the words in the conflated passage that are taken from Augustine, and I have indicated their relative positions in the two chapters of his text. Augustine's mention of fornication and adultery in the first chapter is part of a *reductio* argument about the gradation of evils or goods. His main point is that both marriage and virginity can be good, even if virginity is better. His argument in the second chapter is that it is less serious to sin by having vaginal intercourse than to sin by having nonvaginal intercourse. Hence, it is less sinful for a wife to permit her husband to engage in nonvaginal intercourse with a prostitute than for her to permit him to do it with her. In neither passage does Augustine say or suggest that nonvaginal intercourse is worse than maternal incest.

That is just the lesson that Paul reads in his legal authorities. It is a lesson more powerful to him than to a modern reader. The medieval Latin church is famous for its preoccupation with avoiding incest. Much of the ecclesiastical regulation of marriage was concerned to map out the exact limits of permissible kinship between spouses. The kinship could often be quite remote, as it could be spiritual. Various marriage taboos were created by baptismal sponsorship or other sacramental performance. Recall Peter Damian's horror at the "incestuous" copulations of priests who seduce those whom they have baptized. Within this realm of fear over remote possibilities of incest, Paul of Hungary reads that nonvaginal intercourse is worse than the worst imaginable incest—the physical incest of son and mother.

Paul carries the comparison with incest into his next section, on the gradation of sins. A sin may be great because of its horror and cruelty, such as murder, or because of its stench and stain, as fornication, or because of detestation, abomination, and penalty, as with the vice against nature.

12 Adulterii malum vincit fornicationem, vincitur autem ab incestu *Peius est cum matre, quam cum aliena uxore concumbere* Sed omnium horum pessimum est quod contra naturam fit, ut si *vir membro mulieris non ad hoc concesso voluerit uti*. . . Usus enim naturalis si ultra modum *prolabitur, in uxore quidem veniale est, in meretrice dampnabile Iste, qui est contra naturam, execrabiliter fit in meretrice, sed execrabilius in uxore Tantum valet ordinatio creatoris et ordo creaturae, ut in rebus ad utendum concessis, etiam cum modus exceditur, longe sit tolerabilius, quam in eis, que concessa non sunt.*

"Because we never read in the Old or New Testament that any sin was so gravely punished, and no one doubts that something more wicked has been committed when it is more gravely punished."[13] A bit later he emphasizes the point from another direction: "Note the degree in fornication, because an adulterer sins more gravely than a fornicator, and someone committing incest than an adulterer. But graver than all of this is the delinquent against nature. Thus it is less a sin to know your own mother than to sin against nature, as Augustine expressly says."[14] The conflated passage in Gratian is cited again.

Paul has made his view of the gravity of the sin clear enough, but the reader should still be surprised that the sin against nature comes to fill almost half of the whole treatise of vices. Indeed, it makes up the treatise's latter half, because Paul's arrangement of the capital vices puts *luxuria* last among the seven. The sin against nature comes last in *luxuria*. None of its other species merits more than a few words. Even incest is treated in three lines of simple definition. By contrast, the sin against nature requires more than three hundred lines. So the final, the lengthiest, and the most vehement words that the reader hears on the matter of human vice are an attack upon this one sexual sin.

Paul announces that he will divide his discussion according to four topics: how detestable the sin is, what evils arise from it, what punishments are assigned to it, and what its cause was. As it turns out, Paul interpolates between the second and third topics an unannounced section explaining "the water of Sodom and Gomorrah." He also prefaces the discussion with a definition: "The vice or sin against nature is when someone spills semen outside the place specified for this."[15] This definition is, of course, much wider than the definition used in Paul's authorities. Even the "Augustinian" passage had counted as sin against nature nonvaginal heterosexual intercourse. Paul's definition includes any seminal emission outside the vagina—with or without partners, whatever the sex of the partners. It is clear, I think, that Paul himself recognizes the shift in definition, because when he now quotes the "Augustinian" passage, he omits the phrase "as when a man would want to use a woman's member not given for this" (*ut si vir membro mulieris non ad hoc concesso voluerit uti*). He omits the heterosexual specification. The deliberation blurring of definitions is essential to Paul's strategy in the attack on the sin against nature.

13. Paul of Hungary *Summa* (p. 199a).
14. Paul of Hungary *Summa* (p 199a).
15. Paul of Hungary *Summa* (p. 207b): "Vitium sive peccatum contra naturam est quando aliquis extra locum ad hoc deputatum effudit semen."

There are, he begins, five reasons for detesting this sin. The first is that it is worse than incest with one's mother—here figures the abbreviated quotation from Augustine. The second reason is that the sin ruptures the community (*societas*) that we ought to have with God. The authority here is another passage from Augustine via Gratian. This time the passage is taken more or less whole from the *Confessions,* though again out of context.[16] The decisive thing is that it introduces the Sodomites, who have so far been absent: "Crimes against nature are everywhere and always to be detested and to be punished, as the Sodomites were." If Augustine invokes the punishment of the Sodomites as an indication of the severity of punishment, Paul will use it as grounds for equating crimes against nature with the crimes of the Sodomites simply speaking. The third reason for detesting vice against nature is that it cannot even be spoken without polluting the mouth of those speaking and the ears of those listening. Paul invokes through Gratian a passage from Jerome.[17] He adds that he remembers hearing that some saint wrote that good angels flee as far away from those speaking about this sin as the sound of their voices carry. This is connected with the fourth reason. The sin against nature cannot be forgiven anyone unless it is confessed by name, and yet its acts are so bestial that they can hardly be named. As Haymo of Auxerre says, they are left unnamed even by nature.[18] Not to speak them is to entomb oneself in hell, and yet nature itself seems to abhor the speaking. So, fifth, the Epistle of Jude speaks of the eternal burning of those who go after "alien flesh"—a burning just like that of the cities of Sodom and Gomorrah. Paul adds a gloss: "alien flesh" means "man polluted with man, woman with woman."[19] If traditional, the gloss is still necessary. The copulation of same with same would hardly seem to be the embrace of "alien" flesh. On the contrary, it would seem to be less "alien" than the flesh of the opposite sex.[20]

Such is Paul's list of reasons for detesting the sin against nature, now

---

16 Augustine *Confessiones* 3.8.15 (Skutella-Verheijen 33:56 16–22) I will discuss this passage at greater length below, in connection with Thomas Aquinas's use of it.

17 Paul of Hungary *Summa* (pp. 207b–208a) The reference is to Gratian *Decretum* 2.32.4.12 (Richter-Friedberg 1:1130).

18 Paul of Hungary *Summa* (p. 208a). The reference is to Haymo's commentary on Rom 1·26, as in Migne *PL* 117 376.

19. Paul of Hungary *Summa* (p 208a) The reference is to Jude 7.

20. The passage in Jude is notoriously difficult. Bailey suggests that it might be connected, through intertestamental rabbinic traditions, with the equally obscure passage in Gen 6:1–4 on the copulation of between "sons of God" and "daughters of men." See Bailey, *Homosexuality and the Western Christian Tradition,* pp. 10–18.

revealed as the sin of the Sodomites. It is not clear for whom the list is intended. Are these reasons meant to supply the confessor with arguments for use in the confessional, with terrifying scriptural passages and *exempla* involving the revulsions of angels? Or are they meant to prove for the confessor that the sin is a serious one? Paul had conceded in his first paragraph that "some count the sin as nothing and . . . in some regions men are abused almost publicly as if from a sort of urbanity (literally, "courtliness," *curialitas*), and those with whom they perpetrate this terrible and abominable vice are called charming (*gratiosos*)."[21] Note the implications. There is a world in which the sin against nature is publicly accepted and freely spoken. Far from being silent, it speaks artfully and even coyly about itself. Moreover, the sin is the sin of those who master speech, the learned, the inhabitants of courts. If "terrible and abominable," it is also worldly and attractive.

If Paul's concern is to rebut these views, to root them out in the mind of any of his readers, then the context suggested by the original "Augustinian" sense of sin against nature has been entirely reversed. Paul is worried not about nonvaginal intercourse between married couples, but about what seems to be either a common opinion or a public and perhaps privileged practice. The opinion is unspecific enough to cover a number of sins. The practice, as he describes it, is concerned only with men. The reference to "certain regions" might suggest that he has in mind non-Christian regimes, perhaps especially Islamic ones. But then this is a confessor's manual, not a missionary handbook. If the opinion and the practice stigmatized here were only distant threats, there would be little reason to digress at such length on the reasons for detesting this sin. And since the whole of the treatise is directed to the confessor rather than to the penitent, we must assume that some of the urgency in Paul's arguments is an urgency about convincing confessors to treat the sin as the serious thing it is.

Paul turns to evils that have arisen and that "arise daily" from the "sin of Sodomy." Two things are striking. The first is the presence of the sin from day to day. The second is that the sin has now changed its name from the sin against nature to Sodomy. The scriptural associations invoked in the five arguments are now made into an equation. The equation makes it possible to transfer to an unspecified variety of nonprocreative sexual acts the full force of the biblical description of the judgment on the cities of the plain. It gives to these sins an apocalyptic dimension. This makes some-

21. Paul of Hungary *Summa* (p. 207a)

what plausible Paul's list of evils resulting from the sin of Sodomy. It was one of the causes of the Flood.[22] It destroys humankind by destroying semen, as Onan did. Its denial of life so outraged God that he turned Sodom and Gomorrah into a sea within which nothing can live and over which no manned boat can cross.

This third evil resulting from Sodomy seems to be what launches Paul into his unannounced discussion of the properties of the water of Sodom and Gomorrah.[23] It is a discussion that he places explicitly between the evils that arose from Sodomy and that evils that daily arise from it. The properties of the Sodomitic water are so many metaphors for the unnaturalness, sterility, and repulsiveness of Sodomy itself. The water over the burned-out cities bears up pieces of iron while a feather sinks. Alongside it are found apples that are beautiful on the outside but filled inside with cinders and ashes. Other trees bear apples that disappear at the touch, exploding into dust and yet more cinders. The imaginary botany concedes again how attractive the allegedly repulsive act of Sodomy is. The apples may be cauterized inwardly; outwardly they are beautiful. Beautiful enough to attract touch, because it is only when touched that they explode.

The fate of Lot's wife should remind us that God wants no trace of this sin to survive because it is the greatest of all sins. "[Sinners] of this kind are hepatic and enervated weaklings (*epatici et enervati molles*), and are effeminate, as if reserved to the delicacies of Pharaoh." They are "hepatic" because in the medicine that Paul knows the liver is the principal organ of the system of "natural" powers within which generative power is included. Sodomites seem to have a disordered reproductive desire, correlated with a dysfunction of the liver. They are "enervated" because they exhibit a physiological susceptibility associated with women—here it becomes clear that Paul is thinking of male Sodomites. Finally, their effeminacy is associated with that of the Egyptian court, known in the medieval imagination for its oriental luxury and its calamitous punishment by the God of Israel. As an Oriental court, Egypt was also imagined to house eunuchs.

From the continued presence of sinners against nature there come in the present any number of catastrophes. "The [church] law says that because of this crime there come about famine and plagues, and earthquakes. . . . Again Sodomites are the adversaries of God, and murderers and destroyers of humankind. They seem to say to God, 'You created human beings to

---

22. Paul cites Methodius *Historia Scholastica* cap. De causis diluvus The same passage is understood by Peter of Poitiers to refer to male-female copulation with the woman on top See his *Compilatio praesens* cap 12 (ed Longère p. 16, lines 41–43)

23 Paul of Hungary *Summa* (p. 208b)

multiply. But we work so that your work may be destroyed.'"[24] The Sodomite is the anticreator, the one who spurns God's offer of the power of procreation. Of course, the same charge, if not the same speech, could be imputed to any vowed celibate. Anyone who freely renounces procreation would seem to reject God's command to multiply—indeed, would seem to reject God's gift of a sexed body. This is a point to which we will return.

The radical rejection of God makes it fitting that Sodomy be punished by the maximum penalty. According to Paul, both divine and human law make the sin a capital offense. He links Leviticus 18:22 with a passage from legislation attributed to Constantine. There may be some mitigation for partial or incomplete acts. Someone who corrupts a youth "completely" is to be executed, but if the corruption is only incomplete, then the penalty is exile to an island. The canonical penalty for this is perpetual penance in a monastery. Paul also notes that deposition is for clerics what beheading is in civil law. But none of these is comparable to the divine punishment of the Sodomites. God's patience exhausted, God burned them alive in this life and then cast them down into hell where they could be punished without end.

Paul turns finally and at greatest length to the cause of "the Sodomitic sin." A number causes are given without any attempt to explain their connection. The first cause, supported by Ezekiel, is that of abundance of food, wine, oil, leisure, foreign foods, and pride of life.[25] The second cause, described by St. Paul and noted by two commentators on him, is idolatry.[26] But then Paul of Hungary seems to change direction. He uses a quotation from Gregory the Great to suggest that the sins of Sodom were so novel and outrageous that God was somehow surprised by them. God had to go down and look at these incredible events.[27] The mention of Genesis leads Paul to list the four sins that cry out to heaven: Sodomy, homicide, oppression, and bribery (or perhaps usury). Each is a violation of nature, but the worst violation is that of Sodomy.

Paul returns to the question of its causes, but he speaks now not so much from scriptural authorities as from "learned men and those who are experienced in hearing confessions."[28] We presume that what follows is grounded

24 Paul of Hungary *Summa* (pp 208b–209a)
25 Paul of Hungary *Summa* (p 209a). The reference is to Ezek 16:49
26 Paul of Hungary *Summa* (p 209b). The reference is to Rom 1:26, with the commentaries of Haymo (Migne *PL* 117:376a–b) and Ambrose *De Abraham* (Schenkl 536–539)
27. Paul of Hungary *Summa* (p 209b) The reference is to Gen 18·21, with Gregory's remark on it in at *Moralia in Job* 19 25 (Adriaen 992)
28. Paul of Hungary *Summa* (p. 210a)

in observation of the prevailing reality in Christendom. Sodomitic sin is typically found in two groups. The first is certain courtiers (*curiales*) who are not strong enough to have a quantity of women (*copiam mulierum habere non valentes*). I take Paul to refer to the effeminacy of the Sodomite. These half-men do not have the physiological desire or stamina for promiscuity with women. Hence they practice the (less demanding?) sin of Sodomy. The second group comprises clerics and the cloistered who have little devotion in prayer and who detest discipline of the flesh. The association of Sodomy with clerks and monks is hardly novel. We have seen it at least from Peter Damian forward. But Paul wants to explain it in more detail by associating it with lack of spiritual and physical asceticism. So he repeats from Jerome and Matthew that there is no triumph over the flesh except by prayer and fasting. The devil will fight this, of course, by sending stronger temptations. But one ought not to despair; the helping hand of God is omnipotent. Having failed, turn to God through penance.

Paul does not end the chapter or his discussion of Sodomy with that call to repentance. He goes on to restate his conclusion: the vice is most grave. One should reject out of hand the excuse or mitigation of those who say that it is only a kind of pollution, like a nocturnal ejaculation. "It is indeed a pollution that pollutes the soul and the body. Nor is it done in the body of one who sleeps, but rather in one who is awake." It does not have the excuse of sleep. The confessor ought to apply this rule: Any emission outside of the natural vessel, however it is brought about, is a vice against nature, and anyone who commits such an act is to be considered a Sodomite.

With that severe censure, we come to the end of Paul's long digression—and indeed, to the end of his confessional manual. However much he has dilated on the sin of Sodomy, he has said rather little about how the confessor is to address it in the conversation of the confessional. Indeed, it has remained unclear whether Paul is trying to instruct the confessor how to treat the sin or to convince him that it is a sin. The length and vehemence of his digression suggest the latter.

If the scope of Sodomy is so large, and the judgment on it so severe, the confessor will certainly want to exercise care in approaching the topic. On the one side, he will not want to suggest such terrible practices to those who might never have thought of them. On the other side, he will want to ferret out those who have practiced such acts but who would hesitate to admit them. Paul of Hungary does give some general directives for proceeding about sins in general. The confessor is to "lead out the twisted serpent with an obstetric hand." [29] He is to ask about any of the principal sins "under a certain covering" (*integumentum*, the word used by Alan of Lille for poetic fiction). But the confessor is also to ask after much of the penitent's biography, after his friends and customs, and especially after his temptations. How were these resisted? What thoughts accompanied resistance or succumbing? By such indirect means, the confessor may be able to proceed with sufficient indirectness and caution. More is needed for confidence. We have not heard in any detail how the confessor is to converse with the Sodomite.

CONFESSIONAL INQUIRIES

Cautions to confessors appear in a number of other texts, if not always where or as we might expect them. Robert of Flamborough's *Penitential Book* was written a few years before Paul's *Summa* (probably 1208–1213). [30] It became one of the most widely diffused confessor's manuals of the thirteenth century. Robert of Flamborough provides in his section on *luxuria* one of his usual schemata for questioning a penitent. [31] The confessor is to ask whether the penitent has ever committed *luxuria* against nature. If so, with a man? A cleric or a layman? If a layman, married or single? In what ecclesiastical state was the penitent when committing these acts? And so on. The inquiry proceeds only under the general cautions about confession. Matters change when Robert of Flamborough directs the confessor to ask whether the penitent sinned in some other way against nature, whether he "had someone" in a manner out of the ordinary. If the penitent asks for clarification the confessor is not to respond. "For I never make mention to him of something from which he can take the occasion of sin, but only of generalities which all know to be sins. But masturbation (literally, 'softness,' *mollitia*) I extract painfully (*dolorose*) from him, and similarly from a woman, but the manner of extracting it is not to be written down." [32] The anxiety over provoking sin seems for Robert of Flamborough to be most intense around the act of masturbation, not around that of same-sex intercourse. The *Penitential Book* does provide penalties for masturbation, and recognizes that it is typically a sin of boys, but it never reveals the

---

29 Paul of Hungary *Summa* (p. 195a).
30 Robert of Flamborough *Liber poenitentialis* (Firth 9).
31. Robert of Flamborough *Liber poenitentialis* 4.8 (Firth 195–196, sec. no. 223)
32 Robert of Flamborough *Liber poenitentialis* 4 8 (Firth 196–196, sec. no. 224).

secret of how to extract the confession of masturbation from the penitent.[33]

Peter of Poitiers's *Compilation* also has a chapter of general advice on questions about sexual sins. "Unusual sins, namely against use and nature, are certainly not to be asked about everywhere and indifferently, nor are circumstances of this kind, especially with young persons, whether men or women, who have not had much experience with sliminess of the flesh (*lubricum carnis*) either as regards time or number of partners."[34] If the confessor suspects that the person is guilty of such crimes but is ashamed to confess them or fearful of punishment, he should ask "more securely and more diligently, thus at once more cautiously and more candidly" whether the penitent sinned with a woman "or in some other way than use or nature requires."[35] If the penitent denies it absolutely, then the confessor should not proceed.

More detailed and more forthcoming instructions for the examination of sexual sins are given in a little work by Robert of Sorbonne. The work may have been written as many as forty or fifty years after Paul of Hungary's *Summa*.[36] The chronological skip need not be too worrisome. We are not trying to construct a narrative history. Moreover, the treatise's interest lies precisely in its author's mediocrity. Robert was a popular preacher, a friend of the royal court, and an academic founder of some ability. He was hardly an original or experimental theologian. If his pastoral works were widely copied and even plagiarized, it is because they spoke well of familiar truths. This is the case with the little treatise on the confession of sins of *luxuria*. It may be a fragment of some larger, lost work.[37] It may have been intended as a freestanding, practical guide to a particularly difficult area. On either supposition, it is extremely revealing of the care Sodomites could expect to receive in the confessional.

The treatise, which is known merely by its opening words as "If the sinner should say," consists of a series of ideal dialogues between confessor and penitent on sins of *luxuria*.[38] The sins are of various kinds. They range from masturbation through same-sex copulation, bestiality, openmouthed kissing, touching the genitals of another, touching one's own genitals with-

33. Robert of Flamborough *Liber poenitentialis* 5 10 (Firth 243, sec no 294).

34. Peter of Poitiers *Compilatio praesens* 19 (Longère 22.1–6).

35. Peter of Poitiers *Compilatio praesens* (Longère 22 9–14)

36. This is the opinion of Glorieux, who places all of Robert's works between 1261 and his death in 1274. See his *Aux origines de la Sorbonne*, 1:54

37 Glorieux, *Aux origines de la Sorbonne*, 1 57 The work's authenticity is also accepted by Diekstra, "The *Supplementum*," p 24

38 I use the text printed as a work of William of Auvergne in *Guilielmi Alverni   Opera omnia*, 2:231b–232b

out ejaculation, to showing one's penis to another. The center of concern is clearly the sin of the Sodomites, which serves as a threat in the analysis of lesser sins.

Robert avoids the issue of how to interrogate penitents about sexual matters by having the penitent begin the imaginary dialogue. The penitent admits to have ejaculated by touching his "nature" (*natura*) with his own hands. (The use of "nature" for penis is a startling reminder how difficult it is to give any strict philosophical sense to this term.) The confessor is to reply as follows: "You sinned most seriously, and it seems more serious to sin by doing this than by knowing one's own mother; for it is more serious to know a relation than to know a stranger, and the closer the person is as relation the more serious the sin done with that person. So someone who pollutes himself in this way sins most seriously." Here Robert transfers the false Augustinian passage from same-sex copulation, where Paul of Hungary had attached it, to masturbation. Quite ingeniously, he makes one's relation to oneself the worst case of incest. Because you are closer to yourself than to anyone else, having sex with yourself is the worst kind of incest.

Robert is not alone. A similar logic about self-relation in masturbation can be found earlier in the pastoral tradition. In the *Compilation*, originally composed just about 1216, Peter of Poitiers devotes a separate chapter to the "monster of masturbation" (*mollitia*).[39] The sin is to be inquired after cautiously, but once it is confessed, it is to be judged harshly. The confessor is to say that this sin is so terrible that it is never plainly named, but rather always referred to under a certain euphemism (*pallatio*) as "softness." It is different from the Sodomitic vice in that it corrupts only one person, but it is also more monstrous than that vice. In masturbation, the same person is both active and passive. The masturbator is "as if man and woman, and as if a hermaphrodite." What is worse, the ordinary advice about sins of the flesh does not work in this case. The confessor can advise in others cases that a penitent avoid bad company or places of temptation. In the case of masturbation, you cannot avoid yourself nor the domestic situations in which the sin is likely to happen.

Turn back to Robert's exemplary dialogue between masturbator and confessor. Once the fact of a single instance has been established, the confessor is to ask whether this sin has been confessed before. If so, no plea of ignorance is to be accepted. The next question is whether the penitent has ejaculated semen outside a womb in some way other than by contact with

---

39. Peter of Poitiers *Compilatio praesens* (Longère 18–19). For the work's dating, see pp xiv–xv Longère dates the revisions to the *Compilatio* by James of St.-Victor shortly after the original composition, that is, around 1220 (p. xviii)

himself. There is contact with the hands of another, which is detestable and worse than masturbation. Then there is same-sex copulation or copulation with an animal, "and so on," all of which are enormous crimes brought together under the term "abuse," and all of which corrupt nature. Those given to such vices are punished with sudden and horrible death. Robert adds a verse: "The bestial man who touches sacred things and who spills semen, rejecting [all] warning, will die a sudden death." The death of the unclean who touch the sacrament is inferred from 1 Corinthians 11; the sudden death of those who emit semen, from the story of Onan. Other cases of immediate death for sin are mentioned from both Old and New Testament. Even if civic and church law were not to count the vices as capital crimes, God does and punishes accordingly.

Robert's confessor is then instructed to add the comparison with maternal incest and the equation with murder. The usual scriptural verses of condemnation are included, along with a traditional etymology that makes "Sodom" mean "mute." Those guilty of the sin that cannot be named, that makes them less than human, are rendered mute as animals before God. So the confessor is to say, "Friend, you should thank God much in so far as you have escaped this [fate], and you should love Him who liberated you from such a passion and from hellish death." The rhetorical strategy here is that of pretending to presume that the sin will be avoided once its full horror has been described. The confessor is to speak as if any sane person would henceforth flee from something so horrible. That is why no particular therapies are suggested for dealing with any relapse.

The treatise moves on to what are presented as male-female sins. First there is disordered kissing—that is, kissing women openmouthed, with the use of the tongue or with nibbling. Next comes touching of the genitals in order to produce lust in a woman. The confessor is instructed to ask whether the penitent has ever touched himself without ejaculating. He is to be warned that this leads very quickly to fornication. Finally the confessor is to ask whether the penitent has ever displayed his "nature" to his companions or to anyone else. If he has, he is to be warned that this is at least a sin of fornication, since it is so obviously productive of lust. The confessor may also add the following admonition, though it is to be used cautiously: "It is the custom of Sodomites to show each other their male members (*virilia*), and they know each other by this sign, and it is most vile to become like the Sodomites." But Robert adds immediately that this is best said only to those who desire women vehemently and who have often sinned with them. The caution suggests that only very virile men,

men excessively attached to women, can safely hear about the practices of the Sodomites. Anyone else might learn from the confessor that there is a community of Sodomites with its own customary signals. We see again the anxiety that Sodomy is in fact not repulsive—that it is immensely attractive. We also learn that Sodomites seek each other out in typical ways, that they pass down from generation to generation a language of recognition. The confessor is warning his penitent to avoid places used for cruising.

PLACING SODOMY

Robert of Flamborough insists at the beginning of his *Penitential Book* that confessions should be conducted according to a rationalized system of sins. He says in the prologue that the penitent should confess "by steps and in order about all of the seven capital vices, first about the first, second about the second, and so on about single ones according to the single pattern (*propter compendium*)."[40] A little later he speaks more personally: "Almost everyone confesses in a disorderly way. Setting aside the order of vices, they follow the order of age, places, and times. . . . In this way they confuse both themselves and the memory of the priest. I prefer that you confess single vices in sequence together with their species so far as one is born and proceeds from another, starting from pride, which is the root of all evils."[41] Adequate confession depends on an adequate moral theology. It ought ideally to follow the causality of sins, their pattern of genesis.

Confession must then depend upon the preaching of that moral theology. This much is clear already in the decrees of the Fourth Lateran Council. Bishops who are, for one reason or another, unable to meet their pastoral obligations are to appoint assistants to help them both in preaching the word of God and in hearing confessions and assigning penances.[42] The juxtaposition of preaching and confessing is hardly coincidental. If the faithful needed to be taught the rudiments of the creed, they also needed to be taught the outlines of Christian morality. So the conciliar decree emphasizes that the preachers must show in their lives what they speak in their sermons. But if the preachers are going to teach a rational pattern of morality, much more if they will live it, then they themselves must be taught. This need was recognized early on. Obviously Paul of Hungary's *Summa* combines instruction in confessional practice with a review of the

40. Robert of Flamborough *Liber poenitentialis* prologue (Firth 55.27– 28)
41. Robert of Flamborough *Liber poenitentialis* 3 (Firth 62.68–76).
42. Lateran IV *Inter cetera* (Alberigo 239–240).

vices and virtues. So it is in earlier and contemporary confessor's manuals. But there was also need for fuller treatments of moral life, treatments that would somehow combine the traditional doctrine of the virtues and vices with the more specific "cases of conscience" that were increasingly discussed among moralists.

Organizations of the virtues and vices reach back through the Eastern monastic traditions and the Fathers to pagan mythographers and philosophers.[43] No exact knowledge of the stages of transmission and elaboration is presupposed by the confessor's books. It is enough to know that by the twelfth century, catalogues of virtues and vices were well established, though the order of their elements was not fixed. Theological variations on these treatises lengthened the catalogue by adding other elements in sequence—virtues, vices, gifts, beatitudes one after another, as in Alan of Lille's *Summa*.[44] The sequences lengthen again as later writers distinguish more carefully between theological and cardinal virtues and as they continue to add new elements, such as the commandments. So William of Auxerre considers in turn the virtues as such, the theological virtues, the cardinal virtues (with their annexes), the gifts, the beatitudes, the properties and comparisons of the virtues, and finally the commandments, with corresponding sins and cases.[45]

The appearance of cases in William of Auxerre, early in the thirteenth century, is significant. Alongside the sequential treatments of academic theology, there had developed the "summa of cases" or confessor's studybook. An early example can be had in the sprawling *Summa of Sacraments and Counsels of the Soul* that goes under the name of Peter the Chanter.[46] The last part of this *Summa* is a *Book of Cases of Conscience* in 64 "chapters." Some of the chapters do report particular cases calling for delicate moral judgments.[47] Others deal with fundamentals—the virtues, merit, and sin as such.[48] The variety of Peter's material is exceeded by its disorder, which worsens near the anthology's end.

By contrast, and with the benefit of intervening decades, the Dominican Raymund of Peñafort codifies the casuistic material by applying a schema of crimes. Crimes are committed either against God or one's neighbor, and

---

43. The best introduction to the medieval organizations of virtues and vices is now Newhauser, *The Treatise on Vices and Virtues.*

44. See above, chapter 4.

45 William of Auxerre *Summa aurea* 3 11, 12–16, 19–29, 30–34, 35, 38–43, and 44–55, respectively

46 It was finished by his colleagues and students shortly after his death in 1197

47 Chapters 5, 29, 37, 44, 59, and 61

48 Chapters 20 and 58, 49, and 60 and 63, respectively

they are fully direct, less direct, or indirect.[49] Raymund then establishes order within each title, usually by adopting some of a standard list of questions: What is it? Why is it called that? How many senses does the name have? How is it distinguished? What are its kinds? What are its punishments? What doubtful cases are there? Raymund's order is an achievement, I think, and is directly connected with his work as a decretalist. The achievement has its price. The crimes here categorized do not even constitute a complete list of sins, much less a frame for a full account of the moral life. There is no special section on sexual sins. Raymund does mention very briefly Gregory's list of the seven capital sins and their "daughters" or consequences, but he does not even provide a list of their subspecies.[50] The only discussion of Sodomy seems to be one in the discussion of penances to be imposed in confession.[51] The authoritative texts adduced by Raymund are familiar from Paul of Hungary. Indeed, much of Raymund's language echoes Paul or some common source. It is as if Raymund had taken Paul's topics without taking his discussion of them. Thus we have the comparison with matricide, the argument from divine punishment of Sodom, the claim that many evils follow from Sodomy, and the assertion that it includes every kind of act except male-female copulation "in an orderly way" and in the right receptacle. Raymund's only personal note concerns the care to be used in discussing the matter: "Among all crimes, I believe that this one needs inquiries with caution and speaking with fear." However brief the discussion, this caution seems to be required. The fear of Sodomy is omnipresent.

A full account of the sin, indeed a summary of all previous accounts, is given by William Peraldus, whose combined *Summas of the Vices and the Virtues* must count as the great work of Dominican moral systematization before Thomas Aquinas. The combined work is large—about 11 percent longer than the moral section of Thomas's *Summa*. Peraldus returns to the consecutive or sequential treatment of moral topics, but with extraordinary thoroughness. He likes to argue by accumulating authorities, whether from Scripture, the Fathers, the nearly contemporary Masters of Theology, or ancient poets and philosophers. Peraldus deploys these texts so that those

49 Direct crimes against God are simony (1.1–3), simple unbelief (1 4), heresy (1.5), schism (1 6), and the combination of these last two in apostasy (1.7) Less direct crimes against God are breaking vows (1.8), breaking oaths and other perjuries (1.9), mendacity or adulation (1.10), divination (1 11), and disrespect for solemn feasts (1 12) Indirect crimes against God are sacrilege (1.13), crimes against Church sanctuary (1 14), refusal to give tithes, firstfruits, and oblations (1.15), and violations of the laws of burial
50 Raymund of Peñafort *Summa* 3 tit 34 "An sit facienae interrogationes " (p. 432a–b)
51 Raymund of Peñafort *Summa* 3 tit 34 De mensura poenarum (p 437b).

in sin might be converted, those struggling to live virtuously be confirmed. The result is rich in superlatives and in particular pleas: "Eight points that ought to hold men back from the office of lawyer," "The multiple evil that comes from carnal love in the church of God," "The twelve stupidities of propertied religious."[52] He finds room for every topic within his scheme.

Peraldus's *Summa of the Vices* is organized around the seven capital or "deadly" sins, with pride allotted almost as many sections as the rest combined.[53] A host of lesser sins is attached to the seven. There is also a long appendix on sins of the tongue. In the *Summa of the Virtues,* William Peraldus adopts a familiar serial order: the virtues in common, theological virtues, cardinal virtues, gifts, and beatitudes. There is a regular sequence of subtopics. Each cardinal virtue, for example, is given its several senses, then described, next commended and divided into parts. Before or after the division, mention is made of helps and hindrances to the particular virtue. All of this is not so much a guidebook for use in confessional inquiry as it is a moral teaching within which confessional topics can be properly placed and thoroughly analyzed. The confessor is not to have a copy of Peraldus on his knee in the confessional. He ought to have absorbed its teaching, in whole or in part, through long study before entering the confessional.

Within Peraldus's ample doctrine, there reappear most of the pieces we have seen in the other confessional works. New pieces are added. For example, *luxuria* as such brings in its train seven "worries" or "anxieties," including "stench, filthiness, infamy" (*fetor, foeditas, infamia*).[54] This is the threat of exposure. The sin is repugnant and displeasing to the angels, most damaging to the sinner. And so on. *Luxuria* loosely considered is divided into five species, ranging from soft clothing and bedding to sin with "the members assigned to generation." Only the last are *luxuria* strictly speaking. The species of generative sins is broken down into five subspecies: "simple fornication," "illicit deflowering of virgins," "adultery," "incest," and "sin against nature."[55] The last receives the fullest treatment, though nothing nearly so disproportionate as the tirade in Paul of Hungary.

Peraldus begins blandly enough. "Sometimes [the sin] is against nature as regards manner, as when the woman is on top or when it is done in the

---

52. *Summae de vitiis* (Venice 1497), folios 235rb [#365], 240vb [#377], 252rb [#403], respectively The numbers in brackets are sequential chapter numbers assigned according to the divisions of this edition.

53. The sections are allotted as follows: gluttony, 8; luxury, 36; avarice, 96; acedia, 49; pride, 138; envy, 4; and anger, 25.

54. William Peraldus *Summa de vitiis* tract. de luxuria (folio 201vb)

55 I will discuss the genealogy of this standard list below, in chapter 7.

animal manner, but still in the proper vessel. Sometimes it is against nature as regards substance, as when someone procures or consents to spilling semen elsewhere than in the place assigned to this by nature."[56] We recognize the inclusive definition of sin against nature as any ejaculation outside a womb. Having introduced the definition, William adds immediately, "This vice is to be spoken of with great caution, both in preaching and in hearing confessions, so that nothing be revealed to men that might give them occasion to sin." The warning applies to both preaching and confession. It thus poses in acute form a problem that has threatened all of the discussions from Paul of Hungary's *Summa* on.

If the sin against nature is only to be spoken of with great caution, elliptically or not at all, how are the faithful to be instructed about it? How are they to learn about the importance of avoiding it? One answer might be that since the sin is against nature, nature itself teaches that it is not to be done. But if the lessons of nature are so clear, so convincing, then there need be no fear of mentioning what has already denounced by nature. Again, if nature itself teaches that the sin should avoided as something horrible, then there need be no fear of contagion by suggestion—no fear that the least suggestion of the activity will incite to its practice. We have here the paradox of a deadly sin that must be condemned without being mentioned. There is no other sin like this in confessional practice—or Christian theology. With good reason: to hold that there is a very important sin against which the faithful cannot be warned is to make preaching and confession a game of charades.

Peraldus goes on, as is his custom, to offer scriptural and patristic proofs. They are divided into eight ways of showing that sin against nature "is the greatest." Peraldus does not make clear whether he means the greatest sin among sins of *luxuria* or the greatest simply. Some of his arguments go to the second conclusion. His proof texts are those we have already seen in various other authors, here gathered and systematized. Peraldus is able to mobilize so many texts because he assumes two identifications. He first identifies the sinner against nature with the Sodomite. He then finds the Sodomite in any ambiguous mention of heinous crime.

As he deploys the proof texts, Peraldus stresses two consequences of the sin of Sodom. The first is a double silence. This sin of Sodom is "an abomination," that is, "ineffable."[57] It should not be spoken. Again, and Peraldus here invokes the traditional etymology, Sodomy renders its per-

56 William Peraldus *Summa de vitiis* tract de luxuria (folio 203vb)

57. William Peraldus *Summa de vitiis* tract. de luxuria (folio 204rb)

petrators mute before God at the last judgment. "They cannot seek to excuse themselves on account of ignorance since nature itself taught the law
that they transgress to brute animals." The voiceless animals do not do
what Sodomites do, so the voices of Sodomites are taken away. The second
consequence that Peraldus emphasizes is the destruction of human nature.[58]
By choosing to make himself into a woman, a Sodomite shows complete
disregard for the nature God has given him. This is the nature for which
the Son took flesh and suffered. Sodomy not only denies God's creative
intention, it denies God's love as expressed in the incarnation.

Peraldus has offered no startling innovations of classification or condemnation. He does not intend to innovate. The aim of the *Summa* is to
collate the traditions of confessional writing in order to provide an exhaus-
tive and systematic teaching on the moral life. It would seem to do just that
with regard to the earlier texts on Sodomy. But the reader must wonder
after a time whether Peraldus has been as complete as he has promised.
What has been omitted from the *Summa* is not only the problematic analyses of the causes of Sodomy, but the problem of clerical Sodomy. Peraldus
nowhere suggests that Sodomy is a sin to which confessors themselves
might be particularly prone. In a book for clerical readers, he remains silent
about the danger to the clergy of this lethal sin. Is the silence deliberate?
Is it required as part of the caution he has so often invoked?

These questions would not be so important if Peraldus did not include
within his treatment of *luxuria* three sections on the problem of sexual sins
among the clergy and members of religious houses.[59] The chapters speak
only of sexual sins between men and women. Peraldus quotes Seneca, for
example, on the brutishness of giving in to fornication. He quotes Genesis
6 on the "sons of God" who take "wives" from among the "daughters of
men." The "sons of God" are, of course, understood to be males under
religious vows. Peraldus even gives the reader two long moral stories. Both
tell of the demons tempting male clerics to sin with women. In the second
story, some demons are overheard boasting to one another about their
wickedness.[60] One has spent thirty days killing various men in a province.
Another has devoted twenty days to drowning; a third, ten days to killing
newlyweds. Then the fourth demon boasts that he has spent eleven years
inciting a single monk to sin and just that night he has led him to commit
fornication. Satan crows over the fourth demon, saying, "You have done
something great."

58 William Peraldus *Summa de vitiis* tract de luxuria (folio 204va).
59 William Peraldus *Summa de vitiis* tract de luxuria (folios 205vb–206vb)
60 William Peraldus *Summa de vitiis* tract de luxuria (folio 206rb–va)

Nowhere in these longish chapters does Peraldus suggest that priests, monks, or nuns are tempted by masturbation or same-sex copulation. Yet Paul of Hungary, his Dominican predecessor, singled out priests and monks as a class in which Sodomy was most often found. He claimed for his evidence the testimony of experienced confessors. Paul even explained the causes for this—and they did not include eleven years of demonic enticement. Does Peraldus not know this? Or does he think it imprudent to say it? The silence of the confessional may have become the silence of the confessor's guide to moral theology.

I have so much emphasized the silences because they are so troubling. They are typically justified by appeal to pastoral need. Confessors are not to mention any of the forms of Sodomy for fear of encouraging them in those who might not know about them. This justification is incoherent as regards its assumptions of sins against nature. It is further incoherent as an expression of pastoral concern. The fear of Sodomy ends up by undoing the pretense of spiritual care for Sodomites. Their sin cannot be spoken plainly. It cannot be preached against. It cannot be broached even within the confession except with utmost indirection. The fanciful etymology recalled by Robert of Sorbonne and William Peraldus claims that "Sodom" means mute. In fact, it is Robert and William who have been made mute on the subject of Sodomy. Incoherent fear of sin has taken away the voice of confessors and preachers. Their silence is an ironic, an unintended testimony to the power of Sodom over the clergy.

SIX

Albert the Great

The Sodomitic Physiology

Albert of Lauingen was first called "Albert the Great" not by historians, but by his thirteenth-century contemporaries.[1] With the title went a reputation for unequaled scientific learning. It was well deserved. More than any of his contemporaries, Albert had scaled the steps of the complete hierarchy of pagan learning, from grammar and logic through the various branches of physics to metaphysics and ethics. The most impressive evidence of his climb was a set of paraphrases of the corpus of Aristotle. Written over a period of about twenty years, Albert's paraphrases added to the underlying Aristotelian text whatever else Albert had learned or could discover of the topic at hand. Throughout the paraphrases, Albert digresses from page to page to explain a fact or raise a question suggested to him by Aristotle. In some paraphrases, Albert will add whole books to what he receives. If he knew only the title of a missing Aristotelian treatise, he would attempt to reconstruct its content on the basis of his personal knowledge of its subject matter.[2]

At the top of the hierarchy of sciences, Albert placed and practiced the various studies of Christian theology. He wrote several different kinds of theological summas and a number of specialized treatises on doctrinal topics. We also have from him a number of scriptural commentaries, works of spiritual edification, and vernacular homilies. The variety of genres reminds the reader of the many posts that Albert occupied in his long life. He was a secular university student of liberal arts, a Dominican friar and preacher, a master of theology, one of the pioneering Dominican prior provincials, and finally a bishop. By his vocation as a Dominican, Albert shared

1 See Weisheipl, "The Life and Works of St Albert the Great," at p. 46. A more recent and more elegant English biography by Simon Tugwell can be had in *Albert and Thomas*, pp 3–39

2 For the chronology and character of Albert's paraphrases, see Appendix I in Weisheipl, *Albertus Magnus*, pp 565–577

pastoral concerns with the authors of confessor's manuals. He shared with others the most innovative projects of learning in philosophy and theology. He was great indeed in his intellectual passions and his polymathy.

Now Albert inherited as one part of his erudition teachings in medicine and natural science on human sex generally and same-sex copulation specifically. These teachings sometimes came with moral judgments, but often only as physiological or behavioral observations, as problems or puzzles in need of natural resolution. Why do some men experience erotic desire more often for other men than for women? Why do some men regularly want to be the passive partner in anal intercourse? These questions and other like them arise from the observation of human society and in medical practice. The answers they demand are not so much moral judgments or legal prescriptions as explanations of natural causes, explanations apparently like other physical explanations in so far as they presume that there are natural causes for these things.

More than any of his Latin contemporaries, Albert was in the position to appropriate for Christian moral theology the medical or scientific explanations of same-sex passion. He did not carry out this appropriation. Indeed, he seems to have turned away from scientific explanation just at the point of treating same-sex desire. Albert is sometimes willing to appeal to medicine in order to mitigate prescriptions about sexual activity between a man and a woman. He is never willing to acknowledge that same-sex activity is a medical problem. Albert refuses this acknowledgment while he makes general concessions about the influence on human character of involuntary bodily dispositions. There is a place for medicine in his theology, but not when it is a question of Sodomy.

MEDICINE FOR THEOLOGIANS

Medical learning was taught and learned in Latin during the thirteenth century not so much through translations of bodies of works by Galen and Hippocrates as in synoptic texts that digested them. This was especially true for nonphysicians who wanted to learn something of medicine without submitting to the curriculum of practical studies. They went not so much to specialized treatises as to the standard overviews. The three most influential synopses of theoretical medicine during Albert's career were the *Articella* (itself an anthology of shorter texts), the *Pantegni* of Constantine the African, and the *Canon of Medicine* by Avicenna. The list is overwhelmingly Arabic in origin. If the *Articella* may contain some works translated from the Greek, the *Pantegni* is a paraphrase of an Arabic original, the

Royal Book of al-Majusi, and the *Canon* was known of course to be the
richest fruit of Arabic medicine. Medical learning came with the attraction
and the danger of an Islamic origin. Beyond these synthetic works, there
were of course more specialized texts on sexual matters. They include short
works on sexual intercourse (such as Constantine's *On Coitus* or the allied
Smaller Book on Coitus),[3] on gynecology (such as the pseudo-Constantinian
On Genital Members),[4] and on the "secrets of women" (such as the famous
treatise by that name once attributed to Albert himself).[5] But medical theory about sex was most available to Christian theologians through the synoptic works, and it was in fact to them that Albert regularly turned.

Each of the three synopses of medicine suggests something about genital
acts between members of the same sex, though the teaching is explicit only
in Avicenna's *Canon.* The first text in the anthology called the *Articella,* the
Introduction or *Isagoge* of Johannitius, gives only the sketchiest account of
the physiology of sexual difference and copulation.[6] Little more is found in
Hippocrates' *Aphorisms,* which also belongs to the anthology. *Aphorisms*
does contain a sequence of sayings on menstruation and pregnancy, punc-
tuated by a single remark on difficult ejaculation in the male.[7] Elsewhere
male semen is used as a diagnostic indicator.[8] But these aphorisms presup-
pose a sexual physiology; they do not teach one. The outline of a physiology is presented in Galen's *Tegni,* as the medieval Latins called the *Art of
Medicine.*[9] But the *Tegni* ends by pointing the reader to other works in an
ideal medical curriculum.[10] The theologian would find little more than this
in all of the pieces of the *Articella* combined.

Constantine the African's *Theoretical Pantegni* treats the same matters
somewhat more fully. In it, biological sex is universally correlated with ele-
mental or humoral properties: masculinity with what is hot and dry, femi-

3 Constantine the African *Liber de coitu,* edited by Cartelle as *Costantini Liber de coitu*
4 See Monica Green, "The *De genecia* attributed to Constantinus Africanus"
5 See Kusche, "Zur 'Secreta Mulierum'-Forschung", and Lemay, "Some Thirteenth and Fourteenth Century Lectures on Female Sexuality" (which treats lectures on the *Secreta mulierum*) For a
translation of *Secrets* with excellent annotation, see Lemay, *Women's Secrets*
6 Johannitius *Isagoge* 20 [in the Latin numeration] (De sexu), 30 (De coitu) I consider here the
Articella of six elements (Johannitius's *Isagoge,* Hippocrates' *Aphorisms* and *Prognostics,* Galen's
"Tegni," Theophilus on pulses, and Philaretus on urines), but without the commentaries of Galen on
Hippocrates or Haly Abbas on Galen This uncommented *Articella* of six represents the basic canon
for the earlier thirteenth century, that is, for the period before the ascendancy of Avicenna's *Canon*
7 Hippocrates *Aphorismata* 5 29–63
8 For example, Hippocrates *Aphorismata* 6 1
9 Galen *Ars medica* 13
10 Galen *Ars medica* epilogue

ninity with what is cold and wet.[11] These properties occur in many combinations and degrees. So the physician must be taught to diagnose the exact mixture of properties or "complexion." For example, the complexion of the testicles must be inferred from the amount and kind of pubic hair, sperm, and sexual desire as evidenced by erection.[12] If the complexion is hotter and drier, male children will be produced; if the opposite, females. But these qualities are scalar, as is shown particularly in cases of multiple births of mixed gender.[13] There is no sharp separation between male and female. Constantine undoes the binary opposition of sexes in favor of a dialectic of qualities subject to any number of qualifications.

Constantine further suggests ways of thinking about copulation apart from its reproductive function. If he begins his chapter on copulation by stressing the teleology of reproduction, he ends it by recounting at length the physiological consequences of too much or too little sexual activity on various kinds of bodies.[14] Moreover, the "causes" of copulation or its absence include certain foods, alcohol, baths, hard labor, visual stimuli, and cognitive aversions. Sexual activity thus serves Constantine as both a symptom and a cure for various medical conditions. It is not far from this to a view of copulation as just another element in a healthy regime—something to be increased or decreased depending on bodily needs and circumstances. Indeed, very little speculation is required to step from the text of Constantine to a medical consideration of nonreproductive sexual activity between members of the same sex. The step is taken in Avicenna's *Canon of Medicine.*

The *Articella* and Constantine's *Pantegni* were rapidly displaced in thirteenth-century Latin medical teaching by the *Canon.* It is easy to see why. The *Canon* is not only much more detailed than either of the other synopses, it deploys a fuller range of medical authorities. In reviewing contrary medical opinions, Avicenna will narrate competing views of the different medical and philosophical schools. He shows himself well versed

11 Constantine the African *Pantegni theorica* 1 "De mutatione complexionis propter sexum". "In omnibus animalibus calidiores et sicciores sunt masculi quam femine. femine ergo frigidiores et humidiores" I follow the text in Erfurt, Wissenschaftliche Bibliothek der Stadt, MS Amplon Q 184 (dated 1147) There is much more to the medieval teaching on sexual differentiation For a survey of it, see Cadden, *Meanings of Sex Difference in the Middle Ages* Cadden discusses Constantine's teaching in other texts on pp 62–63

12. Constantine the African *Pantegni theorica* 1 "De testiculis" "Testiculorum complexio de pilis intelligimus, vel de substantia spermatica aut de actionibus"

13 *Pantegni theorica* 4 "De spermate" (folios 21vb–22vb)

14 *Pantegni theorica* 5 "De coitu et eius causa" (folios 39ra–39va)

not only in Galen, but in Aristotle. Moreover, he was already known to Western readers as an eminent philosophical author. The superiority of the *Canon* is borne out in the discussions of sexual matters. Avicenna provides an enormously detailed account of the topics already mentioned and much more besides. He is careful to note disagreements within the medical or philosophical traditions, as on the role of the female seed in conception or the physiological source of desire.[15] Most important, the *Canon* contains what amounts to a full treatise on copulation, its perils and pathologies.[16] Within this treatise there is explicit discussion of same-sex activity. The discussion is not so clear in the Latin translation as in the Arabic, but it is clear enough.[17]

Same-sex coupling is first mentioned by the Latin Avicenna at the end of a chapter on the harms done by intercourse.[18] He argues that certain copulatory positions are to be avoided since they might damage the penis or its spermatic vessels. He then compares the physiological effects of copulation with boys and with women. Copulation with children (*infantes*)— their sex is not immediately apparent—is counted disgusting by many peoples (*fedus apud multitudinem gentium*) and is prohibited by Qur'anic law (*prohibitus in lege*). Medically considered, however, it is both more and less harmful than copulation with women. It is less harmful because the ejaculation it produces is less intense. It is also not so much attended by self-consciousness as is copulation with the vulva—only here does the sex of the "children" become unavoidably clear in Latin.[19] Note in this passage the complex play between customary religious discourse and medical teaching. The double condemnation by widespread custom and revealed law is set forth clearly and then set aside. Avicenna proceeds on the as-

15. Avicenna *Canon medicinae* 3 20 3 and 3.20 (folios 352rb and 352ra)

16 Avicenna *Canon medicinae* 3 20–21 (folios 351vb–378ra). Fen 20 treats the "men's dispositions for generation," fen 21 women's. It is hardly surprising that the most extended discussion of "sexual" matters occurs in the first treatise of the section on men.

17 In what follows, I will consider only the Latin text, since this is the text known to Latin theologians. For the Islamic context of Avicenna's discussion, see Bellamy, "Sex and Society in Islamic Popular Literature," especially pp 37–38, and Bouhdiba, *Sexuality in Islam* No help is to be had from Daniel, "Arab Civilization and Male Love"

18. Avicenna *Canon medicinae* 3.20 11 (folios 352vb–353rb).

19. Avicenna *Canon medicinae* 3.20.11 (folio 353ra–b) "Et coitus quidem cum infantibus est fedus apud multitudinem gentium et prohibitus in lege et est ex parte nocibilior et ex parte minus nocivus ex parte quidem quia natura indiget in ipso motu plurimo et educat sperma est nocibilior sed ex parte alia quoniam sperma non expellitur cum / eo expulsione plurima sicut fit in mulieribus est minoris nocumenti et comitatur ipsum de iudicio presente minus quam vulva." But perhaps the Latin is not entirely clear, since some Latin commentators on the *Canon* found its necessary to construe the sense of the last phrase See Jacquart and Thomasset, *Sexuality and Medicine in the Middle Ages*, p 156, at note 53

sumption that medicine can say something positive about acts strictly prohibited under religious law.

Something similar, though much more confusing, occurs in Avicenna's principal discussion of same-sex copulation. It constitutes a chapter nearer the end of the treatise on copulation, a chapter wedged between discussion of those who lose control of the anal sphincter while copulating and several definitions of hermaphrodites.[20] In Gerard of Cremona's Latin version of the *Canon* the chapter has a nonsense title: "*De aluminati*," "On *aluminati*," which would mean—if it meant anything—"Concerning those tinctured [*or* covered] with alum." The Latin title here corrupts the Arabic *al-ubna*, which is usually rendered into English as "Sodomy." The rendering is inexact. There is an Arabic term for same-sex copulation that refers to the Qur'anic depiction of Lot; it is the term *al-liwat*, "Lotism."[21] That term is not used here. Here Avicenna speaks of *al-ubna*, that is, of desire for the passive role in anal intercourse. Having no comparable term in Latin, Gerard of Cremona merely transliterates *al-ubna* into a term that his Latin copyists read as *aluminati*. For a Latin reader without access to the Arabic, the mysteriously titled passage would read something like this:

> *Aluminati* is according to truth a disease (*egritudo*) occurring in him who is accustomed to have men lie on top of him. And he has much desire, and there is in him much unmoved sperm, and his heart is weak. And his erection is weak in the root, or it has become weak now that he is habituated to copulation. So that it affects him and he has no control over it. Or else a meditative power (*potentia meditativa*) has control over him, which is why he desires to see copulation happening between two people, and he is nearer who is with him. Then his desire is moved, so that he emits sperm when someone copulates with him, or his member goes out from him [*i.e.*, becomes erect while someone is copulating with him?] and then the task is to complete his desire.
>
> Now there is a group (*secta*) of those in whom desire is not begun or moved except when someone copulates with them; and then the pleasure of the emission of sperm comes to them, either with his operation [i.e., masturbation?] or without effect. And there is another group of them who do not emit sperm when someone copulates with them: rather they wait until they copulate with another. And they have in truth a prostrate spirit and a wicked nature and bad custom and the complexion of women.
>
> And sometimes their members have more sustenance than the members of men.
>
> And you should know that everything said beyond this is empty.

20 Avicenna *Canon medicinae* 3 20 40–43 (folios 357vb–358ra) "De alacuoth," "De regimine eius," "De aluminati," "De hermaphrodito"

21 See *Encyclopaedia of Islam*, s v "liwat," 5:776b–779b, at 776b

And men who wish to cure them are stupid. For the beginning of their sickness is meditative, not natural. If there is a cure for it, then it is what breaks their desire by sadness and hunger and sleeplessness and prison and beating.

And some say that the cause of *aluminati* is that the sensing nerve that comes to the penis splits in them into two branches, of which the subtler one connects with the root of the penis, while the thicker one goes down to the penis's head: so that the thinner one needs strong friction in order to sense. Which is why it is showered on the man himself [An erotic idiom?]; and then there comes to him the filling [fulfilling?] of desire (*libido*); and this thing is like that which was taken away [i.e., like the penis of the other man?].

And the first [part of the passage] is to be relied on: and what is added is from those by whom a wicked part of science has entered into the art [namely, of medicine]; and the words of all of them were verified concerning what they spoke about.

I have underlined two sentences that serve as brackets to mark off a part of the text. I do not know whether they represent an interpolation in Gerard of Cremona's copy of the Arabic original or in his Latin. I also do not know whether the end of the last sentence is an emphasis on the character of Avicenna's sources or an allegation that "wicked science" was taught by some of those suffering from *aluminati*. What is clear enough is that someone has found the discussion of the passage dangerous—dangerous enough to require immediate erasure or qualification in the text itself. The erasure rubs out Avicenna's own argument against attempting to cure *aluminati* by various traditional therapies. It also rubs out an anatomical explanation that would render moral condemnation problematic. So the Latin reader of the *Canon* is left with an explicitly self-negating passage that seems both to affirm and to deny an untreatable origin for the desire to be the passive partner in same-sex copulation.

Even without the erasure, the passage is difficult Latin, both syntactically and conceptually. Its difficulty is eased in part—but only in part—by placing the passage next to one of its sources. This source lies in a rambling compilation of naturalistic *Problems* that was once attributed to Aristotle.[22] *Problems* was not available in Latin until the end of the thirteenth century, but it was well known to Avicenna. The author of the *Problems* argues that men desire to be passive partners in intercourse because of an accumulation of semen around the anus. Many causes can bring this about: damaged or malformed spermatic ducts, a physiology too close to the female, an excess of semen produced by diet or thought, even long habit. Those who are

22 Compare ps-Aristotle *Problemata* 4 26 (879a36–880a5).

both lustful and womanly in physiology are particularly likely to suffer the condition. However the semen is brought to accumulate, once accumulated it produces a desire for release. Release can be obtained by friction around the anus.

The passage from pseudo-Aristotle's *Problems* attracted the attention of a number of Arabic-speaking physicians.[23] Avicenna does not approach it unaided. But the text of his *Canon*, so far as it appears in Latin, hardly makes easy or familiar sense of the received text. Avicenna seems to teach three things. First, *aluminati* is a disease or more exactly an ailment (*egritudo* as against *morbus*). Hence, and whatever else is said within the chapter, *aluminati* is a condition subject to medical analysis. Indeed, it is here located in a section on constitutional problems affecting copulation, not in the following section on specific diseases of the genitals. By context, then, the desire to be passive in same-sex copulation would seem to be a constitutional condition or affliction. In fact, however, it does not fit neatly within the most common Hippocratic or Galenic definitions of disease, since it does not clearly progress towards the impairment of activities in the whole organism. On the contrary, it seems for some organisms to be the very fulfillment of natural activity. So the status of *aluminati* as disease is unsettled, indistinct.

Avicenna seems to teach, second, that *aluminati* is a condition with an overdetermined causality—which is to say, a dialectically undecided one. At least four kinds of cause are mentioned in this chapter of the *Canon*. *Aluminati* results from (*a*) an excess of desire or of spermatic material; (*b*) an overpowering mental affliction, that is, an overpowering desire to see copulation that leads the sufferer to get as close to it as possible—namely, by putting himself into it; (*c*) a degenerate custom linked to depravity; and (*d*) anatomical irregularities in the system of nerves running through the penis (though this explanation falls within the section put under erasure). It is not clear how these four causes stand with respect to each other, or which of them makes the condition incurable. The meditative cause of a man's wanting to be mounted is "unnatural" and mostly incurable.[24] But the meditative cause is ambiguously related to alternate physiological and anatomical explanations. Is it their cause, their effect, or a parallel effect of

23. Rosenthal, "Ar-Razi on the Hidden Illness," pp 48–49

24 The notion of a mental or "meditative" cause has already been used by Avicenna Among the causes that interfere with copulation are "meditative things" such as horror of copulation or shame about it or the tyranny of the intellect over the heart (*Canon medicinae* 3 20 15 [folio 353va]). And the remedies for a distaste for copulation include direct addresses to the mental—for example, the use of stories and pictures about copulation (*Canon medicinae* 3 21.17 [folio 354rb])

higher causes? Here Avicenna seems just to reproduce the fundamental ambivalence of the pseudo-Aristotelian *Problems*. On the one hand, the passage in *Problems* begins with a physiological cause for desire: the accumulation of semen around the anus. It entertains several anatomical explanations for it. On the other hand, the passage wants to shift the desire into the realm of moral evaluation and education. A single fact, the fact of a physical accumulation, is explained simultaneously on two different causal planes.

Third, the most extended explanation, that of the meditative cause, is clearly incoherent, so far as it can be construed in Latin. Someone with *aluminati* wants to get as close as possible to the sight of intercourse. Presumably he would be just as close to it while being the male partner in other-sex copulation as while the passive partner in same-sex copulation, unless Avicenna means that the copulation which the sufferer has seen is same-sex copulation—a sort of contagion by sight. Or perhaps he means that the desire for copulation is acted out with the first object at hand, in this case, a male companion. On any of these construals the subsequent explanation in terms of nerve misplacement is clearly empty, because it suggests that the sufferer is doing what it takes to fulfill desire given the oddity of his genital construction.

The most confusing part of Avicenna's chapter, the excised or erased remarks on cure, are not aimed at the pseudo-Aristotelian *Problems*. They seem rather to be aimed at Avicenna's predecessor, ar-Razî. Ar-Razî is pessimistic about the success of any treatment for those who have long suffered *ubna*, especially if they are effeminate.[25] (He has already given tests for determining effeminacy by examining the penis and testicles.) Still ar-Razî goes on to describe therapies that can be tried for those who are not effeminate and who want to be cured of the condition. These include manipulation of the penis and heating it in various way so as to draw the semen away from the anus. The patient is also urged to try to engage in active intercourse—and never to submit to passive anal intercourse. Such suggestions Avicenna ridicules. The only treatments, he suggests, would be "sadness and hunger and sleeplessness and prison and beating." In short, it would be, not a regime of medical therapy, but of punishment aimed at breaking desire itself. Does Avicenna mean to suggest that the cause of *ubna* is irremediable because it is physiological? Or that it is essentially imaginative, moral, and so subject to correction? The ambivalence expressed in these questions can be connected with broader issues in Avicen-

25 I follow the translation in Rosenthal, "Ar-Razi," at pp 56–57.

na's discussion of madness.[26] It does not become any less troubling for being connected with them.

However one resolves these difficulties of reading, this much is clear: Avicenna undertakes a medical analysis of same-sex copulation. His analysis would see it as a syndrome associated with a morbid mental condition. But his critique of alternate views suggests alternate analyses, perhaps especially to the Latin reader who confronts the text's self-erasure. It suggests, for example, that being a Sodomite might be due to a naturally occurring anatomy or physiology. It raises the possibility that the appropriate response to the Sodomitic condition, if any is needed, would be medical rather moral or legal. The possibility was deeply submerged in Peter Damien's medical metaphors. It came nearer the surface of the text in Alan of Lille's description of the disorder in sexual nature. But here, in the Latin text of Avicenna's *Canon*, the medical and natural analyses lie right on the surface. There is no need to wait for the nineteenth-century "homosexual" in order to have some same-sex behavior reduced to a medical identity.

This passage from the Latin *Canon* suffered different fates in the hands of different Latin commentators. Some medical writers passed over it in silence; others took it up only to magnify the elements of moral reprobation in it.[27] After Albert, one eminent medical author, Pietro d'Abano, would reconsider the causal explanations in the pseudo-Aristotelian *Problems* and conclude against Avicenna. But let me turn from the medical history of the text to its reception by Latin theologians, for whom the passage from Avicenna could have served as an emblem for the whole of the medical teaching on same-sex copulation. Now most thirteenth-century authors have fewer pretensions to universal knowledge than their modern advocates. Their possession and use of medical knowledge is varied. Bonaventure, for example, refers to scant medical teaching, perhaps less than one would expect in a university-educated writer. Aquinas, who uses rather more, seems to borrow whatever he has from Albert the Great. The case is different with Roger Bacon, who can serve as a useful contrast with Albert.[28] Both Roger and Albert know a great deal of medicine, and they

26. Dols, *Majnun· The Madman in Medieval Islamic Society,* p 97 The Latin text of the *Canon* is not so clear in denying a genetic explanation as Dols would make the Arabic text be.

27 Jacquart and Thomasset, *Sexuality and Medicine in the Middle Ages,* pp 156–159 Of course the *Canon* was not typically received as a single text, but as an assembly of more or less independent texts. Only two sections of it were generally known to everyone who knew something of medicine— namely 1.1 and 4 1.

28 There is another important exception in Peter of Spain, who was a master of medicine and a writer of theological treatises, not to say a logician and a pope. I cannot find in the printed Peter any approach to the topic of same-sex copulation

know it first hand. In Roger, as in Albert, we might well expect a full engagement with the medical doctrine on the causes and character of same-sex copulation. In fact, there is no engagement—though Roger declines engagement differently than Albert will.

The last and longest section of Bacon's masterpiece, the unfinished *Opus majus*, or *Greater Work*, is a hortatory argument that means to show how moral teaching is the highest and most useful knowledge. In this argument, same-sex copulation is mentioned only once, in a subsection on human legislation. Here Bacon explains that cities must regulate reproduction by establishing laws on marriage. These laws should above all seek to exclude from cities "fornicators and Sodomites" who lead citizens away from what is noblest in the city, namely marriage.[29] Bacon quotes Avicenna—not the Avicenna of the *Canon of Medicine*, but the censorious Avicenna of the Latin *Metaphysics*.[30] Perhaps this is understandable, given that the context is not physical or even individual so much as civic. What is not so easy to understand is the absence of any medical consideration in the next section of the *Opus majus*, which treats personal morality. There is no medicine and no explicit mention of same-sex copulation. There are frequent discussions of self-discipline in matters of sexual pleasure, each of which commands the rejection of unspecified unclean acts. Most of this section is made up of quotations from approved moral authors, pagan and Christian. So, for example, Bacon quotes the persona of Philosophy from Boethius's *Consolation:* "Is [a man] to be immersed in filthy and unclean desires?"[31] Still the most prominent authority on illicit sexual pleasure is "Aristotle," that is, the pseudo-Aristotelian author of the book known as the *Secret of Secrets*.

Bacon elsewhere dignifies this pseudonymous book by making it the object of detailed commentary. Here in the *Opus majus* he quotes it at some length against carnal pleasure. One of the quotations describes "bestial pleasures" as the source of a cascading series of other vices, from avarice to unfaithfulness.[32] "Bestial" here need not refer to unusual sexual couplings, since male copulation with women is just below called "a property

29 Roger Bacon *Opus majus* 7 2 1 1, in *Rogeri Baconis Moralis Philosophia*, edited by Delorme and Massa, p 39, lines 2–9

30 Roger Bacon *Opus majus* 7 2 1 1 (Delorme-Massa 39 7–9), with the reference to Avicenna *Metaphysica* 10 4 (*Liber de philosophia prima*, edited by Van Riet 544 94–100) Note the differences between the Latin and the Arabic recorded in the apparatus

31 Roger Bacon *Opus majus* 7 3 1 3 7 (Delorme-Massa 57 17–18) = Boethius *Philosophiae consolatio* 4 3 17

32 Roger Bacon *Opus majus* 7 3 2 2.3 (Delorme-Massa 66 11–19) = *Secretum secretorum* 1 8

of pigs," "a vice of irrational beasts," and "an act of brutes."[33] But same-sex copulation is certainly counted among these piggish properties, beastly vices, and brutish acts, not the least sign of which is that they produce "feminine manners."[34] Then there is the guiding Stoic principle, quoted here from Seneca, that "desire was given to man not for pleasure, but for the propagation of the species."[35] In his separate gloss on the *Secret of Secrets*, Bacon adds little to these two passages, beyond a clarification of the causality of vice in the first and a cross-reference in the second.[36]

Neither in the *Opus majus* nor in the gloss is there any reference to medical doctrines. There is no complication of the duality of genders, the physiology of desire, or the consequences for sexual behavior of miswiring of the nerves. It is all and only a simplistic appeal to notions of purity. But then these notions of purity are found in pagan authors, especially Seneca, in whom there are a number of passages referring to same-sex copulation, as well as to cross-dressing and other putatively related vices.[37] Bacon chooses to condemn such things not by Christian Scripture, but by pagan moralizing. There are, then, two discourses missing in the *Opus majus*—the medical teaching on one side, the scriptural condemnations on the other. Bacon wants to construct the moral condemnation of sexual irregularity from pagan ethics alone. We might see this not only as an exercise of his skillful classicism, but as a desire to take the least complicated approach to the task. Bacon wants to keep the condemnation simple because any complicated condemnation tangles itself, either in scriptural exegesis or the ambiguities of medicine.

THE LAW OF PROCREATION

We come now to Albert the Great himself. It is important to begin by repeating that his reputation for medical learning was well earned, not least in sexual matters.[38] It is all the more remarkable, then, that he suppresses

33 Roger Bacon *Opus majus* 7.3.2.2.11 (Delorme-Massa 69.2–4) = *Secretum secretorum* 1 13.

34 Roger Bacon *Opus majus* 7.3 2 2 11 (Delorme-Massa 69 6) = *Secretum secretorum* 1 13

35 Roger Bacon *Opus majus* 7 3 2.2.11 (Delorme-Massa 69 8–9) = Seneca *Ad Helviam* 13 3.

36 Roger Bacon *Secretum secretorum cum glossis et notulis* 1.8 and 1 13 (*Opera hactenus inedita*, ed Steele, p 46, notes 1 and 2, and p 51, note 4)

37. See, for example, the discussion in Dalla, *"Ubi Venus mutatur,"* pp 17–26.

38 See, for example, Brandl, *Die Sexualethik des Heilige Albertus Magnus,* Shaw, "Scientific Empiricism in the Middle Ages", and Jacquart and Thomasset, "Albert le Grand et les problèmes de la sexualité" Of these, the last is by far the most helpful and the most reliable

medical doctrine in discussions of same-sex copulation and that he does so in a way that makes the suppression clear. There are references to Sodomy throughout Albert's corpus, from the earliest extant work to the latest.[39] The three most extended discussions of the topic occur in works separated by about fifteen years. They show remarkable similarities, not least in the exclusion of all pertinent medical knowledge.

The first discussion comes in an early question on *luxuria*, that is, on the master vice of self-indulgence that comprises what modern readers call "sexual" sins.[40] The transformation of *luxuria* from a shameful weakness in the civic piety of Republican Rome to a perversion of human nature in Christian theology has been recounted briefly above. Albert replays the story's end with particular emphasis. He defines *luxuria*, characteristically, as "fleshly commingling with someone not his own (*non sua*) by an act of the reproductive power."[41] He then generalizes: "*Luxuria* is an experience of pleasure according to the reproductive power that does not comply with law." The most striking feature of both definitions is the restriction of reproductive power within human law. The power of reproduction is for the good of the species, and the human legislator acts on behalf of the species in establishing monogamous unions of one man with one woman. Individual genital organs are to be used only for a power of the species. The organs are, as it were, on loan from the species and—more important—subject to an exercise of eminent domain by the city.

Albert's understanding of *luxuria* has innumerable consequences, one of which is to make same-sex intercourse a particularly serious sin. It is, says Albert here, a sin against grace, against reason, and against nature.[42] This triple formula is so important for Albert that he repeats it verbatim in several later works, down to his last.[43] The triplet means something like this. Sodomy is a sin against grace because it is a sin especially condemned by God in both the Old and New Testaments. Sodomy is a sin against reason because it overrides reason. It is, finally, a sin against nature because it contradicts the natural impulse to species continuity. As Albert had already

---

39 Some early examples include Albertus Magnus *De natura boni* 2 1.2 2 (Cologne *Opera omnia* 25/1:25 79–83), written before 1243 or 1244, and *Summa de bono* 5.1.3 (Cologne *Opera omnia* 28.274 22–26), written 1244–1245. The latest example would be *Summa theologiae* 2 18 1.1 (Borgnet *Opera omnia* 33·394b–395c) I will discuss these treatments where they are thematically related to the three main texts from Albert

40 I take the *Quaestio de luxuria* as genuine and accept the dating to the years just before 1249. For the arguments, see the "Prolegomena" to Cologne *Opera omnia* 25 2:xxvii–xxix.

41 Albertus Magnus *Quaestio de luxuria* 1 sol. (Cologne *Opera omnia* 25/1 147 49–50)

42 Albertus Magnus *Quaestio de luxuria* 3 sol (Cologne *Opera omnia* 25/1 151 8–9)

43 For example, Albertus Magnus *Summa theologiae* 2 18 1 1 (Borgnet *Opera omnia* 33 401a)

said elsewhere, sin against nature is sin against "nature's order in the manner of generation, which is the starting point for the whole of nature."[44]

Albert can sustain this triple condemnation only if he can resist an objection that regularly threatens discussions of *luxuria*. Isn't the reproductive power to be treated on analogy with other biological powers, such as the power of nutrition? If so, why can't we reason about sex the way we would about food—for example, that an individual has an extralegal claim on food, even someone else's food, because of the end of individual survival? Albert raises and responds to such questions several times in the question on *luxuria*.[45] He argues, as one might expect, that the nutritive power is for the sake of the individual, while the generative power is for the sake of the species. His reponse ignores the medical teaching that genital organs are individual and function within the temperament of the individual organism. This exclusion of medical knowledge is deliberate. Albert will, in these same pages, invoke other medical doctrines. For example, he reasons from a Peripatetic account of conception that polygamy is sometimes permissible, polyandry never.[46] What is perhaps more bizarre, he argues here as elsewhere that a woman who has intercourse with more than one partner risks becoming sterile because of excessive wetness in the womb.[47] The argument is incoherent, but it suggests how far Albert will reach for medical doctrine when it suits him. It is all the more striking, then, that he excludes what physicians and philosophers teach about the role of genital organs in the health of the individual.

Beyond the local inconsistencies of silence and citation, there are deeper oscillations in Albert's understanding of *luxuria*. The oscillations are caused by the effort to keep the category of *luxuria* together around the law of procreation. We tend to overlook them because we assume that there is behind the category of *luxuria* something like our modern idea of the sexual. But "sexual sin" is not a term of Albert's vocabulary. It is certainly not the basis for his understanding of *luxuria*. The oscillations in his understanding will appear in attempting to answer questions like the following: What, if not "sexuality," is the subject of the vice of *luxuria*? What is the underlying thing to which the sin attaches? What good is damaged by whatever is sinful in sins of *luxuria*?

44. Albertus Magnus *Summa de bono* 5.1.3 (Cologne *Opera omnia* 28:276.41–45).

45. Albertus Magnus *Quaestio de luxuria* 2 obj. 1 (Cologne *Opera omnia* 25/1·149 10–16), and 4 obj. 1 (152:10–13)

46. Albertus Magnus *Quaestio de luxuria* 4 ad 4 (Cologne *Opera omnia* 25/1 152.65–73).

47. Albertus Magnus *Quaestio de luxuria* 4 ad 4 (Cologne *Opera omnia* 25/1:152 74–153 1), to which compare *Commentarii in I–IV Sententiarum* 4 26.B sc 1–2 (Borgnet *Opera omnia* 30:104b–105a).

Albert, with most of his contemporaries, is willing to describe *luxuria* with varying degrees of strictness. His strictest definitions, given above, make *luxuria* a sin "through" or "according to" the "generative power." Pleasure appears in the definitions as a concomitant effect, not as an essential element. Albert's first technical definition does not even mention pleasure. He is of course willing to define *luxuria* more loosely as an appetite for the pleasure to be had in "venereal things," that is, in the things having to do with Venus.[48] Albert insists that the experience of these things produces a particularly violent pleasure, one that overwhelms reason and disorders the soul. But appetite for pleasure is a general feature of sin. What distinguishes *luxuria* is that it is an appetite for pleasure that works itself out in an illicit use of the power to procreate. Indeed, it is an illicit use of generative power in its first phase, that of placing and preparing the matter that will become the embryo.[49]

By making *luxuria* a sin of misusing preembryonic matter, Albert has much restricted its traditional range. That is why he is careful to rewrite or reject a large number of traditional definitions for it. They are definitions of something else—say, of a sin against justice. Or they refer to the accidental features of the sin. *Luxuria* is properly defined only as a sin of misusing the matter for human generation. So female masturbation, which for Albert does not involve any generative matter, he holds elsewhere not to be intrinsically sinful. The sinfulness of male same-sex copulation will lie principally in the misuse of semen, which is being placed where it cannot actualize menstrual fluid. This argument applies equally, of course, to nonprocreative practices between a man and a woman.

It is important in all these cases, as in the case of Sodomy, that Albert be able to assert that any ejaculation of semen is only a first phase of a complete action of generation. Before the semen comes in contact with the menstrual fluid from which the embryo will be produced, it must already and always be understood in relation to that contact. Albert settles this issue quickly, as if in passing, because uncertainty here would be lethal to his argument. If his argument for a first phase does not hold, any number of nonprocreative acts could be counted as not being acts of *luxuria*. Indeed, his argument could be turned exactly around. Precisely because semen by itself is not generative, an objector could argue, ejaculation outside a fertile womb cannot be a sin against generative power.

Beyond the misuse of the matter for procreation, *luxuria* involves a

48 Albertus Magnus *Quaestio de luxuria* 1 sol (Cologne *Opera omnia* 25/1:147 31–42)
49 Albertus Magnus *Quaestio de luxuria* 1 ad 9 (Cologne *Opera omnia* 25/1·148 50–54)

transgression of what is spoken of as a law. It is the law that has been enacted to govern human reproduction on behalf of the species. Fertile couplings outside of marriage or against it are sins of *luxuria* for this reason. Now legislation about reproduction is legislation of reason, not of unreasonable custom or whim. It must have some comprehensible basis in facts about what is required for reproduction. Albert offers two facts. The first, as noted, is that copulation with many men makes a woman sterile.[50] The second is that fathers do not care for children begotten outside of a proprietary, monogamous relationship. It is only by means of such facts that Albert can condemn as nonreproductive the various sins traditionally classed under *luxuria*. If promiscuity had no adverse consequences for reproduction, it would not fall within Albert's strictest definitions of *luxuria*. To say this differently, Albert must find something antireproductive in heterosexual promiscuity or else the principle used to condemn Sodomy will not work as a general argument against sins of *luxuria*. Because Sodomy is condemned as nonreproductive, something nonreproductive must be found in heterosexual fornication and adultery. Monogamy must serve a patently reproductive end. So Albert stretches the sense of reproductive teleology not just to include the possibility of female infertility from too much copulation, but to require a commitment to child rearing from both parents. The breadth of the latter argument is troubling. It would make into a sin of *luxuria* the marriage of a woman to a man negligent of children. So too the marriage of a fertile man to a woman known to be infertile.

I conclude that *luxuria* is not for Albert a sexual sin in any modern sense. It is not a sin that has to do with sexuality as an element of personality. *Luxuria* is only a reproductive sin. It attacks the first phase of human reproduction by lodging semen elsewhere than in a fertile womb. In order to work against Sodomy, the argument must suppose, among other things, that the quantity of semen is roughly proportional to reproductive need, else its being wasted would not affect reproduction. This supposition is not backed by clear medical doctrine, as Albert knows. His argument against Sodomy must also suppose that no individual can be subtracted from the service of procreation—that no good is served by having some individuals not reproduce. This is an argument contradicted by both philosophical and Christian doctrines of voluntary celibacy, dcotrines that Albert otherwise approves.

These tensions and others like them show the difficulty of using procreation as the single principle to construct the category of *luxuria*. The law

---

50 Albertus Magnus *Quaestio de luxuria* 3 sol. (Cologne *Opera omnia* 25/1:151.30–35).

130 / CHAPTER SIX

of procreation as common good for the species rules out prohibited ejaculations only on a tenuous theory of the teleology of the matter for generation. It excludes fornication and adultery only on the supposition of controversial or too expansive facts. It condemns Sodomy only on the assumption of a naive account of the requirements for species reproduction in large, mixed populations. Albert knows these difficulties, and so he attempts to supplement the law of procreation with an appeal both to the purposes of genital organs and to the dangers of pleasure. With them he hopes to strike a better balance between the arguments against infertile Sodomy and the arguments against fertile fornication.

ORGANS AND PLEASURES

Not more than a few years later, Albert comes back to the question of same-sex copulation in the more familiar framework of a commentary on Peter Lombard's *Sentences*. Here Albert begins by teaching that God created sexual difference for the sake of generation.[51] Human reproduction would have occurred in paradise, but with a true pleasure that did not suffocate reason and without any pains in parturition.[52] The reasoning here on both sides is medical, and Galen is cited explicitly in the very next article, where the issue is whether matrimony is a medicine for the disease of disordered desire.[53] The question of same-sex copulation is broached five sections later—but indirectly, in an article on whether there can be anything against nature in proper copulation, that is, in copulation between a man and a woman who are married.[54]

Albert cannot even begin to discuss this question without exclaiming that such filthy matters have nowadays to be treated because of the monstrous things one hears in confession.[55] He then distinguishes two kinds of unnaturalness, both based on a strict teleology of genital organs. The more unnatural is when such an organ is not used for the act for which it was

51 Compare Albertus Magnus *Commentarii in I–IV Sententiarum* 4.33 3 sol (Borgnet *Opera omnia* 30:295a), and *De anima* (Cologne *Opera omnia* 7.1 94.11).
52. Albertus Magnus *Commentarii in I–IV Sententiarum* 4 26 B 7 resp and ad obj (Borgnet *Opera omnia* 30:105b–106a).
53 Albertus Magnus *Commentarii in I–IV Sententiarum* 4 26.B.8 obj 2 (Borgnet *Opera omnia* 30 106b)
54 Albertus Magnus *Commentarii in I–IV Sententiarum* 4 31.G 24 (Borgnet *Opera omnia* 30·262a–263b)
55 Compare Albertus Magnus *Summa de bono* 3.3 6 contra 3 and 3.3 7 contra 1 (Cologne *Opera omnia* 28 163 38–42 and 165 77–83), with the brief discussion in Brandl, *Die Sexualethik des Heilige Albertus Magnus*, p 207

formed—that is, when the organ is put into an inappropriate vessel. The less unnatural is when it is used for its proper act, but not in the way intended by nature—that is, when something other than the frontal, male dominant position is used. Only the more unnatural act is necessarily a mortal sin. Some variety of positions is permissible on medical grounds, for example, because of obesity or during pregnancy. But any use of the organ other than for copulation with one's wife is intrinsically and lethally sinful. The anatomical arguments in excuse of alternate positions are detailed, and so they make the absence of analogous arguments in excuse of same-sex copulation more striking.

A number of different notions about organ formation are invoked here. One notion is just that any operation by which the organs can accomplish their ends is legitimate. So any kind of married copulation that gets the semen into the womb is legitimate.[56] A second notion is that organ teleology is reciprocal. The penis and the vagina being made for each other, any copulation that unites the two adequately is acceptable.[57] A third notion is that variation from the typical use of organs can be excused in the case of some interfering cause.[58] To these notions Albert opposes a fourth, taken from Aristotle's *History of Animals*. The notion appears in an objection, but Albert approves it in his response.[59] The notion holds that the teleology of human reproductive organs is to be inferred from what is different in human beings. Since only human females have vulva presented frontally, human copulation must take place from the front.[60]

The moral inference is not Aristotle's. Indeed, Aristotle discusses animal copulations partly to show their variety, their obscurity. But Albert takes up the Aristotelian material to make law of it. What is distinctive is obligatory. In the same way, Albert arranges these notions as a scale of proximity to nature. "[A sin] is more unnatural when the act of the instrument formed for this by nature is not accomplished. It is less unnatural, when the act is accomplished in a way that does not agree with the way of nature, which

56. Albertus Magnus *Commentarii in I–IV Sententiarum* 4 31.G 24 obj. 1 (Borgnet *Opera omnia* 30:262a)

57 Albertus Magnus *Commentarii in I–IV Sententiarum* 4.31.G.24 obj. 2 (Borgnet *Opera omnia* 30:262a).

58. Albertus Magnus *Commentarii in I–IV Sententiarum* 4.31.G.24 obj 3 (Borgnet *Opera omnia* 30 262a)

59 Albertus Magnus *Commentarii in I–IV Sententiarum* 4.31 G.24 resp. (Borgnet *Opera omnia* 30:263a).

60. Albertus Magnus *Commentarii in I–IV Sententiarum* 4.31.G.24 arg. 3 (Borgnet *Opera omnia* 30·262b). Albert seems to have in mind several different sections of *History of Animals*, perhaps especially 3 1, 5 2.

is understood from the natural disposition of the members." It is more unnatural to ejaculate semen outside the womb than to ejaculate it within the
womb in a position other than the "missionary." The end for which the
organ was formed takes precedence over inferences about the action from
the physical disposition of the organ.

It is important to see that these arguments from organ teleology or disposition are much richer in moral consequences than arguments from an
abstract generative power ordered to the good of the species. The generative power is too far from the individual to allow easy deduction of moral
rules for the individual. But the teleology of organs can be used to bind
any organism with the organs in questions. If the teleology of an erect penis
is just to ejaculate semen into a properly disposed womb, then no other use
of the erect penis will be according to nature. The organ is quite strictly
the "instrument" of a teleology according to which its every operation can
be judged. "Nature formed" the organs for an end that must govern their
every use. This is Albert's appropriation of natural philosophy.

Similar notions about teleological ordering are used by Albert in understanding sexual pleasure. His notion of pleasure is a strong generalization
of certain remarks Aristotle makes in the *Nicomachean Ethics.* What produces pleasure, Aristotle says, is the best natural operation of a power or
organ in relation to its best object.[61] But pleasure does not act on the organ
or power in the way that is proper object does. Pleasure is not another color
for sight, not another sound for hearing. It is an epiphenomenon of the
proper activity, an accompaniment to it. "Pleasure completes the activity
not as the inherent state does, but as an end that supervenes, in the way the
bloom of youth comes to those in the flower of their age."[62] For Aristotle
here, and for Albert following him, pleasure is understood in relation to
natural activity. It is defined in terms of that activity. So it is that Albert
can contrast the disordered pleasure of a sexual ardor that overcomes reason with "the greater and more honest pleasure" that would have accompanied copulation in paradise.[63] Pleasure then would have been under the
command of reason. However intensely it would have been felt, it would
always have allowed the contemplation of "immutable first good." In other
words, copulation in paradise would have been more pleasurable than copulation now precisely because its pleasure would have included contemplation of the final end for which the copulation was undertaken. This claim
will seem silly unless it is remembered that Albert has defined pleasure in

61 Aristotle *Ethica Nicomachaea* 10 4 1174b17–23
62 Aristotle *Ethica Nicomachaea* 10 4 1174b31–33
63 Albert the Great *Commentarii in I–IV Sententiarum* 4 26 B 7 (Borgnet *Opera omnia* 30 106a)

terms of the best operation of a natural power. The best operation of the acts of procreation is in relation to their end, which is reproduction of the species for the sake of obedience to God.

The moral use of Aristotelian natural history must point up the persistent inconsistency in Albert. The moral use is extraordinarily selective. It requires not only a rewriting of some pages in Aristotle; it requires the suppression of whole topics in the natural history or medicine. There is in Albert the Great's texts on Sodomy a series of dissociations by which he refuses to engage the analyses of same-sex copulation in his own scientific or medical authorities, and this despite his regular appropriation of their teaching on other topics. At the same time, Albert fails to correct the medical or scientific analyses of same-sex copulation—even though he is eager to correct errors elsewhere. His refusal to discuss even to the point of refusing to correct shows quite plainly a now familiar feature of the theological artifact that is the conception of "Sodomy": the desire to exclude it from speech altogether. Albert here enacts that desire with regard to medicine and natural philosophy. Where he will not engage, he keeps silence.

The silence is not sufficient to cover Albert's refusal to think coherently the cause or causes of the thing named. The confusion built into the category of "Sodomy" is not just a confusion about which acts the word names, though Albert is reticent on this point as well. He nowhere offers the kind of definitions of Sodomy with which Peter Damian begins the *Gomorran Book*.[64] Albert is willing to speak in detail only when he is directed to do so by the Christian Scriptures. He speaks there with his back turned on what he knows of natural science.

THE RETURN OF REPRESSED SCIENCE

There is no application of medical learning whatever in the third and last text, which might be considered Albert's fullest explicit discussion of same-sex copulation as sin. It comes in a Gospel commentary written at least fifteen years after the last part of the commentary on the *Sentences*.[65] Albert is explicating Luke 17:28–29. He justifies the vehemence of the divine punishment on the Sodomites by arguing that four features distinguish "this wicked sin" (*in nefando isto peccato*), which has been described only as "a

64. Albert rarely gives a list more detailed than this early one in *De bono* 5.1 3 arg.14 (Cologne *Opera omnia* 274.24–25): "ut sodomiam, mollitiem, incubationem vel succubationem iumento et huiusmodi."

65 Meersseman, *Introductio in opera omnia B Alberti Magni*, pp. 94–95 and 111–113

burning and flaming desire beyond what the natural order permits."⁶⁶ The first is its flaming (*ardor*), which overwhelms reason. The second is the stink of its infamy, which rises up like the stink of corpses. "And it is well said that the stink rises," adds Albert, "because this wicked vice is found to reign more in high persons than in the humble."⁶⁷ The third feature of the vice is its persistence, "since it almost never deserts one whom it has captured."⁶⁸ Hence Genesis tells us that Sodom was located in a valley filled with pits of tar, the strongest glue. Finally, this vice—mind you, it has still neither been named nor described—this vice "is said to be a contagious disease, and from one it infects another."⁶⁹

The fourfold description is drawn from no earlier source that I can find. The stench and the flame are mentioned in a passage that an authoritative reference tool, the *Ordinary Gloss* on the Bible, borrows from Gregory the Great's *Moral Readings of Job.*⁷⁰ The connection between Sodom and the tar pits Albert could have learned not just from Scripture, but from ancient naturalists.⁷¹ Still, what is most striking about Albert's passage is how it echoes certain themes from Avicenna—excess of desire overcoming reason, connection with putrefaction in the body, incurability, even contagion—without once allowing the kind of medical teaching represented by Avicenna to be heard.⁷² It is as if we have here Albert's reply to the medical analysis that he never explicitly engages.

The features of Albert's fourfold description are fixed elements of the theological treatment. We have heard often enough how much Sodomitic desire disorders the soul. We have heard how it persists, how it afflicts especially the highest strata of medieval society, even the stratum of the

66 Albertus Magnus *In evangelium Lucae* 18 29 (Borgnet *Opera omnia* 23 488a), especially "ignitam et exardescentem ultra fas naturalis ordinis habebant concupiscentiam."

67 Albertus Magnus *In evangelium Lucae* 18.29 (Borgnet *Opera omnia* 23 488a) "Et bene dicitur foetor iste ascendere, quia infandum istud vitium plus in aliis personis, quam in humilibus invenitur regnare"

68 Albertus Magnus *In evangelium Lucae* 18 29 (Borgnet *Opera omnia* 23.488b)· "quod eum quem capit, vix umquam deserit"

69 Albertus Magnus *In evangelium Lucae* 18 29 (Borgnet *Opera omnia* 23 488b): "quod dicitur esse morbus contagiosus, et de uno inficere alium."

70 *Glossa ordinaria* on Genesis 19 [24] "Igitur dominus pluit super etc." (Strasbourg 1485 p 55) "Sulphur fetor carnis Ignis ardor carnalis desiderii cum dominus carnis scelera punire decrevisset qualitate ultionis innotuit macula criminis Sulphur enim fetet, ignis ardet, qui ergo ad perversa desideria carnis fetore arserant. iure sulphure et igne perierunt"

71 For example, Pliny *Historia naturalis* 5 15 15–16 15

72 It would be difficult to prove or disprove that Albert knew directly the passage from the *Canon* on *aluminati* All the arguments would be both general and circumstantial For example, Siraisi counts Albert one of "the pioneers in the Latin West in the use of Avicenna as a medical authority" See her "Medical Learning of Albertus Magnus," p 392.

clergy. We have seen often enough the appearance of medical images in descriptions of the vice. It would be easy enough, then, to take Albert's remarks here simply as a repetition of theological commonplaces. What makes it difficult to do so is the presence in the passage of terms or notions that also figure in the bodies of scientific knowledge that Albert has worked so hard to establish for the Latin world. When Albert writes of differences between male and female, of contagious disease, or even of the forfeiting of human nature, he cannot be entirely innocent of the technical senses of these terms. He has, after all, labored to incorporate medical and scientific discourses within the discourses of Christian theology. He has, in this sense, "medicalized" the theological treatment of human nature by placing theology in a hierarchy that also encompasses a highly articulate medicine. How can he then cut free theological language, even the language of scriptural commentary, from any responsibility for precision? I am not suggesting that Albert cannot engage in allegorical reading, as he plainly does here. I am suggesting that his explanations of the allegories cannot be entirely segregated from what he says elsewhere on the same topics. The excluded topics of medicine and natural philosophy trouble what would otherwise be simply another allegorization of Genesis 19. They trouble it precisely because Albert has brought medicine and natural philosophy into a single hierarchy that also contains, if eminently, the Christian scriptures.

Medicine and natural philosophy present to Albert the paradox of conceiving a naturally occurring unnatural desire. The threat of this possibility is the real threat of the return of the scientific topics that Albert has wanted to exclude. The return is not merely a topical echo, it is the insistence of the underlying paradox. The paradox is contained in the statement, Some men are constructed so that they can exercise their reproductive power only with other men, that is, only in circumstances making reproduction impossible. This statement produces certain equivocations in the medical categories of disease and deformity. It posits the genetic undoing of certain natural operations. But it produces greater and more crucial equivocations in theological uses of the category of nature. If the fact of Sodomitic physiology threatens the distinction between disease and natural disposition, it seems to block theological appropriations of philosophical definitions of nature altogether. These appropriations figure centrally in Albert's most famous student, Thomas Aquinas. They are the more visible in Thomas because he prunes away most of Albert's medical and naturalistic knowledge. In Thomas, the problem of Sodomitic physiology is all too plainly caught up in the larger problem of the usefulness for theology of any natural conception of human sex.

SEVEN

Thomas Aquinas

The Sin against Nature

Thomas Aquinas is not so often read as brandished. He has become more emblem than author. It is very difficult to read Thomas as the medieval author of certain remarkable books. He is consulted as the guarantor of Catholic orthodoxy, say, or reviled as the ideologue of papal tyranny. And on too many gay readings he is just accused of having sanctioned centuries of homophobic repression.

The cause of these misreadings is not hard to find. Thomas had the misfortune of being adopted first by his order, the Dominicans, and then by the papacy as a preferred theologian. He was adopted by the Dominicans not just because he was a loyal member of their Italian province, but because he was a prominent theologian who was attacked publicly by the strongest competition, the Franciscans. It is harder to say why Thomas was adopted by the papacy. The reasons had something to do with favoring Dominicans, something to do with Thomas's teaching on disputed questions of interest to the papacy—say, on papal power. And it may have been that Thomas seemed to offer a reasonably coherent and clear teaching on the traditional range of doctrinal topics.

Whatever the causes, the effects of Thomas's adoption are notorious and unhappy. By the sixteenth century, Thomas's *Summa* had become a most potent authority. It displaced Peter Lombard's *Sentences*, on which it depended, as a central text in the university faculties of theology. Most important, it was used by the Council of Trent both as a ready reference and as the source for compromise language in its extensive doctrinal legislation. Two centuries later, Thomas's authority pervaded Catholic thought. St. Alphonsus Ligouri, the architect of modern Catholic moral theology, begins his masterwork with a reverent acknowledgment of Thomas. In fact, St. Alphonsus's method is antithetical to Thomist teaching, and many of his conclusions differ from Thomas's. But St. Alphonsus assures the reader that he has spent years studying the texts of Thomas. Indeed, Thomas is the only patristic or medieval theologian mentioned by name.

Little more than a century ago, a number of administrative actions before and after Leo XIII's encyclical *Aeterni Patris* (1879) gave fresh force to the study of Aquinas. There followed decades of feast and famine—the feast of remarkable historical and conceptual discoveries about Thomas, the famine of an enforced and mechanical Thomism. All of this ended about thirty years ago. The decline is frequently connected with Vatican Council II, but that council only registered what was in fact a widespread distaste for Thomisms old and new. Thomism has since suffered an eclipse as rapid and complete as that of state Marxism. If Thomas is studied today by non-Catholic as a figure in the history of thought or even as someone with interesting thoughts, he is still either exalted or rejected by Catholics on the basis of rumor alone. Within the highly politicized discussions of Catholic theology, Thomas remains a potent force for imagination. He is sometimes cited nostalgically as an answer to present "confusion." He is often excoriated as the source of lingering repression. In the meantime, the gains of the last century of close exegesis have been scattered.

I rehearse these stages of Thomas's afterlife in order to set them aside. I am for the moment not interested in Thomism, but in Thomas. I want to read Thomas's reconstruction of the theological treatments of Sodomy. The reconstruction will reveal a last set of instabilities in Sodomy as a theological authority. These are embedded within the teaching of Thomas's greatest achievement in morals, his *Summa of Theology*. Having traced the instabilities in this teaching, I will turn at the end to a single aspect of Thomas's posterity—the way in which his achievement as a moral teacher made the authoritative misappropriation of his teaching easy. Precisely because Thomas was such an extraordinary teacher of morals, his texts lent themselves to abuse. Instead of becoming the occasion for rethinking the teaching on Sodomy, the *Summa* became an occasion for concealing the paradoxes of Sodomy under an apparently simple explanation of the sin.

THE SUMMA AS MORAL TEACHING

What can be discovered about the origin of the *Summa* suggests that it was a masterful improvisation in the face of very particular circumstances for the teaching of Christian theology. Near the end of 1259, at the age of thirty-four or thirty-five, Thomas Aquinas left Paris to return to his ecclesiastical home, the "Roman" or Italian province of the Dominican order.[1] He had behind him a brilliant if occasionally controversial career as a student and master of theology at the University of Paris. But his work in Italy would be within the houses of his order and not at a university. Six years later, in September of 1265, Thomas was assigned to open a house of studies for Dominicans in Rome. There was no university there and no previous academic establishment for the order.[2] Thomas's new *studium* was also to see the inauguration of a new curricular project very much dependent on his personal activity as *lector* or teacher. Thomas was given full authority by the provincial governing body to send back those who proved negligent in their studies.

What did Thomas teach? The prevailing curriculum in Dominican houses relied on Scripture and books of scriptural history, of course, but also on collections of texts for sacramental theology, manuals of the moral life, and some reference works of canon law and the church Fathers. Thomas seems to have had other plans at Rome from the start. During his first year, he tried revising his earlier, Parisian commentary on the *Sentences* of Peter Lombard. He began not with the fourth book, often used by Dominicans for teaching on the sacraments, but with the first book, with its doctrine on God as unity and trinity. After revising and supplementing parts of the first book, Thomas seems to have set the project aside.[3] He turned instead to the *Summa*, which begins much as Lombard's *Sentences* does, but goes on to a more rigorously ordered consideration of the whole of theology. In short, the evidence we have of Thomas's teaching and writing at Rome suggests that his main effort was directed at expanding the pastoral and practical curriculum of Dominican houses by placing it within the frame of the whole of theology.

Thomas tells us as much in the prologue to the first part of the *Summa*. He begins with a verse from 1 Corinthians, "as little ones in Christ, I gave you milk to drink, not meat" (3:1–2). The prologue's first section interprets

1   The standard English biography for Thomas remains Weisheipl, *Friar Thomas d'Aquino*. Besides the biographical account, this volume also provides a brief catalogue of Thomas's works (pp 355–405, with corrections pp 478–487) The catalogue is the best guide to the works of Thomas available in English as of 1983   A newer biography is available in French: Torrell, *Initiation à saint Thomas d'Aquin*

2   The best description of the evidence for Thomas's teaching at Rome, and for its importance to the understanding of the *Summa*, is Boyle, *The Setting of the Summa theologiae of Saint Thomas*.

3   The evidence of Thomas's revision of the commentary on the *Sentences* is contained in a manuscript at Lincoln College, Oxford. The manuscript gives the Parisian version of Thomas's commentary as the main text, then enters alternate or supplementary texts in the margin   The marginal annotations are concerned at greatest length with Trinitarian questions, but there are also new treatments of the nature of theology, divine simplicity, and the names of God, among other topics   There is as yet no edition of the text, but for a discussion of its authenticity see Boyle, "Alia lectura fratris Thome"

THOMAS AQUINAS / *139*

the verse as it applies to "the teacher of Catholic truth," who ought to instruct not only advanced students, but also "beginners" (*incipientes*). The intention of the *Summa*, Thomas says, is to hand on what pertains to "the Christian religion" (*religio*) in a manner suited to the instruction of beginners. Who exactly are these beginners and what is the religion they are to learn? The obvious reading supposes that they are beginners in the study of university theology. In fact, the *Summa* is not fully appropriate as an aid to university theology, since it follows the order of none of the standard medieval academic texts and is not nearly as complex as comparable academic disputations. A second look at the prologue shows that the key words can be understood in a quite different sense. "Beginners" will later refer in the *Summa* itself to those who stand lowest in the hierarchy of spiritual learning, and "Christian religion" will refer not to religion in the modern sense, but to life in a religious community under the vows of poverty, chastity, and obedience.[4] The prologue of the *Summa* can also be taken as addressing beginners in spiritual learning who hope to progress through the discipline of the vowed life. It addresses just such beginners as were Thomas's students in Rome. The reading is strengthened in the second section of the prologue, which is a triple complaint against the prevailing forms of academic writing and teaching. Those new to the study of "this doctrine," Thomas continues, are impeded by a multiplication of useless material, by an order tied rather to textual exposition or formal dispute, and by tiresome repetition. The *Summa* promises, by contrast, to give only what is essential, to give it in the pedagogical order required by an introduction, and not to repeat itself.

Of course, this way of reading the prologue to the *Summa* does not mean that the work is only a temporary solution to a particular problem in teaching. The situation that Thomas faced in Rome is a perennial problem for Christian teaching. It is the problem of bringing together happily and clearly the creed's truths with the daily life of faith. Or, again, it is the double problem of seeing the implications of doctrine for life, and of seeing the need to ground particular habits of life in the whole of Christian revelation. Thomas addressed the perennial problem masterfully and generally. His aim was not limited to a particular pedagogical problem; it reached out toward a structure of learning that could ground theology on a much larger scale and in many different contexts. But there is still something to be remembered from the particular origin of the *Summa*. The text is not simply another academic work. That is why it differs in so many respects from the

4. *Summa theologiae* 2–2 qq 186–189

synthetic works of Thomas's predecessors and successors. There are many summas in the thirteenth century, but none quite like the *Summa of Theology* in simplicity, scope, and rigor of organization. Thomas offers in the *Summa* a way into the whole of Christianity, dogmatic and moral, by means of a structure of inquiry. Indeed, the achievement of the *Summa* lies not so much in its particular arguments or doctrines as in its arrangement of arguments and doctrines. Its mastery shows up most in its structure. It is the structure that makes Thomas's teaching on Sodomy so interesting.

The *Summa* was never completed. Thomas stopped writing it—and anything else—in December of 1273, after the experience of a vision. He died within four months. We do not know exactly how he would have arranged the end of the work in detail, or what improvements of clarity he would have introduced in discussing the topics he never reached. It is particularly unfortunate that Thomas was not able to write the section on the sacrament of marriage, since this had long been one of the most poorly ordered sections of medieval theology. It had also been a section requiring much subtlety in the handling of sexual matters, as we learn from Albert. But we can know how Thomas ordered moral teaching, because he did complete the center of the *Summa*, its *pars secunda*. This is the "moral part" of the *Summa*. It is Thomas's rewriting of Christian moral theology.

The second part of the *Summa* is divided into two sections. The first section speaks more universally of the kinds and starting points of human acts. The second section speaks more particularly of virtues and the states of human life.[5] This division merits long reflection. The distinction between universal and particular, for instance, is relative, because moral science always remains universal in its terms and arguments. Again, the distinction between universal and particular is here curiously paired with a distinction between elements and compounds. The more universal consideration treats as if analytically the end, elements, and causes of human acting. The more particular consideration treats as if synthetically concrete actualizations in durable dispositions and choices about ways of life. Whatever the end of these reflections, the distinction between the first section and the second section of the second part is the original and presumably the most fundamental distinction that Thomas wishes to make in moral science.[6] It makes the second section of the second part, the particular and

5 *Summa theologiae* 1–2.6 prol, 2–2 prol
6 Despite that, the distinction has not been well explained by scholarly commentators on the *Summa* Sometimes it is collapsed into other distinctions that are presumed to be more fundamental, as that between *exitus* and *reditus* See Audet, "Approches historiques de la *Summa theologiae*," p. 15; and

synthetic consideration of moral actions, into a variation on traditional treatises of the virtues and vices.

We have seen something of these traditions in Alan of Lille and the confessors' manuals. The lists of virtues and vices are augmented more or less haphazardly, while specific cases submitted to moral analysis are accumulated in no particular order. Thomas inherits these problems together with efforts by some of his immediate predecessors to remedy them. Thomas obviously knows the schema of crimes used by the eminent Dominican jurist Raymund of Peñafort. Indeed, Thomas will sometimes borrow verbatim from Raymund in the course of the *Summa*. But Raymund's schema achievement has its price. The crimes here categorized do not even constitute a complete list of sins, much less a frame for a full account of the moral life.

William Peraldus and his *Summae of Virtues and Vices* are also on Thomas's mind, though not as an authority to be emulated. Thomas begins the second section of the second part with an unusually discursive explanation of his intention. He wants to avoid the needless repetition required by sequential treatment. It is better—more intelligible, more pedagogical, more persuasive—to cluster in one inquiry a virtue, its corresponding gifts, its opposed vices, and the entailed positive and negative commands. But Thomas also insists that the table of the vices should itself be constructed by real differences rather than by accidental ones. He writes, "Vices and sins are distinguished by species according to their matter and object, not according to other differences of the sins, such as 'of the heart,' 'of the mouth,' and 'of the deed,' or according to weakness, ignorance, and malice, and other such differences" (1–2.prol).

The immediate references are to two distinctions passed down by Peter Lombard.[7] Both distinctions are used by Thomas in other texts, even within

---

Hankey, "The *De Trinitate* of St. Boethius and the Structure of the *Summa Theologiae* of St. Thomas Aquinas" Or else the two parts of the *pars secunda* are likened to parts of a syllogism, with their connection being something like that of deduction. See, for example, Grabmann, *Einführung in die Summa theologiae des heiligen Thomas von Aquin*, pp. 84–88; Ruello, "Les intentions pédagogiques et la méthode de saint Thomas d'Aquin"; and Philippe, "La lecture de la *Somme théologique*," p 904 Even book-length studies of the *Summa's* organization refuse to enter into the plan or position of the *secunda secundae* See, for example, Lafont, *Structures et méthode dans la Somme theologique de S. Thomas d'Aquin*, p 262 The single best discussion on the sequence of the *par secunda* I know is the obscure note by Tonneau, "Le passage de la *Prima Secundae* à la *Secunda Secundae*"

7 The division according to "heart, mouth, and deed" is from Jerome *Commentaria in Hezechielem* 43 23–35 (Glorie 75:642), as reported by Peter Lombard *Sententiae* 2 42 4 (CSB 1:569); according to "weakness, ignorance, and malice," from Isidore of Sevilla, *Sententiae* 2 17.3–4 (Migne *PL* 83 620a–b), as reported by Peter Lombard, *Sententiae* 2.22.4 (CSB 1:445)

the *Summa,* though he is always careful to point out that they are not classifications by genera or essential species.[8] What is more important, both triplets are akin to the sorts of classifications in Peraldus's *Summae* and other works like them. Thomas's criticism would surely apply to Peraldus's addition of a special supplement on sins of the tongue. It must also count against Peraldus's practice of distinguishing sins by their external occasions.[9] But the force of Thomas's criticism is felt most by the main principle of Peraldus's *Summas,* namely the order of the seven chief vices.

One of the effects of Thomas's organization of the second section of the second part is to push the seven capital vices to the margin.[10] They appear, each in turn, but without obvious connection or special importance.[11] Now this might seem odd, because Thomas himself uses the list of seven in arranging his disputed questions *On Evil.* Indeed, the two articles in the *Summa* that introduce the seven vices are extremely close to the parallel article in *On Evil.* But a study of either text will show that Thomas makes very limited claims for the division by capital vices. Thomas insists that the seven are not the "roots" or "starting points" of all sins. They are, in *On Evil,* those ends to which desire is ordered "principally" or "for the most part."[12] They are, in the *Summa,* those vices from which others arise

8 For the use of the first triplet see, for example, *Scriptum super libros Sententiarum* 3.37.1 2 sol. 3 (Mandonnet-Moos 3·1242), and *De malo* 9.2 sc. 3 For its qualification, see *Scriptum super libros Sententiarum* 2.42.2 sol. 1 (2:1072–1074), 4.16.1.1 sol. 3 ad 1 (4:775), and *Summa theologiae* 1–2.72 7. For the use of the second triplet, see *De malo* 3.6–12, and *Summa theologiae* 1–2 76, 1–2 77.3, 1–2 78, where the three are classed among the causes of sin

9 As, for example, the multiplication of types of pride by types of ornament or, indeed, by subtypes, such as horse trappings, buildings, books, singing, and so on (William Peraldus *Summa de vitiis* [folios 293ra–299rb and 304ra–306vb, respectively])

10. Thomas is not unique in this regard. See Wenzel, "The Seven Deadly Sins. Some Problems of Research," p. 14 One other instance of a return to old ways after Thomas's innovations is the compiling from the *Summa* of a treatise on the seven capital sins—for example, MS patr 122 (Q V 12), folios 220r–225v, as described in Dondaine and Shooner, *Codices manuscripti,* 1 48, no 113

11 *Acedia* and *invidia* appear together as vices opposed to *gaudium* (1–2 35–36), which is one of the acts or effects of charity. *Avaritia* is one of two vices opposed to liberality (2–2 118), which is itself a quasi-integral part of justice *Inanis gloria* is one of the vices opposed to magnanimity (2–2 132), itself a part of fortitude. The other three sins are listed among the vices opposed to subject and potential parts of temperance *Gula* is opposed to abstinence (2–2 148), *luxuria* and its species to chastity (2–2 153), wrathfulness (*iracundia*) to mercy (2–2.158) Thomas asks in each case whether the sin is a capital vice (2–2 35 4, 36.4, 118 7, 132 4, 148 5, 153.4, 158 6) In each case, the *sed contra* is a reference to Gregory's *Moralia* He is well aware that there are other authorities with other lists (2–2 36 4) but is willing to follow Gregory Indeed, he follows him so faithfully that he refuses to identify *superbia* with *inanis gloria* or to call *superbia* a capital vice (2–2.162.8) Thomas defends Gregory's list as a suitable classification of these final causes (1–2 84.3–4), but he explicitly denies that the classification by final causes—or any causes—ought to count as an essential classification (1–2.72.3 corp and ad 3)

12. *De malo* 8 1 ad 1, "principaliter" (LE 23:195.370), 8.1 ad 6, "in pluribus" (195.402), and 8 1 ad 8, "in pluribus" (196 432).

"most frequently," but not exclusively.[13] For Thomas, then, a treatment of sins and vices organized around the Gregorian list of seven is fundamentally misleading.

The second section of the second part of the *Summa* innovates when it replaces the serial order with a more compendious, "simultaneous" order according to virtue. That is not all. The change in order requires that the list of virtues be traced back from accidental or causal classifications to an essential one. The result is not only greater clarity or compression, but a theoretically justified form within which to arrange the sprawling matter of both the moral catalogues and the "summas of cases." Within this new form, under its precise logic, Sodomy makes its discreet appearance as a subspecies of a familiar vice.

Luxuria and the Violation of Nature

Sodomy appears in Thomas's *Summa theologiae* within two questions on the vice of *luxuria* (2–2.153–154), which is to say, some considerable way into Thomas's rewriting of the confusion of theological instruction in morals. The first question, in five articles, begins by restricting received notions of *luxuria*, and next defends an authoritative teaching about how *luxuria* causes other sins. *Luxuria* is, Thomas says, properly a vice of excess in "venereal pleasures" (*voluptates venerei*), though it is secondarily applied to a number of self-indulgent excesses such as drinking too much wine (153.1 ad 1 and ad 2). The restriction is meant to discipline lax uses of a term that had ranged in Peraldus over that host of pleasures, from soft clothing to hot baths.[14] For Thomas, as for Albert, *luxuria* is to be understood as principally concerned with venereal pleasures. It is a vice so far as it is an excess of pleasure. There is no sin in the "use of venereal things" (*usus venereorum*) according to proper manner and order, that is, as directed to the end of human generation (153.2 corp). There are qualifications here, of course. The "use of women" (*usus feminae*) is a lesser good that bars one from complete virtue (153.2 ad 1). (Beyond underscoring the quoted phrase, I will not insist further that Thomas's texts speak only and always with a male voice.) The present intensity of venereal pleasure is a penalty for the Fall (153.2 ad 2, ad 3). These explicit qualifications belong to the evidently dialectical structure of the question. Having said that *luxuria* is an excess of venereal pleasure, Thomas argues that a "venereal act" (*actus*

13 *Summa theologiae* 1–2 84.4.ad 5: "ista vita dicuntur capitalia, qui ex eis ut frequentius alia oriuntur. Unde nihil prohibet aliqua peccata interdum ex aliis causis oriri."

14 William Peraldus *Summa de vitiis* tractatus de luxuria pars 1 (folio 203va).

venereus) is not always sinful, but that it often is—and, indeed, that excess in this kind of act is an important cause of other sins. The question ends just by defending Gregory the Great's teaching that *luxuria* is a capital sin with a number of "daughters," including hatred of God and despair (153.5 corp).

Thomas's next question proposes a division of *luxuria* into six kinds: simple fornication, adultery, incest, deflowering (*stuprum*), abduction (*raptus*), and vice against nature. Thomas cites as his authority for this division a text from Gratian. But Gratian is there distinguishing not six kinds of *luxuria*, but five kinds of "illicit intercourse" (*illicitus coitus*), and he does so in a different order and without mention of a vice against nature. Thomas is in fact choosing a variation on several divisions of *luxuria* current in the Parisian faculty of theology,[15] which divisions themselves had derived from Gratian through Peter Lombard.[16] Here and elsewhere Thomas defends the accuracy of the list of six against authoritative alternatives, including four passages from Paul.[17] Thomas also follows the received order of the list, though it conforms neither to his own logical derivation of the species (154.1) nor to his assessment of their gravity (cf. 154.12).[18]

The body of question 154 runs through the six species of Thomas's list in the received order.[19] The only significant addition to the taxonomy is the subdivision of the vice against nature. This vice comprises procuring pollution without "sleeping together" (*concubitus*), doing so by sleeping with a member of another species, doing so by sleeping with someone not of the proper sex, and doing so in other than the natural way, either by using an improper instrument or by using certain "monstrous and bestial manners" (154.11 corp).[20] The question ends with an article on the relative

15. See the order *fornicatio, adulterium, stuprum, sacrilegium, incestus, peccatum contra naturam* in the prologue to *Summa Halensis* 2/2 3 4 2.2 1.7 9, published as Alexander of Hales *Summa theologica* 3·604; and the order *simplex fornicatio, stuprum, adulterium, incestus, peccatum contra naturam* in William Peraldus *Summa de vitiis* tract. de luxuria pars 1 (fol 203vb).

16 Peter Lombard's *Sententiae* 4.41.5–9 (CSB 2:500 no 2) is a close paraphrase of Gratian's *Decretum* 2.36 1 2 (Richter-Friedberg 1 1289) Thomas knows both texts directly, of course.

17 The Pauline passages are 2 Cor 12:21, Eph 5·3, Col 3 5, and Gal 5·19, on which see *Summa theologiae* 2–2 154 1 arg.5, arg 6, ad 5, ad 6, especially in comparison with *Scriptum super libros Sententiarum* 4 41.1.4b arg.1–3 and ad 1–3 (Busa *Opera omnia* 1:625a–b).

18. Earlier Thomas had argued that the traditional list is an order of gravity, though he added even then that the order could be much varied by circumstances See *Scriptum super libros Sententiarum* 4.41 1.4c corp (Busa *Opera omnia* 1·625b)

19 There are two articles on simple fornication, two interjected articles on noncoital pleasures, then one each on the remaining species, with an interjected article against taking sacrilege as a separate species—as it is in the *Summa Halensis* 2/2 3 5 2 1 7 (CSB 3:648–653).

20 It seems to me that Thomas does not mean to use *concubitus* as a synonym for *coitus*. He reserves *coitus* for penile-vaginal intercourse between humans, as would be suggested by Gratian and

seriousness of the kinds of *luxuria*. The most serious is the vice against nature, the least serious simple fornication (154.12 corp). Of vices against nature, the worst is bestiality, the least serious, solitary uncleanness (154.12 ad 4).

If you recall scholarly narratives about Thomas's importance in the history of Christian intolerance,[21] you may be surprised to learn that the article on vice against nature is one of the shortest in these two questions. Indeed, it is about a quarter of the length of the longest article, which is the article that argues for the sinfulness of simple fornication. This crude, quantitative comparison would seem to suggest that the matter of the article on vice against nature is either not particularly important or not particularly difficult for Thomas. It does not require a complex set of distinctions or the defusing of difficult authorities. Hence there is no reason, on the surface of the text, to think that the discussion is tense or that there is any particular importance being attached to vice against nature.

Nor is there any reason on the surface of the text to think that particular emphasis is being put on the sleeping together of persons of the same sex. The language used to describe it is colorless. Indeed, the very term "sleeping together" (*concubitus*) is rather prim. The only phrase of invective in the whole article is used to describe improper manners by which members of different sexes lie together. These manners are "monstrous and bestial"; the others are merely practices of an unemphatically named "Sodomitic vice." The derogatory Pauline term "softness" (*mollities*) is used for what we would call masturbation (154.11 corp).[22] Nor, as I have said, is the Sodomitic vice singled out for its gravity: although the whole class of vices against nature is the most serious in the category of *luxuria*, the Sodomitic vice is not the worst of that class.

This impression that Thomas fails to emphasize the Sodomitic vice is strengthened by looking to the larger structure, which is the conclusion and the means for Thomas's rereading of moral traditions. Within that rereading, *luxuria* is given no particular prominence. If one of the best-calculated effects of Thomas's organization of the moral part of the *Summa*

Peter Lombard He is authorized in using *concubitus* for illicit sexual activity by the Vulgate, which uses *concubitores* only in the phrase "concubitores masculorum" (1 Cor 6 19, 1 Tim 1 10) That is how the Latin renders Paul's *arsenokoitai*, for which see Boswell, *Christianity, Social Tolerance, and Homosexuality*, pp. 341–353. The Vulgate uses *concubitus* twice neutrally (Gen 38 16, Rom 9 10), twice in contexts of excess ("concubitus concupiscentiae" at Sirach 23·6, "insanivit libidine . . super concubitu eorum" at Ezek 23:20).

21. Signally, Boswell, *Christianity, Social Tolerance, and Homosexuality*, pp 318–330.

22. On the difficulties of translating the Pauline *malakoi* (1 Cor 6·9), see Boswell, *Christianity, Social Tolerance, and Homsexuality*, pp 338–341

is to push the seven capital vices to the margin, *luxuria* is pushed there with the rest of them. It might be argued, even so, that *luxuria* remains most prominent among the seven once they are dispersed throughout the *Summa*. It merits two questions, after all, and by far the most extended discussion. But that is due, I think, to the number of species and "daughters" of *luxuria*. Sloth and envy have neither species nor daughters. Avarice and vainglory have daughters but not species. Gluttony and wrathfulness have both daughters and species, but their species are fewer and less confusing than those of *luxuria*. The extent of the treatment of *luxuria* is determined by taxonomy, not by gravity. Nor is the presence of an article on whether *luxuria* is the greatest of sins particularly significant. The same issue is raised with respect to three other of the capital vices.[23] The determination in each case is negative. None of the capital vices is the gravest or greatest sin. That distinction is reserved, even within Gregory's scheme, for pride, which is the gravest sin, the first sin, and the ruler of the capital sins.[24]

With all of this contextual reinforcement for the relative unimportance of *luxuria* and any of its species, the attentive reader of Thomas will be puzzled to recall one remark in the question on *luxuria*—a remark connected to other, much more emphatic references to the Sodomitic vice, though it is not elsewhere called by that name.[25] The remark is this: "Just as the order of right reason is from man, so the order of nature is from God himself. And so in sins against nature, in which the very order of nature is violated, an injury is done to God himself, the orderer of nature" (2–2.154.12 ad 1). What is peculiar about the remark is that the same syllogism can be constructed for any sin whatever. Every vice or sin is against nature, hence against God.[26] More superficially, Thomas himself uses sins of *luxuria* as a clear example of "sins against self" when these are to be contrasted, according to a different schema, with "sins against God."[27]

Now Thomas does explain in what way it is justified to single out one vice as the vice against nature. He notes, in an article on the inclusiveness of natural law, that "the sleeping together of men" (*concubitus masculorum*) is said especially to be a vice against nature because it controverts the

23. With respect to *avaritia* (*Summa theologiae* 2–2 118 5), *gula* (148 3), and *iracundia* (158 4)

24 See *Summa theologiae* 2–2 162 6, 162 7, and 162 8 respectively

25. Thomas speaks of *vitium sodomiticum* only in the *Summa*'s question on the species of *luxuria*, 2–2.154.11 corp, 154 12 ad 4, and in the commentary on Isaiah 4 (Leonine *Opera omnia* 28:33 43) In the latter, it is used as an example of an act that can never be ordered to the end of generation

26 This is the principal argument of *Summa theologiae* 1-2.71 2

27 *Summa theologiae* 1–2 72 4 corp "Et quando in his peccatur, dicitur homo peccare in seipsum, sicut patet de guloso, luxurioso et prodigo"

"commingling" (*commixtio*) of men and women that is natural to human beings and animals (1–2.94.3 ad 2). This is not an admission, frank or otherwise, that the terminology "is a concession to popular sentiment and parlance."[28] It resonates too strongly with other passages in which the vice against nature is seen as a violation of a fundamental teleology. In *De malo*, for example, every act of *luxuria* other than the commixture of men and women is said to be against the nature of any animal as such (15.1 ad 7). Again, in the *Summa contra Gentiles* sins against nature are coupled with murder so far as they prevent human conception.[29] So too Thomas follows Aristotle in using desire for such copulation as an example of an unnatural desire—as unnatural as the desire to eat coal or dirt.[30]

On the one hand, then, Thomas's rereading of the moral traditions places the Sodomitic vice as a middling species of a subsidiary class of sins, which cannot, as carnal, be among the gravest. On the other hand, the vice against nature is the eponymous denial of the order of animal nature, hence of nature's God. What is it that makes this vice at once a circumscribed self-indulgence and a radical denial of human purposes? What makes it, to pervert Eve Sedgwick's categories, at once minoritizing and universalizing?[31]

CARNAL, BESTIAL, UNNAMABLE VICE

Three descriptions of the vice enact this oscillation with great energy: they teach that it is a carnal vice, a bestial vice, and a vice that cannot be named. Each of these descriptions is justified by what I will begin by calling a "misreading" of an authoritative passage.

A carnal sin is, says Thomas, a sin that is consummated in a turning towards, a cleaving to some bodily good.[32] It arises from and is partly mitigated by the violence of our "concupiscence of flesh." Sins of *luxuria* are eminently the carnal sins in part because of the violence of concupiscence evident in them.[33] On Thomas's account, *luxuria* is a sin because it permits

---

28. Boswell, *Christianity, Social Tolerance, and Homosexuality*, p. 328.

29. *Summa "contra Gentiles"* 3.122 (Marc no 2955)

30. *Summa theologiae* 1–2.31.7 corp, 2–2.142 4 ad 3, to which compare Aristotle *Ethica Nicomachaea* 7 4 (1148b26) and Thomas *Sententia libri Ethicorum* 7.5 (Leonine *Opera omnia* 47·400.80–82). I will come back to Thomas's transposition of cannibalism in these contexts

31. Sedgwick, *Epistemology of the Closet*, pp. 40,41, and the review in her *Tendencies*, pp xii–xiii.

32. *Summa theologiae* 1–2.73 5 corp

33. *Summa theologiae* 2–2.153.1 corp: "Maxime autem voluptates venereae animum hominis solvunt"; ad 1, "luxuria principaliter quidem est in voluptatibus veneris, quae maxime et praecipue animum hominis resolvunt."

concupiscence to command what is against the common good, that is, against the conservation of the human species. But this account oscillates between two diagnoses of *luxuria*. The first diagnosis discovers a sin of self-indulgence that issues immediately in the dissolution of the soul. The second discovers a sin that imperils the future of the species by misusing its powers of reproduction.

The resulting instability can be seen quite plainly in Thomas's misreading of the familiar quotation from Augustine's *Confessions*. Recall what Augustine says: "Disgraceful acts (*flagitia*) against nature are everywhere and always to be detested and punished, as those of the Sodomites were; if all people did these, all would be held guilty of the same crime by the divine law, which did not make human beings that they should use each other in this way. Indeed the society that we ought to have with God is violated when the nature of which He is the author is polluted by perversity of lust."[34] Thomas quotes this whole passage, rather unusually, in replying to an objection that sins against nature are less serious than adultery, deflowering, or abduction because they do not harm one's neighbor. He replies with the quotation that sins against nature are the more serious because they are done against God.

The authoritative passage from Augustine becomes pertinent only after two misreadings. The first misreading, the explicit one, moves the accent in the passage from the perversity of lust—*libido*, the great word of Augustinian spiritual diagnosis—to the misuse of created bodies. The second misreading, the implicit one, changes the allusion to the Sodomites from the ferocity of their punishment to the (presumed) species of their crime. With the Old Testament prophets, and much patristic exegesis, Augustine takes the destruction of Sodom as a type for the ferocity of divine judgment. Aquinas, with much medieval exegesis, takes it as a type for a certain kind of sin.

There is nothing in the *Confessions* to make clear what Augustine has in mind when he speaks of "disgraceful acts against nature" (*flagitia contra naturam*). Augustine has here fallen into the hissing cauldron of lust, but not it would seem into acts that we would call homosexual. Moreover, the immediate context for the passage is an argument against the Manichaean charge that the God of the Old Testament changes his laws. Augustine is seeking to distinguish crimes that are always punished by the divine law

---

34 Augustine *Confessiones* 3.8 15 (Skutella-Verheijen 35 3–9). Thomas's version (as in the Leonine) differs only in punctuation and in reading "omnes eodem" for "eodem." A truncated version of the passage is used by Peraldus in the parallel discussion See his tractatus de luxuria 1 (folio 204va)

from crimes that can be punished or not depending on particular historical circumstances. The "disgraceful acts against nature" are everywhere and always to be punished in the way that the Sodomites were punished. What are these disgraces? They are specified only by the remark that human beings were not intended to use one another in such a way. There is no reference to the thwarting of reproduction or to the teleology of reproductive organs. Indeed, the Augustinian sense of "use" as the counterpoint for "enjoyment," and the teaching that all creatures are only to be used, would lead one to conclude that the passage in the *Confessions* is not about physical *usus* at all. Yet Thomas's argument will hold only if the passage refers to sins against nature understood as misuse of reproductive powers. He specifies this reference by relying on the now traditional misunderstanding of "Sodomites." That misunderstanding permits the transfer of Augustine's opprobrium—indeed, the full force of prophetic invective—to a particular set of acts, which it then understands as a misuse of the natural power of reproduction.

Another kind of misreading supports Thomas's description of the Sodomitic vice as a bestial vice. In the explicit taxonomy of the *Summa*, it is by no means the only one. Every carnal sin is bestial so far as it privileges the bodily delights that we share with other animals, thus rendering us "in some way . . . animal-like" ("quodammodo . . . brutalis," 1–2.73.5 ad 3). But the explicit taxonomy is again broken here by particular associations between Sodomitic vice and animality. On the one hand, the vice is consistently linked with cannibalism and what we still call bestiality.[35] On the other, it is inserted into an Aristotelian discussion of bestial vice, namely, vice that falls below the level of the human. Both associations are misreadings.

The association of an erotic desire for members of the same sex with cannibalism seems to come by misremembering Aristotle's discussion of unnatural desire. As Thomas tells it in his literal exposition of the *Ethics*, Aristotle distinguishes brutish desires from unnatural desires due to illness or to custom.[36] Examples of the brutish states are atrocities that include cannibalism. The examples of morbid desire resulting from custom include erotic activity among men.[37] It is Thomas who collapses Aristotle's distinc-

35. *Summa theologiae* 1–2.31.7 corp, "in coitu bestiarum aut masculorum", 2–2.142.4 ad 3, "in coitu bestiarum aut masculorum"; 2–2.154.11 corp, "Alio modo, . . bestialitas. Tertio, . . sodomiticum vitium"; 2–2.154.12 ad 4, "Post hoc [bestialitas] autem est vitium sodomiticum."

36. Aristotle *Ethica Nicomachaea* 7 5 (1148b15–30).

37. Aristotle speaks of "*hē ton aphrodisíōn toîs árresin*," which Thomas's Latin renders quite literally as "quae venereorum masculis." Compare Aristotle's *Ethica Nicomachaea* 7.5 (1148b29) with Thomas's *Sententia libri Ethicorum* 7.5 (Leonine *Opera omnia* 47 398). In Grosseteste's version of the anonymous

tions by connecting cannibalism, bestiality, and same-sex copulation under the notion of bestial desire.[38] He makes this clear in letting stand an objection according to which "the vice against nature is not contained under malice, but under bestiality, as is clear from the Philosopher in *Ethics* 7."[39] The misreading is so strong that it pushes Thomas to intervene untypically in the text of Aristotle's *Politics* as he expounds its letter. In reviewing Lacedaemonian and Cretan legislation, Thomas cannot stop himself from twice inserting the adjective "wicked" (*turpis*) when naming sexual acts between men.[40]

Transferring the erotic acts between men into the Aristotelian category of bestial vice yields both a rhetorical and a conceptual advantage. The rhetorical advantage lies in being able to reinforce the shame produced by Aristotle's having stigmatized, earlier in the *Ethics*, certain kinds of physical pleasures as "slavish" and "bestial."[41] The Sodomitic vice is not merely ridiculous and shameful in the way that gluttony is, it is also disgusting and horrifying in the way that atrocities are. The conceptual advantage comes in pushing this vice outside the boundaries of the discourse of ethics. The horrors enumerated by Aristotle in the discussion of bestial desire lie beyond the realm of rational inquiry. So too, for him, do the exaggerated diseases of desire. These acts are outside correction, hence outside ethical discussion. Thomas's conflation of the Aristotelian categories places the Sodomitic vice as such in this inhuman beyond.

A more dramatic displacement occurs when Thomas appropriates the tradition according to which vice against nature is a vice that cannot be named. He does so explicitly not in the *Summa*, but in his first *Scriptum* on the *Sentences*. "The species of *luxuria* are divided first into lying together according to nature and against nature. But since *luxuria* against nature is unnamable, it will be set aside."[42] The authority for this prohibition is a

<hr>

commentary on *Ethics* 7, the commentator has the same reading for the Aristotelian lemma, but goes on to speak of "abusing" or "corrupting" (*masculis . abuti, masculos corrumpere*). See Mercken, *The Greek Commentaries on the Nicomachean Ethics of Aristotle*, 3 41.95–07.

38. Albert, with whom Thomas studied the *Ethics* intensively, is more careful to distinguish the causality of long habit when raising questions about this passage He also counts *concubitus masculorum* as less unnatural than some of the other Aristotelian instances. See his *Super Ethica, Commentum et quaestiones* 7 5 (Cologne *Opera omnia* 14:545.37–40)

39. *Summa theologiae* 2–2 154 11 arg 2 and ad 2, to which compare *Scriptum super libros Sententiarum* 4.41 1 4b ad 4 (Busa *Opera omnia* 1 625b). Recall also the way in which Aristotle's remarks about the scope of temperance in *Ethics* 3 10 are taken as referring to *peccata carnalia* in 1–2 73 5 ad 3.

40 *Sententia libri Politicorum* 2.13 (Leonine *Opera omnia* 48:A164 140–149), 2.15 (A174.117–123)

41 Aristotle *Ethica Nicomachaea* 3 10 (1118b1–8)

42 *Scriptum super libros Sententiarum* 4.41 1 4b corp (Busa *Opera omnia* 1·625a)

misreading of Ephesians 5:3.[43] In commenting on that passage, Thomas explains that the idiom "are not to be named" means that the Ephesians are "to abstain from deeds, thoughts, and sayings" about a list of sins.[44] But in the *Scriptum* he appropriates the tradition that makes the precept dictate silence with regard to a certain class of sins against nature. Although the precept is not explicitly recalled in the *Summa,* it seems to be practiced. The descriptions of sins against nature are remarkably vague. One may contrast Thomas's reticence, for example, with the enumeration of four kinds of Sodomy by Peter Damian, or with the suggestive metaphors for organ complementarity in Alan's *Plaint* and Albert, or even with the anatomical distinctions in Peraldus.[45]

Of course, Peraldus himself immediately inserts the pastoral caution that would seem to explain the Pauline prohibition: "This vice is to be spoken of with great caution both in preaching and in confessional questioning, that nothing be revealed to men that might give them occasion to sin."[46] Why this caution? If the Sodomitic vice is the eponymous sin against nature, desire for which can be acquired only by long distortion of what is most innate, how can it be so easy to suggest?

The contradiction is a familiar one. It was enacted with particular clarity by Peter Damian in the few lines of his preface, which hesitates melodramatically to name a vice that it then likens to a raging epidemic. There is nothing so obvious in Thomas, and his aversion to gross contradictions may explain the omission of reference to Ephesians in the *Summa.* But in writings contemporary with the *Summa,* Thomas paraphrases and augments Aristotelian accounts of the genesis of the vice that suggest that it is much easier to acquire and perhaps to inculcate than the model of long abuse would allow. Thomas seems to agree with the *Politics* that the vice accompanies warlikeness and that it can be caused or exacerbated by the physiological effects of too much horseback riding.[47] Hence, the vagueness of the *Summa* and its emphasis on the rare conditions under which the vice is generated would seem to indicate something of the traditional reserve.

43. In the Vulgate, "Fornicatio autem et omnis inmundıtia aut avaritia nec nominetur ın vobıs sıcut decet sanctos" Note that the lıst extends consıderably beyond *luxuria contra naturam,* and that the sense ın the ıdıom ıs that these are not even to be mentıoned among Chrıstıans, much less practıced.

44 *Super ad Ephesios* 5.2 (Busa *Opera omnıa* 6·460c).

45. Wıllıam Peraldus *Summa de vıtııs* tractatus de luxurıa pars 1 (folıo 203vb)

46. Wıllıam Peraldus *Summa de vıtııs* tractatus de luxurıa pars 1 (folıo 203vb): "de quo vıtıo cum magna cautela loquendum est et predıcando et ınterrogatıones ın confessıonıbus facıendo· ut nıhıl homınıbus reveletur quod eıs prebet occasıonem peccandı"

47 *Sententıa lıbrı Polıtıcorum* 2 13 (Leonıne *Opera omnıa* 48:A164 140–153), wıth the ınserted reference to the ps-Arıstotelıan *Problemata*

152 / CHAPTER SEVEN

In these three descriptions of the vice as carnal, bestial, and unnamable, Thomas misreads just in the way that produces the duality of the Sodomitic vice as self-indulgence and eponymous crime against nature. But we cannot stop with calling them misreadings. Misreadings are questions, not answers. Why do the oscillations enacted by the category "Sodomitic vice" require such misreadings?

It may be part of an answer to say, in the first place, that the misreadings are justified by appeal to Thomas's largest judgments about the circumstances of moral teaching. These assumptions can be represented compendiously as a master narrative about the history of human learning. The master narrative is the double story of the deepening silence of natural law, caused by sin, and the growing articulateness of divine teaching, the work of grace. The narrative goes something like this: Original sin obscures our access to natural law, which was, in any case, never meant to serve as a guide apart from divine law and human laws in conformity with it. As the effects of sin accumulate, the natural law speaks less and less clearly. Indeed, it can become so inarticulate that whole peoples can forget one or another of its basic teachings. Thomas makes a famous mention of Caesar's claim that the Germans did not regard theft as an evil.[48] The silences of natural law can be filled in only by divine revelation, that is, by the articulation of divine laws of the Old and New Testaments. They make explicit and practicable what the natural law only suggested, when it spoke at all. The progress of Christian moral theology aids the work of articulation, not by adding new laws, but by specifying applications and correcting misunderstandings. Later theologians speak "more cautiously" and "as if selectively" in view of the history of misunderstandings and controversies that is the history of heresy.[49]

In the second place, Thomas presents through the *Summa* the ideal of a set of patterns for the analysis of moral life. What is meant by pattern can be seen in a contrast. One staple of Dominican moral preaching was the sermon *ad status*, the sermon concerned with the perils and patterns of a particular profession or social class. The closest Thomas comes to that kind of direct address is in the final questions of the *secunda secundae*, which concern religious life. Even here, however, the *Summa* keeps itself at considerable distance from the particular. It seems to offer no more than schemata for moral applications or analyses yet to be done. Particular issues are treated, of course. Thus, Thomas considers whether it is licit to baptize

---

48 *Summa theologiae* 1–2 94 4 corp.
49 *Contra errores Graecorum* pars prior prol (Leonine *Opera omnia* 40 A71 39–40)

non-Christian children against the will of their parents (2–2.10.12), how one is to proceed in fraternal correction (2–2.33.7–8), and when one is to fast (2–2.147.57). But the overwhelming majority of questions in this more particular part of the *Summa* concern the classification, causality, order, and opposition of virtues or vices. It is much more taxonomy than exhortation, much more causal classification than spiritual direction. Hence, Thomas's ideal of moral science would seem to be self-limiting in another way: It recognizes the intrinsic universality of moral teaching and does not pretend to annul it by a pretense of particularity. this is all the more striking because the affirmation of personal providence might seem to require that moral theology be more particular than moral philosophy—not less particular.

Then, third, Thomas reminds his readers in the *Summa* of the limitation of any theological teaching about morals. What is required for a complete life of virtue is the personal gift of divine grace. Moral science is bound to offer self-corrections if the activity of teaching it is not to be self-contradictory. What is the point of teaching a Christian moral doctrine if the enactment of that doctrine will depend utterly on God? Thomas knows one formulation of this puzzle in Augustine's anti-Manichaean writings.[50] What is more striking, the *Summa* itself contains at least two explicit correctives to any overestimation of the value of human teaching.

The first comes, prominently, at the end of the *Summa*'s first part (1.117.1). It is the first article in a set of three questions (1.117.prol). Thomas argues that a human teacher can do no more than minister externally to the learner. The ministry is of two kinds. The human teacher can provide "helps and instruments," such as examples, analogies, disanalogies, or more proximate propositions. And the human teacher can propose an order of learning—can trace out a path for the learner's work of understanding. That is all.

The *Summa*'s second reminder about teaching comes at the end of the *secunda secundae*. In the final questions on special graces and conditions of life, the issue of human teaching appears and reappears. There is, for example, the freely given grace of the "word of wisdom" or "of knowledge" (*sermo sapientiae, scientiae*, 2–2.177.1)—a gift of speaking persuasively about God by which the human teacher becomes an instrument for the Holy Spirit.[51]

50 See, for example, Augustine *De correptione et gratia* 1 2.3–6 9 (*PL* 44 917–921)

51 *Summa theologiae* 2–2 177 1 "Ad quod quidem efficiendum Spiritus Sanctus utitur lingua hominis quasi quodam instrumento, ipse autem est qui perficit operationem interius." Compare the remarks on teaching for the sake of saving souls in 181.3, 187 1, and 188 4–5.

The remarks on teaching are not casual asides. They are deliberate reminders of Thomas's ideal of moral science as embodied in the *Summa*. The *Summa* is neither scriptural exegesis nor preaching. It is intermediate between them—dependent on Scripture, intended for the formation of preachers. To say this again, the *Summa* is intermediate between divinely inspired books that embrace every important genre of teaching and the specialized genres of direct spiritual formation. The *Summa* is at once a clarifying simplification of Scripture for the sake of preaching and confessing, and a clarifying generalization of pastoral experience brought back under the science of Scripture, which is to say, under the whole of theology. Nothing more ought to be asked of a theologian's moral teaching. The ideal of *scientia moralis* ought to insist first and last that it is ancillary to the workings of divine grace in individual human souls.

The narrative of moral darkening is easier to tell than the ideal of a theological *scientia moralis* is to imitate. The ideal requires of Thomas both that he speak what is silent in natural law and that he speak most judiciously about matters liable to cause scandal. He must both strengthen the voice of nature and conceal how often the voice has been unheard. Most particularly, since the *Summa* teaches "Christian religion" to those who would learn it in the school of religious life, he must present these "Sodomitic" sins as remote ones, beyond the border of nature, and hence much more outside the cloister, even as he omits to mention that the history of the church has shown this vice to be a peculiarly clerical "contagion"—I use one of the recurring metaphors for it.

This account of the circumstances of Thomas's teaching justifies the misreadings of Sodomitic vice as carnal, bestial, and unnamable by presenting them as corrective rereadings. It would be easy to show that Thomas regards this kind of correction as an essential part of the theologian's work. But in doing so we would lose the specific problematic of the Sodomitic vice in a general account of theological procedure. We have not yet got what it is about the category of this vice that causes it to oscillate. We have not, because it is here that our conflicts of motives and surplus of stories diverge irremediably from Thomas's. I will end by trying to say how this is so.

MORAL THEOLOGY AND AUTHORITY

I suggested above that the oscillation in the category of Sodomitic vice, by which it swings from a middling sin of *luxuria* to the eponymous sin against natural teleology, was somewhat like Sedgwick's dialectic of minoritizing

and universalizing accounts of homosexuality. But whatever the cause of
the oscillation of Thomas's category might be, it cannot be the dialectic
that Sedgwick describes. It cannot, because there is nothing resembling the
categories "homosexual" and "heterosexual" in Thomas. Thomas cannot
responsibly be made even to speak in debates where homosexuality and
heterosexuality serve as categories for personal identity. When Thomas
talks about the Sodomitic vice, he is talking about a vice. The vice is precisely not a physiological disposition or its behavioral consequences. Neither is it an identity determining the whole of a person's action. Nor does
the vice have anything specifically to do with gender inversions or exagger-
ations.[52] Indeed, so far as I can see, there are no references to gender at all
in Thomas's passages on same-sex copulation.

It does not follow that Thomas regards nothing beyond acts of copulation. A vice is never the sum of acts. It is rather their cause and ground.
The Sodomitic vice is meant to explain why certain people do acts that are
against their natures as reasonable animals. Part of the explanation reaches
downward to particular circumstances. Part runs backward to personal history or physiology. Part spreads out into the network of a person's other
vices and virtues, into passions, dispositions, character. But these explanations cannot be mapped onto the theories embedded in the term "homosexuality."

If the dialectic of homosexual/heterosexual cannot be the deep cause of
the conceptual oscillation that we have traced through textual anomalies
and acts of misreading, what is the cause? I am not content to answer that
it is stupidity or a mere sloppiness in the use of basic terms, as if the matter
could be solved by "being clear" about the meanings of "nature." Nor do
I want to conclude that the oscillations are the most visible effects of an
ideological abuse of discrepant conceptual schemes. I want to say, rather,
that the oscillations of the category of Sodomitic vice arise from what must
appear to us as a paradox in the notion of unnatural pleasure—a paradox
glimpsed in the category of *luxuria* but observed most strikingly in the persistent fact that some people derive pleasure from unteleological copulation.

The paradox is this: For Thomas, true pleasure is the effect of natural
completion, of the fulfillment of natural teleology. The Sodomitic vice rad-
ically disrupts the most obvious continuities of animal nature. Yet the cause

---

52 Thomas does follow old traditions, both pagan and Judeo-Christian, in associating all *luxuria*
with effeminacy. Thus, following Hos 4:11, he holds that fornication and drunkenness make a man
effeminate (2–2 153.5 ad 2). On Thomas's view, the adulterer or rapist is just as likely to be as effeminate as a man who copulates with other men.

of this violently antinatural sin is the intensity of pleasure it yields—a pleasure so intense that it "dissolves the soul." But it is not only the intensity
that is troubling: Thomas here confronts a kind of pleasure that cannot
be divided without remainder into teleological sequences. He confronts a
pleasure without end. He names the possibility of this pleasure the antithe-
sis of nature. Much more than thieving Germans, the fact of Sodomitic
pleasures threatens to assert that a large group of moral arguments from
natural teleology is specious.

Just here we are prevented from pursuing the paradox further. Indeed,
we must wonder whether the paradox is not our misapprehension. We are
up against what seems to me the most startling divergence between our
stories and Thomas's, his motives and ours. For Thomas, the assertion that
venereal pleasures are for the sake of reproduction is not an assumption,
but a tautology. It is the way of picking out certain pleasures as venereal.
The category of *luxuria* is constituted by its relation to the teleology of
reproduction. There is no other way of distinguishing the class of acts,
pleasures, and sins as venereal. For us, on the contrary, the category of the
"erotic" or even the "sexual" is constituted by the assertion of that there is
a distinctive class of pleasures whose members exceed—indeed, precede—
the relation of the pleasuring organs to reproduction. For us, the restriction
of sexual or erotic activity to procreation seems at best quaint, at worse
tyrannical. For Thomas, there is no category of the sexual apart from animal teleology.

This divergence between our terms and Thomas's does confirm, in a
small way, Foucault's assertion that our category of "sexuality" is itself a
fairly recent invention. It also and immediately provokes another question:
What was there before the category of "sexuality"? In Thomas, there is
sex (*sexus*), the complex of anatomical and physiological features that distinguish male and female. There is the right use (*usus*) of procreative
power, of copulation and any necessarily connected acts, for the reproduction of the species. And then there is *delectatio,* dangerous pleasure, with
its threats to the soul's rational order. These terms, whether taken singly
or together, do not map onto the objects or reasons implied by our term
"sexuality." We begin again to diverge from Thomas.

Is there another way forward? Texts, like traditions of inquiry, carry
unactualized possibilities. Might there be in Thomas principles or procedures or materials for constructing something more like the modern notion
of sexuality? More specifically, might there be in Thomas a potency for
something akin to one of the modern notions of homosexuality?

The question demands three different answers. The first is that no exegetical strategy has done more violence to Thomas's texts than the strategy of trying to guess what he might have said to some modern dilemma. Thomas ends up saying what his readers wanted to say before turning to him. This is called "Thomism."

The second answer is that Thomas's teaching on human *sexus* is one of the thinnest and least reflective parts of his moral doctrine. He worked much harder to clarify or to construct other moral teachings. What he did achieve by giving the sins of *luxuria* a reasoned placed within the structure of the *Summa* was undone by the kind of oscillations already described.

The third answer, the most interesting, is that there are in Thomas at least two principles that might have been used to great effect in constructing Christian discourses about same-sex desire. One principle holds that a virtue infused by God can require different actions than the corresponding natural virtue. Divine law can overrule any limited calculation of human goods or ends. Thomas uses the example of fasting. Natural temperance condemns severe fasting as a denial of the mean in nutrition. Infused temperance, the temperance of divine law, commands us to chastise and subjugate the body.[53] The principle is applied by Thomas repeatedly in his defense of virginity. The physical teleology of reproduction is suspended in particular cases by the higher call of divine law, which proclaims that there is something more than the imperatives of the body.[54] So Thomas argues in the pages of the *Summa* immediately before the questions on *luxuria*. Why not extend the principle to the consideration of human sex generally and to same-sex copulation in particular?

The other latent principle is one that Thomas invokes rarely if at all in moral matters, though it is his chief principle in the rest of theology. It is the principle of *apophansis*, of negation: we speak more truly about God and divine things when we negate human categories than when we apply them. Theological discourse ought to be—and is in much of the *Summa*—the precise arrangement of strings of negations. These strings lead the reader, again and again, to the point at which human language fails to capture divine truth. They lead the reader back to the decisive questions on the "divine names," that is, on the possibilities for speaking about God by negation. There is no stricter theological principle for recognizing the "other" as other.

Imagine, then, the principle of negative theology applied to the teaching on *luxuria*. Would it not require that the Christian theologian suspect easy

53 *Summa theologiae* 1–2 63 4 corp
54 *Summa theologiae* 2–2 152.2 corp

applications of prevailing categories for human actions? That she examine attentively any proposed deductions from comprehensive accounts of "nature"? That she wonder whether the divine teaching about human things might not be as offensive to societal prejudices as the doctrine of the Trinity is offensive to prevailing human arithmetics?

I do not find that Thomas considers these injunctions or the possibilities of the apophantic principle in dealing with the morality of human sexes. Nor were they considered by Thomas's students and later readers. Just here the history of Thomism becomes important. Because Thomas was adopted by church power from its own interests and for its own purposes, Thomist moral teaching could never explore antinomian consequences of its own first principles. It could never inquire into reformulations of moral theology that would cut against the interests of its patrons. For this reason, Thomas's extraordinary achievement in moral teaching remains imperfectly understood and perpetually stunted. It has not been possible, under the historical circumstances of Thomism, to rethink Thomas's rather superficial teaching on Sodomy in light of his deeper teachings. It has not been possible to stop the oscillations in the category of Sodomy by reference to the powerful principles that structure the whole of the *Summa*.

The power of those principles was used in the opposite direction. Because Thomas reasons clearly and synthetically, his *Summa* was all too easily confused with the systematizations of canon law. Indeed, it seemed to fulfill a canonist's fantasy—the extension into every detail of human life of universal legal principles. Far from being an invitation to reconsider teachings about human sex, for example, the moral part of the *Summa* seemed to promise the imposition of exceptionless norms of behavior across Christian living. So St. Alphonsus may not have been disingenuous in acknowledging Thomas at the start of his deeply juridical treatment of moral theology. The use of Thomas's *Summa* as a quasi-legal system of moral theology did in fact prepare the way for the sterile systematization of moral theology in the past three centuries. Whether Christian theology could take advantage of the collapse of official Thomism to carry forward a genuinely Thomist project of moral theology is another question. It is the question of how present-day thinkers can appropriate moral theology's long and checkered past. The question is nowhere more urgent than with regard to the checkered theological category of Sodomy.

A Postlude after St. Ambrose

The Responsibilities of a Theology of Sodomy

At a moment full of consequences for the history of Christian teaching—just before he will adopt Cicero as an authority in morals, just after he has anguished over whether, when, and how to speak about moral matters—Ambrose offers this double analogy: "As Cicero wrote to educate his son, so I too write in order to form you, my children; nor do I love you less for having begotten you in the Gospel than if I had gotten you by marriage."[1] This gives a first test for Christian moral teaching. Its motive must be love, a love as strong as the intertwined loves of philosophic pedagogy and a parent's anxiety for education, and its address must be to those who are bound to the speaker in a community of love.

Having applied this test to himself, Ambrose still hesitates to begin speaking about Christian duties. Another sort of test remains. Ambrose must ask himself, whether the Ciceronian word that will be his topic, the word *officium*, "duty," is a philosopher's word only or also a scriptural one. Do the Scriptures authorize his thinking with the help of the category "duty"? Ambrose receives an answer, providentially, in his daily reading of the Gospel. It comes from Luke's description of the announcement of the birth of John the Baptist, that patron of moral teachers. The Latin version that Ambrose reads continues in this way (Luke 1:23): "It happened that the days of [Zechariah's] *officium* were completed and he went home."[2] The *officium* here is the priestly service of John's father, Zechariah. Ambrose finds in this use of the word sufficient confirmation of his intention to write a Christian treatise on moral duties. He proceeds, at once, to appropriate Cicero's classification of *officia* and so to authorize for the Latin-speaking West the long traditions of moral classification, explanation, in-

---

1 Ambrose of Milan *De officiis* 1 7 24 (Testard 106 = Migne *PL* 16 30c)
2 Ambrose of Milan *De officiis* 1 8 25 (Testard 107 = Migne *PL* 16 31a–b)

quiry, and instruction—of what we have come to call "moral theology" or "Christian ethics."

The authorization supposes that two tests have been met—the test of shared motive and the test of precedent. Each test is complex. The first means, I have suggested, that the motive of Christian teaching must be a special love for the community of those listening, a community constituted by the same kind of love. The second criterion, the criterion of precedent, means at least that Christian moral teaching should intend to speak when and as the Scriptures speak. It should seek to conform its logic of categorization and argument to the logic of the Scriptures. Most important, it should be silent when the Scriptures are silent. There are too many sins in speaking, Ambrose has said, for speech to be undertaken lightly, especially when the topic of speaking is Christian living.

Let me agree with Ambrose that these are appropriate tests for a Christian who wants to speak about morals. Then let me go on to ask a question that presses on all the readings undertaken in this book: Do we meet these tests when we invoke the history of Christian moral teaching to speak about what we call homosexuality? Our readings in medieval texts have suggested that we do not meet them. Indeed, we fail much lesser tests. We typically disregard the most basic rules of respectful reading when arguing about same-sex love. We rip words out of context; we magnify what is microscopic and ignore what is enormous; we refuse to examine the rifts that divide our languages, our discourses, from the patristic or medieval discourses we want to invoke. But there is more. Even when we are most responsible about our readings, we do not speak cogently about same-sex pleasure. There seem to be troubles in what our traditions themselves say. Indeed, the traditions themselves do not pass Ambrose's tests for Christian moral teaching, however much they descend directly from him.

It is time to recall the troubles in our medieval texts at three levels. The first level is that of unstable terms; the second, of unfaithful descriptions; the third, of inconsistent arguments. Unstable terms, unfaithful descriptions, inconsistent arguments—I intend to remind my reader that the concern has been with levels in texts, in moral discourse. I am concerned, as Ambrose was, with failures of Christian speaking. The texts are embedded in any number of contexts, of course—institutional, economic, geographical, literary, personal. But we have concentrated just on the texts, because they have cast such long and gruesome shadows over European and American history.[3]

3 Compare Nietzsche, *Joyful Science* 3 §108 (Colli-Montinari 3 467)

UNSTABLE TERMS

The first challenge in approaching the medieval texts was a problem of language—not the problem of their being written in medieval Latin, but the problem of their employing terms or categories that we cannot get over into modern English, that we cannot easily conceive without provoking serious misunderstandings. The term "Sodomy" is just such a term. It has shown itself to be untranslatable.

We must come to old theological texts on the assumption that we have everything to learn about the meaning of their central terms. So we cannot come to the texts knowing what their authors mean by "Sodomy." The last thing we should do is to translate "Sodomy" as "homosexuality." "Homosexuality" is a term from late nineteenth-century forensic medicine, a diagnostic term for regulating the behavior of the patients or prisoners it presumes to classify. If you ask, What does medieval moral theology have to say about homosexuality? the only precise answer is, Absolutely nothing. "Homosexuality" is no more discussed by medieval theology than are phlogiston, Newton's inertia, quarks or any of the other entities hypothesized by one or another modern science. "Sodomy" is not "homosexuality." What it is, we can learn only from medieval texts. We begin to learn it when we recall that "Sodomy" was coined in medieval theology by derivation or deduction from a previous term, the term "Sodomite."

Peter Damian coins "Sodomy" on analogy to "blasphemy" in a context that means to emphasize the seriousness of both: "If blasphemy is the worst sin, I do not know in what way Sodomy is any better."[4] What is new in this sentence is the abstract noun, the abstraction of an essential sin. To assert that there is an essence, "Sodomy," is to imply that there is one intelligible formula that captures a previously unspecified range of human acts, activities, or dispositions. Remember that this abstraction, this essentializing remains linked to a category of personal identity—the identity of the "Sodomite." "Sodomy" is an essence abstracted from an identity, which has itself been generalized out of the narration of a historical event.

In Peter Damian's *Book of Gomorrah*, the figure of the Sodomite becomes a page on which the troubles of unstable abstraction are written out. Consider the topic of community: The Sodomite ought to be exiled from his homeland as unfit for citizenship, and yet the Sodomite is conceived by definition as a citizen of an ancient, enduring city, the city of Sodom. The Sodomite is unfit for full membership in the church, especially in its minis-

4 Peter Damian *Liber Gomorrhianus* (Reindel 328 2–3).

terial orders, and yet Peter fears that Sodomites have taken over the church, constituting a shadow hierarchy with its own means of recognition and recruitment. Or consider punishment: Sodomy is subject to capital punishment under civil law and to the severest censures of church law, and yet, on Peter Damian's own testimony, Sodomy has greatly increased during the history of Christendom. Most strikingly, the city of Sodom was subject to the worst divine punishment recorded in the Scriptures, and still its citizens multiply. Or consider cure: Peter Damian spends much of his treatise arguing by reason and authority against Sodomy, but he also insists that the Sodomite is a madman beyond reach of reason. The Sodomite is a sinner, but one for whom no repentance seems practicable. Finally, the Sodomite would seem to need the strongest spiritual therapy, the penitential ascesis of the monk's cell, and yet long years in the cell will not cure the most basic errors about Sodomy—as becomes clear in a story of the elderly monk whisked off by demons for misunderstanding masturbation.

We might think of these instabilities, these swings in the abstract term "Sodomy," as playing out certain underlying paradoxes. For example, the crime of Sodomy responds to punishment not as a crime should, but as an involuntary nature does. Sodomy subverts what is supposed to be the foundation of the city, namely the reproductive family, even while it builds enduring communities. While Sodomy should contradict reason by denying nature, it seems marvelously equipped with reasons that speak on its behalf. Finally, Sodomy seems to be an unrepentable sin—that is, either an exception to divine grace or not a sin at all.

These paradoxes are indeed present in Peter Damian's thought. They are intensified, if not constituted, by the very process of abstracting or essentializing as a sin an allegorical reading of the biblical narrative of Sodom. There are two, separate mistakes here. The first is to think that the story of Sodom is centrally about same-sex pleasure—or even a particular kind of same-sex copulation. It is not. Even if it were, Peter Damian's abstracting or essentializing would commit a second mistake. The story of Sodom, like most stories in the Old Testament, should have moral lessons for a Christian reader. Still, the moral lessons discovered in allegorical reading do not have the character of legal definition or prescription. Even if this story were about same-sex pleasure, it would not yield a quasi-legal definition of an abstract act, Sodomy, as the core of an abstract identity, the Sodomite.

The procedures of abstraction are what make the term "Sodomy" so unstable. It contains within itself a mistaken reading and a mistaken way of inferring moral truths. These two mistakes are also why the term "Sodomy" has proved so useful as an ideological or polemical term, that is, as a mask for violent exercises of power. From the beginning, "Sodomy" has meant whatever anyone wanted it to mean. It has been able to encompass very different acts and to project very different identities. It has been able to carry opposed arguments. It has been able to justify a dozen differently motivated oppressions. All this because the term is essentially unstable, not to say unscriptural, in form and content. It pretends to speak a lesson from Genesis 19. In fact, it misreads that chapter allegorically and then illicitly generalizes from allegory to lawlike definition and prescription.

I underline one unintended consequence of the instability of the term "Sodomite." The idea of an identity built around the genital configuration of one's sexual partners is, in our tradition, the product of Christian theology. The rapid acceptance of the term "homosexual" as a term of identity was prepared, long before, by a double mistake in medieval theology. Because Latin theologians thought in terms of Sodomites, we have found it so easy to think of ourselves as *being* homosexuals, as having a lesbian or gay *identity*. When we lesbians and gays think of ourselves as members of a tribe, as a separate people or race, we echo medieval theology's preoccupation with the Sodomites. Perhaps there is some room for gratitude to Peter Damian even here. And room for correcting some pages in the first volume of Foucault's *History of Sexuality*.

Foucault there draws an influential contrast: "The sodomy of the ancient civil or canonical codes was a category of forbidden acts; their perpetrator was nothing more than the juridical subject of them. The nineteenth-century homosexual has become a personage: a past, a history and a childhood, a character, a type of life; also a morphology, with an indiscreet anatomy and possibly a mysterious physiology."[5] We can now say, at least, that Peter Damian attributes to the Sodomite many of the kinds of features that Foucault finds only in the nineteenth-century definition. Indeed, Peter Damian pretends to find these features in the patristic and early medieval "canonical codes." We have also found in other authors remarks on Sodomitic anatomy and physiology, personal history, and secret community. This does not mean, of course, that the Sodomite *is* the nineteenth century's homosexual. The identities are different, as are the notions about identity itself. It does mean that the invention of the homosexual may well have

5 Foucault, *Histoire de la sexualité*, 1 59

relied on the already familiar category of the Sodomite. The idea that same-sex pleasure constitutes an identity of some kind is clearly the work of medieval theology, not of nineteenth-century forensic medicine. So too any rejection of the Christian account of Sodomy may well carry with it the rejection of identity as a necessary category for thinking about same-sex pleasure.

UNFAITHFUL DESCRIPTIONS

The term "Sodomy" makes possible a number of theological descriptions in which the realities of human lives are lied about, are deliberately misrepresented, for allegedly moral purposes. We have seen this differently in the dissembling of the confessor's manuals and the silence of Albert the Great. The dissembling and the silence both occur at another moment full of consequences for Christian moral theology in the Western churches. It is the moment of wanting to give a comprehensive and literal description of how Christians ought to act. The description is to be comprehensive. It will describe not just some virtues or vices, but all virtues and vices, arranged systematically according to cause or seriousness or some other principle. The description will also be literal. It will have neither the multiplicity of a parable or an allegory, nor the rhetorical specificity of a sermon or a prayer. The project is to give, for the first time, a comprehensive and literal moral doctrine.

Albert the Great is rightly regarded as a polymath in whom the natural sciences and medicine entered into various combinations with theology. But we have watched Albert pass over inconvenient science in silence. We have heard from Albert descriptions of Sodomitic nature that omit or rewrite what he knows of nature. This is the more striking because Albert elsewhere seems unconcerned with sexual activities. Female masturbation he excuses as morally indifferent on physiological grounds. He quotes prostitutes for their experience with sexual matters. But the taste for description disappears as Albert approaches same-sex pleasure. He substitutes in its place the repetition of fantastic myths.

Albert is one of the chief agents of the reorganization of moral teaching. Even before a Franciscan team undertook to rework academic theology in the *Summa of Brother Alexander*, Albert was reordering parts of the treatment of virtues and precepts. He performs one of the first rereadings of Aristotle's *Nicomachean Ethics* on the basis of a complete Latin version and with the aid of newly translated Greek commentary. But the efforts at systematization do not extend to same-sex love. Albert refuses over decades to redescribe it within the possibilities opened by Avicenna's medicine or Aristotle's ethics.

In the manuals, we have heard repeatedly that same-sex copulation and related sins are not to be spoken about for fear of provoking them. This suggests that their sinfulness, their unnaturalness, is in no way apparent. For some hearers, at least, a description of same-sex copulation induces not revulsion, but desire. So the confessor's description of human sexual life has to be carefully edited, fortified by frightening examples, made repulsive by analogy. This unfaithfulness of description is already an occasion for sin in the moral theologian. A systematic classification of sins is an essay in extending the Gospel so far as it imports nonscriptural distinctions or causalities or rankings. The temptations in constructing a comprehensive and literal description of sins beyond the Gospel are obvious. One's own sinfulness may all too easily lead to the ad hoc valuation of categories, to mistaking accidental for essential, to confusing private taste with divine ordinance.

Here we see the disparity between the faithful self-description of the penitent and the unfaithful description of the confessor. What is the effect on the confessor of hearing sins of Sodomy described? If these are so highly suggestive, if they are almost instantly contagious, what protection has the confessor? Of course, the confessor is always described as free from the sin. This is another kind of unfaithfulness. We know that the truth is otherwise from the confessor's manuals themselves, in which the sin of Sodomy has been singled out as particularly a clerical sin. The faithful self-description of the penitent may well incite this sin in the confessor, but the confessor will stand behind unfaithful description, behind the mask of hypocrisy. This unfaithfulness, this particular hypocrisy, seems to me to trouble much of the history of Christian teaching on same-sex pleasure. The teaching almost inevitably proceeds where some of those present have the strongest personal interest in seeing that the discussion stops with the briefest, most vehement condemnation of same-sex pleasure. The closet, far from being a construction of the present century, is a very old ecclesiastical dwelling place.

Deep methodological effects follow on clerical hypocrisy. They are effects not in particular rules, but in the tenor of the whole system of rules. They appear most clearly as a willingness to be entirely too confident of one's own ability to capture moral prohibitions. What is signally lacking in the confessor's manuals is a doctrine of negative theology for morals. To say this again, what is lacking is any sense of how the unknowability of God has consequences for the unknowability of God's providence in human lives. In the absence of a sense of the unsayable, the unknowable in morals, Christian moral theology risks becoming something less than Greek ethics rather than something more. It is a common teaching in Greek philosophy that ethical knowledge is not of the same character as knowledge of logic, mathematics, or physics. What is required in a student of ethics is not just brightness or docility, but experience and self-control. To memorize ethical propositions in philosophy without being able to enact them is to be no more than a parrot or a hypocrite.

Surely we should demand at least as much of moral theology. Its truths are not learned if they are merely memorized in the way one might memorize a code of civil or canon law. The truth of moral theology is learned only in the heart's intimate relation with a personal providence, with the indwelling of the Holy Spirit. To think otherwise is to take the analogy implied in speaking of "divine law" as an equation. It is to pretend that God's moral pedagogy is just like any other law.

INCONSISTENT ARGUMENTS

The project of moral systematization in thirteenth-century theology did not exhaust itself in confessor's manuals or efforts to segregate morals from medicine. It also gave birth to the first works of moral theology conceived on analogy to theoretical knowledge. The best known is Thomas's *Summa of Theology*. As we have seen, its triumph is to organize and situate Christian moral teaching between a theology that issues in cosmology and a Christology that issues in an account of the church. The structure of Thomas's *Summa* puts the teaching about Christian living right at the center of a complete pattern of Christian instruction. Just because it is so superbly ordered, Thomas's *Summa* has offered an exemplary text in which to see the third kind of trouble in dealing with Sodomy—I mean the trouble of inconsistent arguments.

The inconsistencies here are not of the kind to be fixed by fiddling with premises. A modern reader cannot step into this or that paragraph, change a word, and emerge with a demonstrative argument. Indeed, the inconsistencies are most often compounded when taken up by modern readers. Many of those who quote Thomas as a moral authority are guilty of this. First, most obviously, it is impossible to condemn same-sex copulation on Thomas's authority without condemning a variety of other sexual practices that we now typically accept. These include masturbation, mutual masturbation, fellatio, cunnilingus, and the use of coital positions other than what we call the "missionary." The centerpiece of Thomas's argument against genital expressions of same-sex love is that they violate the reproductive purpose of the genitals. If you want to borrow his argument, you must be willing also to argue against any nonreproductive use of the genitals, including, I would say, their use with contraceptive intent or in marriages known to be sterile.

Second, less obviously, to pick out Thomas's remarks against same-sex copulation is to redouble the structural inconsistency that troubles him— the inconsistency of giving too much prominence to a middling subset of fleshly sins. I have argued that the vehemence with which Thomas sometimes condemns same-sex copulation is not consistent with the fundamental principles of his moral theology. A similar inconsistency seems to me to appear and reappear in works of the Western Christian traditions. You can witness the distension of Christian moral systems under the pressure to emphasize, to exaggerate the sinfulness of same-sex copulation.

Similar inconsistencies haunt Alan of Lille's *Plaint of Nature*. On one side, Alan wants to show the inconsistency, the inconstancy of Nature herself in sexual matters. She cannot even name, much less argue against, practices that undo her fundamental purposes. On the other side, Alan elsewhere treats the theologian's sin of Sodomy in conventional terms as a sin of *luxuria* specified by its opposition to nature. He unleashes his considerable talent for invective against it, investing it with a horror unmotivated by its place in the list of sins or by the allegory of its ambiguous origin in nature.

What is this pressure? What is it that pushes a theologian as lucid as Thomas Aquinas to contradict his own best principles, to undo his own extraordinary achievement of theological order? What leads Alan to ignore his own subtle discoveries in moral discourse so as to proceed, vehemently, with a simple condemnation? We are not ready to answer these questions on behalf of Christian theology or within it. We have only begun to think about the Christian condemnations of same-sex pleasure with any frankness. We have only begun to take them as questions rather than as evident truths. Moreover, we have no persuasive Christian account of human sex generally, much less of its enactments between members of the same sex or of its categorical applications. The imperative just now is to know what we do not know and to admit what we have not thought.

Above all we should resist the temptation to "answer" questions about same-sex pleasure and Christian theology by fleeing into some ready-made theory. We gain nothing by invoking "homophobia" as an explanation of distensions in the traditions of Christian theology. "Homophobia" is, whenever applied, not an explanation, but a placeholder for an explanation yet to be provided. Nor do we gain by fleeing into one or another psycho-analytic theory in trying to understand the forces that have deformed Christian moral speaking. The theories depend plainly on views of human nature that are alien to the accounts given by the medieval texts. A reader who has already endorsed one of the theories may want to submit the medieval texts to the final judgment of that theory. But this seems to me a way of distancing the texts, of disengaging from them, rather of continuing with them.

If we cannot yet know what forces distend Christian teaching on same-sex pleasure, we can at least note that the forces appear to be connected with three other effects in the language around Sodomy. The disturbances are connections between Sodomy and other, curiously vehement theological discourses. In these discourses, as in the condemnation of same-sex pleasure, Christian theologians speak incoherently, with too much displaced passion, about apparently unrelated moral matters. The first of these disturbances happens around cleanliness; the second, around nobility or aristocratic superiority; the third, around women.

One of the commonest families of words used to describe Sodomy in the theological texts is rooted in the verb *turpo*. Classically the verb takes a wide range of meanings that include what we might render as "to dirty, to befoul, to disfigure." Similar meanings survive into medieval Latin. Now Christian theologians frequently use the related adjective, *turpis*, or the noun, *turpitudo*, when discussing Sodomy. These uses are related to a host of other terms that have to do with uncleanness: *immunditia, inquinatio, obscenus, sordes*. All of these appear in the texts we have been reading—indeed, all appear in Peter Damian, who is a storehouse of moralistic invective. There is also throughout the texts the technical technical use of "pollution" (*pollutio*) for any seminal emission, but especially for emission in solitary or mutual masturbation. What can justify a Christian's invoking notions of cleanliness when condemning a sin? The synoptic Gospels, at the very least, seem unanimous in their refusal of what they take as rabbinic notions of purity. Jesus' ministry presents itself as an insistent violation of various scruples about ritual purity. What warrant is there, then, for a Christian moralist to reintroduce such notions? Isn't this another case of reanimating un-Christian notions that were meant to have been buried with the advent of the Gospel? Isn't the logic of a term like *turpis* formally excluded by the New Law? Yet Paul himself speaks in the Latin versions of uncleanness (*immunditia* = *akathasía*, Galatians 5:19, Colossians 3:5), as well as of the contaminated or profaned (*contaminati* = *bebêloi*, 1 Timothy 1:9).

Similar questions must be asked about terms of opprobrium referring to nobility and its opposite. Nietzsche argues at length in the *Genealogy of Morals* that the origin of terms for moral valuation lies in the tastes of an aristocracy. Even if that were generally true, Christianity would have to declare itself an exception. Surely Christian moral theology cannot reproduce the equation of the good with the noble. Yet that equation is rehearsed ceaselessly in our texts on Sodomy. Sodomy is the *peccatum ignominiosus,* the most ignoble sin. Is that properly a condemnation for a Christian? Again, Sodomy is a *flagitium,* a disgraceful yielding to the heat, the urgency of passion. One should practice instead the autonomy that characterizes the self-control of the aristocrat. After all, one of the names for sexual sins is *incontinentia.* Does Christian revelation authorize the condemnation of passion or self-abandonment in that way? Yet Paul speaks famously of the "ignominious passions" (Romans 1:26, *in passiones ignominiae = eis páthê atimías*) and of those who lose control over themselves (2 Timothy 3:2, *incontinentes = akrateís*).

Related distortions—indeed, the worst troubles linked to condemnations of Sodomy—have to do with misogyny. It is hard to find a single condemnation in the theological tradition that does not rely on misogynistic logic. They condemn violently anything feminine, but especially anything that seems to surrender masculine privilege. A man cannot have sex with another man because to do so makes him less, degrades him, subordinates him. The very logic of the moral category *luxuria* implies a disapproving link with an essentialized feminine. A specific sin of *luxuria* is called *mollities* (softness) and those who practice it are *molles.* Effeminacy of one kind or another is regularly alleged as a consequence of same-sex copulation or of any other form of *luxuria.* These condemnations do not depend for their force on a metaphysical qualm of substantial change, of one thing becoming another. They depend on the familiar male horror about women. Within this horror, to be a woman is to be something defective, something already half-polluted, something disreputable. But this horror is surely not something that Christian theology ought to permit, much less endorse. What warrant could there be in Christian revelation for despising women as such?

The forces that power extreme condemnations of Sodomy seem also to produce condemnations of the unclean, the ignoble, and the feminine. Each of these condemnations ought to be suspect for a Christian. Yet they are allowed to stand in support of the condemnations of same-sex pleasure. This support should be seen as a question, not an answer—as an anomaly, not as a settled fact. The troubles that surround the condemnations of Sodomy are linked to larger patterns of irrationality in Christian moral teaching. Our relation to those patterns and to their implications will require a revaluation of our relation to the Christian traditions of moral teaching.

THE RESPONSIBLE CONSTRUCTION OF CHRISTIAN MORAL TRADITION

Many Christians have come to believe that the official teachings on same-sex pleasure are inadequate both to their own experiences and to the Gospel. They are blocked in any further thinking by what they see as the unanimous condemnation of Christian tradition, whatever they think of the tradition's locus and force. This is not the first time that the body of believers has reached an impasse in moral reflection. Something very similar happened with the question of chattel slavery just over a century ago—as it happened with the doctrine of justifiable war in the 1960s. In every case the question has been the same: How does one honor the tradition while being faithful to the Gospel and to the impulses of God in the present? In every case, the beginning of an answer was the same. Believers had to free themselves from fundamental misunderstandings about the character of Christian moral tradition. Part of freedom is to remember how fragile our relation to that tradition is, so far as it is a relation dependent on the reading of inherited texts.

It is hard to know how to call what we do with old texts of Christian moral teaching, much less how to justify it. Consider the metaphors we use. There is the metaphor of revivifying an ancient text. The classicist Wilamowitz spoke this metaphor grandly in a lecture at Oxford as giving our own blood to ancient ghosts. We speak it less grandly when we describe "conversations" with the authors of the past or "communities" within which the dead are treated as living authorities. But they are not living. They are at best specters given voice to say again what we guess them to have said already.

Or we might want to speak of reactivating the insight adumbrated in an old text. We would mean that a text can help us recreate an experience of an object it wishes to show us. We would be assuming, of course, that we can recognize the object as the same, that we can have what is recognizably the same kind of experience. This is dubious even in the history of mathematics, much more in the history of morals. What, after all, is the object experienced in moral theology? It is not a rule, a proposition, since Christian theology holds typically that rules are at best only instruments for the operation of grace. Nor is the object a thing, a substance, unless it is the substance of God, which cannot be fully experienced under present conditions, much less contained in human texts.

We might instead try to speak of retrieving a theological teaching. The metaphor here suggests that some thing has been lost or forgotten. It is to be found in some definite place, and we will recognize it when we come to that place. How will we? On what grounds are we confident that we will recognize what we seek? And what if the thing to be retrieved is nothing more than a virtuous effect in the best readers of the treatise—not something meant to be spoken so much as something to be lived? Presumably the only way to retrieve a virtuous effect is to experience it. And presumably one can experience it only if one is in the right condition to receive the text's teaching. So we need formation before we can begin to retrieve.

I myself have elsewhere favored the metaphor of joining a work's posterity. I meant that a reader should recognize what kind of community of readers the structure of a work looks to constitute and should then seek to join that community. This metaphor too leads immediately into difficulties. The most obvious candidate for a work's posterity would seem to be the visible communities of serious readers of the work. Who are to count as serious readers? No existing group of readers may be satisfactorily attentive to the ways in which a work attempts to make posterity for itself. Again, none of the historically evident groups of readers may have responded adequately to the work. Frequently read texts generate quarrels among their readers. So, for example, Thomism is not one "tradition of inquiry." It is, at its best, a crowd of alternative traditions, separated by embittered disagreements large and small, often the more bitter for being smaller. Moreover, for some readers all of the traditions of Thomism seem to have been deformed by serious misunderstandings. Étienne Gilson, for example, thought that all readings of Thomas from shortly after his death had mistaken Thomas's essential philosophical insight, namely, the insight into being.

Things are made worse by realizing that a work may intend to make for itself a posterity that flourishes in reacting against it. The best posterity may be continued inquiry or sharp criticism or thorough rebuttal. We certainly have protestations to that effect from any number of ancient and medieval authors, as we have works that seem designed to provoke such a posterity. This is obvious in the structure of Platonic or Augustinian dialogues and of disputed questions. It is implicit in the structure of the Aristotelian treatises, in various genres of commentary, and even in polemic. And almost every work of Christian morals submits itself to correction by better Christians, who are submitted all to the judgment of God.

If we are not revivifying, reactivating, retrieving, or inheriting old texts, might we at least be said to be "encountering" them as something foreign? Of course, but that is only to rename the problem. If we take the foreignness of the texts seriously, then we return again to the now obvious difficulties of translation, which is to say, of reading. There is no guarantee that we could ever translate every important feature of another language, as there is no external check on mistranslation from an old text about obscure and remote matters. There is no group of living speakers to check our renderings, and there is no appeal to practice as a way of testing our understandings. Indeed, "translation" is itself a metaphor that may do us a disservice by oversimplifying. It is not clear that my attempting to paraphrase Aquinas's teaching on same-sex pleasure in English is much like my trying to express my desire for an espresso in Milan's airport.

There is no easy name for what we do when we read older theological texts, as there is no algebra for producing "better" interpretations. Excellence in reading is much like excellence in musical performance—a personal skill valued differently by different audiences, according to competing criteria. The analogy with music is seriously misleading in one respect: the standard of musical performance may be considerably higher than the standard of scholarly "performance." At least, we may suppose that a Baroque composer would appreciate the virtuosity of a modern performer rather more than a medieval master of theology would appreciate the scholarly readings of his texts. With respect to medieval texts, modern scholars show themselves to be at once dunces and jades. They are dunces because they know considerably less than medieval beginners in theological studies. No scholarly expert knows the Latin scriptures or the patristic authorities as immediately and literally as medieval auditors would have known them. But modern scholars are also jades: They know a bewildering variety of texts, notions, languages, and tastes that medieval auditors would neither have known nor relished.

Given these difficulties in our relations to the textual traditions of Christian morals, we ought to engage them diffidently and with a readiness to vary our reading immediately if the texts suggest that we do so. But there is more. If we want to use rather than to abuse the Christian moral tradition, we must undertake a meticulous reexamination of our relation to its texts—a reexamination of what it means to have a tradition. We must escape the most obvious misunderstandings, the most common forms of violence. In what follows, I propose three exercises by which believers can *begin* to do this. Unbelievers may find them helpful too so far as the presuppositions of Christian teaching have grounded secular teaching on same-sex pleasure.

Exercise 1. If Christian theologians have claimed to have a relation to their predecessors that escapes the endless puzzles of interpretation, it is because they can claim a unity with those predecessors in virtue of shared faith. The continuity of Gospel teaching or the rule of faith is thought to provide a connection across history and through the frailty of texts. What kind of continuity is assumed here when we come to morals? What is taken to be continuous in moral tradition? It cannot be the continuity just of statements, since statements are obviously liable to misunderstanding, misapplication, or misdirection in changed practical situations. Moreover, many of the sayings in the Gospel or in the church traditions are not so much statements as exhortations or laments or prayers. The end of Christian moral theology is not to produce a list of stainless steel propositions. It is to help believers to make particular judgments about what is to be done under divine guidance. Hence what makes moral tradition continuous is not the sameness of proposition, the reiteration of certain words, but rather a coherence of purpose, a coherence of helpfulness.

In the passage with which I began this epilogue, Ambrose says, "As Cicero wrote to educate his son, so I too write in order to form you, my children; nor do I love you less for having begotten you in the Gospel than if I had gotten you by marriage." He supposes that one should speak only out of love. That is a rule for testing the coherence of purpose in Christian moral tradition. The same words spoken from some motive other than love are not moral teaching at all, much less continuous with earlier moral teaching. By contrast, different words spoken out of newly discerning love can be entirely continuous with earlier moral teaching.

Exercise 2. There is much to suggest that the condemnation of homosexuality arose not from the Gospel's critique of prevailing social norms, but from those prevailing norms themselves. The Christian condemnation of same-sex pleasure may not be a proclamation in the face of social prejudice as much as a concession to it. Consider that the origin of the misinterpretation of Sodom lies not in the Old Testament, but in the intratestamental contact of Jews with Hellenistic society; that the Pauline condemnations derive from pagan philosophic sources or from the prejudices of certain Jewish communities; that the first Christian legislation against same-sex acts echoes reactionary pagan views of what is proper to masculinity; that the nature arguments against same-sex acts appropriated by Western theology are versions of Stoic or neo-Aristotelian arguments; and so on. We may have here not a courageous Christian witness against the secular, but a cowardly Christian submission to the secular.

This submission is fundamentally connected to the Christian acceptance of un-Christian notions about gender differentiation and reproduction. Condemnations of homosexuality rely quite plainly on pagan notions of bodily fertility that the Gospels want to overturn. Indeed, given the Gospels' views on the priority of spirit over body, the priority of Christian community over natural family, it is extraordinary that so many branches of Christianity should have now degenerated into fertility cults. The Christian criterion of fertility, of parenting, of filiation, is not bodily. That much was worked out with painstaking care in the early Trinitarian debates. So it should be in all our understandings of begetting.

A Gospel understanding of begetting depends on the deeply unbiological character of Christian love. I think of the implications for human intimacy of the character of Christian community. The Christian community ought to undo the great divide of man against woman, the tyranny of man over woman, especially when this is conceived as a direct deduction from the biology of reproduction. Christian relations are not to be enslaved by the tyranny of gender hierarchies. What is most interesting about human bodies in Christian teaching is not the difference that allows for bodily birth. It is the suffering and the affection that grounds evangelization and other expressions of love. Christians ought to want to know not how bodies reproduce, but what they need for wholeness. What they need is both healing and embracing. This much is clear in so many of Jesus' healing miracles as they are retold by the synoptic traditions. Jesus heals by touch, by graphically recounted intimacy, the contact of body with body. In these stories, rather than in scraps of pagan morals, the Christian should find indications for what the body is.

Recall Ambrose again: "As Cicero wrote to educate his son, so I too write in order to form you, my children; nor do I love you less for having begotten you in the Gospel than if I had gotten you by marriage." In that remark, we have both the failure and the promise of Christian moral teaching on bodies. Ambrose conceives himself as a father writing to his son, as a paternal begetter of children that he could have gotten through marriage. Yet what Ambrose means to describe is an essentially ungendered, an essentially spiritual relation of parenting. Ambrose's very writing of a Christian moral treatise is a fertile act of male begetting, of same-sex fertility.

Exercise 3. It is time for the Western Christian churches to "come out." This is nowhere more urgent than in regard to moral theology. The long tradition of Christian moral teaching that runs from Ambrose down through Aquinas is, given the historical circumstances of the Western churches, the expression of an immensely procreative love between men. Here the misogyny of the church turns against itself: the exclusion of women makes it all too clear that there can be, that there are and have always been, familial communities of men who lived together, prayed together, ministered together, and loved one another in complete rejection of heterosexist conceptions of family. Moreover, what scattered evidence we have, despite the extraordinary censorship to which it has been subjected, shows that at least some of these men had erotic and even genital relations. The very continuity of moral tradition in the Western churches testifies against the condemnation of same-sex love in that same tradition.

Recall Ambrose for a third time: "As Cicero wrote to educate his son, so I too write in order to form you, my children; nor do I love you less for having begotten you in the Gospel than if I had gotten you by marriage." The whole question is the delimitation of the love Ambrose invokes. Does it necessarily exclude same-sex love that is erotic? The question cannot be gotten around by pulling in a shopworn distinction between *agapé* and *eros*, between Christian "brotherly" love and non-Christian "sexual" love. There are erotic relations between Christians, and presumably these are subsumed within *agapé*, within the larger notion of the love that constitutes the Christian community. But perhaps here we run across the root of the theological troubles over same-sex love.

The place of the erotic in Christian love is no more settled for other-sex couples than for same-sex couples. In the history of Christian moral teaching, sexual love was permitted for the sake of procreation and on the condition that it be unerotic, that it strive to suppress so far as possible the intensity of passion. This is, at best, a rather restricted license for sexual life among Christians. The vehement denunciations of same-sex pleasure are justified explicitly by appeal to the rule that sex must be procreative. But I suspect that the vehemence is also simply a displacement of the negative judgment on all sex that was suspended in the case of procreative marriage. Most Christian moralists have regarded celibacy as the higher calling, the fullness of Christian response to God. Marriage was permitted, though not recommended, for the continuation of the species and as a concession to human weakness in the present day. But no such concession needed to be made for same-sex love, and so the entire force of condemnation—including the surplus of force left over from the concession to marriage—could be brought to bear on it. The irrational force of the Christian condemnation of Sodomy is the remainder of Christian theology's failure to think through the problem of the erotic.

We might even suspect that Sodomy came into existence as a category just because of that failure. To invent Sodomy was to invent a pure essence of the erotic without connection to reproduction. It was to isolate the erotic in its pure state, where it could be described in frightening colors and condemned without concession. "Sodomy" is a name not for a kind of human behavior, but for a failure of theologians. "Sodomy" is the nervous refusal of theologians to understand how pleasure can survive the preaching of the Gospel.

Works Cited

Acta sanctorum quotquot toto urbe coluntur. Junius, vol. 7. Paris: Palme, 1867.

Adams, J. N. *The Latin Sexual Vocabulary*. Baltimore: Johns Hopkins University Press, 1982.

Alan of Lille. *De planctu naturae*. Edited by Nicholas Häring. In "Alain of Lille, 'De planctu naturae.'" *Studi medievali*, ser. 3, 19/2 (1978): 797–879.

———. *Liber poenitentialis*. Edited by Jean Longère. Analecta Mediaevalia Namurcensia, vol. 18. Louvain: Nauwelaerts; Lille: Giard, 1965.

———. *The Plaint of Nature*. Translated by James J. Sheridan. Mediaeval Sources in Translation, vol. 26. Toronto: PIMS, 1980.

———. *Summa "Quoniam homines."* Edited by Palémon Glorieux. In "La Somme 'Quoniam homines' d'Alain de Lille." *Archives d'histoire doctrinale et littéraire du moyen âge* 20 (1953): 113–364.

———. *Tractatus de virtutibus, de vitiis, et de donis Spiritus sancti*. In *Psychologie et morale aux XIIe et XIIIe siècles*, vol. 6: *Problèmes d'histoire littéraire de 1160 à 1300*, by Odon Lottin, pp. 45–92. Gembloux: J. Duculot, 1960.

Alberigo, Josephus, et al. *Conciliorum oecumenicorum decreta*. 3d ed. Bologna: Istituto per le scienze religiose, 1973

Albert the Great. *Commentarii in I–IV Sententiarum*. In the Borgnet *Opera omnia*, vols. 25–30.

———. *De anima*. Edited by Clemens Stroick. In the Cologne *Opera omnia*, vol. 7, 1963.

———. *De natura boni*. Edited by Ephrem Filthaut. In the Cologne *Opera omnia*, vol. 25, 1974.

———. *De vegetabilibus*. Edited by Ernst H. F. Meyer and Karl F. W. Jessen. Berlin, 1867; reprint, Frankfurt am Main: Minerva, 1982.

———. *In evangelium Lucae*. In the Borgnet *Opera omnia*, vol. 23.

———. *Opera omnia*. Edited by Auguste Borgnet. Paris: Vivès, 1890–1899. Cited here as "Borgnet *Opera omnia*."

———. *Opera omnia*. Edited by members of the Institutum Alberti Magni Coloniense. Munster: Aschendorff, 1951–. Cited here as "Cologne *Opera omnia*."

———. *Quaestio de luxuria*. Edited by Albertus Fries, Wilhelm Kubel, and Heinrich Anzulewicz. In the Cologne *Opera omnia*, vol. 25/2, 1993.

———. *Summa de bono*. Edited by Heinrich Kuhle, Karl Feckes, Bernhard Geyer, and Wilhelm Kubel. In the Cologne *Opera omnia*, vol. 28, 1951.

———. *Summa theologiae*. In the Borgnet *Opera omnia*, vol. 33.

————. *Super Ethica, Commentum et quaestiones*. Edited by Wilhelm Kubel. In the Cologne *Opera omnia*, vol. 14, 1987

Alexander of Hales. *Summa theologica*. Edited by members of the Collegium S. Bonaventurae. 4 vols Quaracchi C. S B., 1924–1930.

Ambrose of Milan *De Abraham* Edited by Karl Schenkl. Corpus Sciptorum Ecclesiasticorum Latinorum, vol. 32/1. Vienna: Tempsky, 1897.

————. *De officiis*. Edited by Maurice Testard. Paris: Belles Lettres, 1984.

————. *Epistulae*. Edited by Otto Faller and Michael Zelzer Corpus Scriptorum Ecclesiasticorum Latinorum, vol. 82, in three parts. Vienna: Hoelder-Pichler-Tempsky, 1968–1982.

————. *Explanatio psalmorum XII*. Edited by M. Petschenig. Corpus Scriptorum Ecclesiasticorum Latinorum, vol. 64. Vienna: Tempsky, 1919.

————. *Hexaemeron*. Edited by Karl Schenkl. Corpus Scriptorum Ecclesiasticorum Latinorum, vol 32/1. Vienna: Tempsky, 1897.

Aristotle. *De interpretatione*. In *Categoriae et Liber de interpretatione*, edited by Lorenzo Minio-Paluello. Oxford: Clarendon Press, 1949.

————. *Ethica Nicomachaea*. Edited by W. D. Ross. Oxford: Clarendon Press, 1925.

————. *Historia animalium*. Edited by Leonard Dittmeyer. Leipzig: Teubner, 1907.

————. *Politica*. Edited by W. D. Ross. Oxford: Clarendon Press, 1957.

ps-Aristotle (Nicholas of Damascus?). *De plantis*. Translated by Alfred of Sareshel. In *De plantis Five Translations*, edited by H. J. Drossaart Lulofs and E. L. J. Poortman. Amsterdam and New York: North-Holland, 1989.

————. *Problemata*. Edited by Pierre Louis. Paris: Les Belles Lettres, 1991–1994.

Audet, Th -André. "Approches historiques de la *Summa theologiae*." In *Études d'histoire littéraire et doctrinale*, pp 7–29. Publications de l'Institut d'études médiévales, vol. 17. Montreal: Institut d'études médiévales; Paris: J. Vrin, 1962.

Augustine. *Confessiones*. Edited by M. Skutella and L. Verheijen. Corpus Christianorum Series Latina, vol. 27. Turnhout: Brepols, 1981.

———— *De bono coniugali*. Edited by Joseph Zycha. Corpus Scriptorum Ecclesiasticorum Latinorum, vol. 41 Vienna: F. Tempsky, 1900.

————. *De civitate Dei* Corpus Christianorum Series Latina, vols. 47–48. Turnhout: Brepols, 1955. Reproducing the text of the 4th edition of Bernardus Dombart and Alphonsus Kalb (Leipzig. Teubner, 1928–1929).

————. *De correptione et gratia*. In Migne *PL* 44:915–946

————. *De mendacio*. Edited by Joseph Zycha. Corpus Scriptorum Ecclesiasticorum Latinorum, vol. 41. Vienna: F. Tempsky, 1900.

———— *Quaestiones XVI in Matthaeum*. Edited by Almut Mutzenbecher. Corpus Christianorum Series Latina, vol. 44B. Turnhout. Brepols, 1980.

————. *Sermo 100*. Edited by Roland Demeulenaere. In "Le sermon 100 de saint Augustin sur le renoncement." *Revue Bénédictine* 104 (1994): 77–83.

Avicenna. *Canon medicinae*. In *Liber Canonis*. Venice, 1507; reprint, Hildesheim: Georg Olms, 1964.

———— *Liber de philosophia prima sive scientia divina V–X*. Edited by S. Van Riet. Avicenna Latinus Louvain. E. Peeters; Leiden: E. J Brill, 1980

Bailey, Derrick Sherwin. *Homosexuality and the Western Christian Tradition* London: Longmans, Green & Co., 1955; reprint, Hamden, Conn : Archon Books, 1975.

Bein, Thomas "Orpheus als Sodomit." *Zeitschrift für deutsche Philologie* 109 (1990). 33–55.

Bellamy, James A. "Sex and Society in Islamic Popular Literature" In *Society and the Sexes in Medieval Islam*, edited by Alaf Luftı al-Sayyıd-Marsot, pp. 23–42. Giorgio Levı della Vıda Conferences, vol. 6. Malıbu: Undena, 1979.

Bıblıa sacra ıuxta vulgatam versıonem. Edited by Robert Weber, with Bonıfatıus Fıscher, Johannes Grıbomont, H. F. D. Sparks, and W. Thıele. 3d ed. 2 vols. Stuttgart: Deutsche Bıbelgesellschaft/Bıblıa-Druck, 1983.

Bıeler, Ludwıg. *The Irısh Penıtentıals*. Scrıptores Latını Hıbernıae, vol. 5. Dublın: Dublın Instıtute for Advanced Studıes, 1963.

Blaıse, Albert. *Dıctıonnaıre latın-françaıs des auteurs chrétıens*. Turnhout: Brepols, 1954.

Boethıus. *Philosophıae consolatıo*. Edıted by Ludwıg Bıeler. Corpus Chrıstıanorum Serıes Latına, vol. 94. Turnhout: Brepols· 1984

Bouhdıba, Abdelwahab. *Sexualıty ın Islam*. London and Boston: Routledge & Kegan Paul, 1985.

Boswell, John. *Chrıstıanıty, Socıal Tolerance, and Homosexualıty*. Chıcago: Unıversıty of Chicago Press, 1980.

Boyle, Leonard E. "Alıa lectura fratrıs Thome." *Medıaeval Studıes* 45 (1983)·419–429.

———. "Notes on the Educatıon of the *Fratres Communes* ın the Domınıcan Order ın the Thırteenth Century." In *Xenıa medıı aevı hıstorıam ıllustrantıa oblata Thomae Kaeppelı O.P.*, edıted by Raymundus Creytens and Pıus Kunzle. 2 vols., 1:249–267. Rome· Ed. dı Storıa e letteratura, 1978.

———. *The Settıng of the* Summa theologıae *of Saınt Thomas*. Étıenne Gılson Serıes, vol. 5. Toronto: PIMS, 1982.

Brandl, Leopold. *Dıe Sexualethık des Heılıge Albertus Magnus*. Regensburg: F. Pustet, 1955.

Bucher, Françoıs. *The Pamplona Bibles*. New Haven, Conn., and London: Yale Unıversıty Press, 1970.

Burchard of Worms. *Decretum*. In Mıgne *PL* 140:549 - 1062.

Bursıll-Hall, G. L. *Speculatıve Grammars of the Mıddle Ages*. The Hague and Parıs: Mouton, 1971.

Cadden, Joan. *Meanıngs of Sex Dıfference ın the Mıddle Ages: Medıcıne, Scıence, and Culture*. Cambrıdge: Cambrıdge Unıversıty Press, 1993.

Cavıgıolı, Gıovanni. "De sententıa s. Petrı Damıanı cırca absolutıonem complıcıs ın peccato turpı." *Apollınarıs* 12 (1939): 35–39.

Chance, Jane. *Medıeval Mythography: From Roman North Afrıca to the School of Chartres,* A.D. *433–1177*. Gaınesvılle: Unıversıty Press of Florıda, 1994.

Colbert, Edward P. *The Martyrs of Córdoba (850–859)· A Study of the Sources*. Washıngton, D C.: Catholıc Unıversıty of Amerıca Press, 1962.

Colombás, García M. *San Pelayo de León y Santa María de Carbajal: Bıografía de una comunıdad femenına*. León: Monasterıo de Santa María de Carbajal, 1982.

Constantıne the Afrıcan. *Lıber de coıtu*. In *Constantını Lıber de coıtu: El tratado de andrología de Constantıno el Afrıcano*, edıted by Enrıque Montero Cartelle. Monografías de la Unıversıdad de Santıago de Compostela, vol. 77. Santıago de Compostela: Secretarıado de Publıcacıones de la Unıversıdad de Santıago, 1983.

———. *Pantegnı theorıca*. Text as ın Erfurt, Wıssenschaftlıche Bıblıothek der Stadt, MS Amplon. Q 184.

Dalla, Danılo. *"Ubı Venus mutatur" Ommossesualıtà e dırıtto nel mondo romano*. Semınarıo Gıurıdıco della Unıversıtà dı Bologna, vol. 119. Mılan: A. Gıuffrè, 1987.

d'Alverny, Marıe-Thérèse. *Alaın de Lılle: Textes ınédıts*. Études de phılosophıe médiévale, vol. 52. Parıs: J. Vrın, 1965.

Daniel, Marc. "Arab Civilization and Male Love." In *Reclaiming Sodom*, edited by Jonathan Goldberg, pp. 59–65. New York and London: Routledge, 1994.

De Sodoma [anonymous poem]. Edited by Rudolf Peiper. *Corpus Scriptorum Ecclesiasticorum Latinorum*, vol. 23. Vienna: Tempsky, 1881.

Díaz y Díaz, Manuel C. *De Isidoro al siglo XI· Ocho estudios sobre la vida literaria peninsular*. Barcelona: El Albir, 1976.

————. "La pasión de S. Pelayo y su difusión." *Anuario de estudios medievales* 6 (1969): 97–116.

————. "Passionaires, légendiers, et compilations hagiographiques dans le haut Moyen Âge espagnol." In *Hagiographie, cultures et sociétés (IVe–XIIe siècles)*, pp. 49–59. Paris: Études Augustiniennes, 1981.

Diekstra, F. N. M. "The *Supplementum tractatus novi de poenitentia* of Guillaume d'Auvergne and Jacques de Vitry's Lost Treatise on Confession." *Recherches de théologie ancienne et médiévale* 61 (1994): 22–41.

Dols, Michael W *Majnun. The Madman in Medieval Islamic Society.* Edited by Diana E. Immisch. Oxford: Clarendon Press, 1992.

Dondaine, H. F., and Shooner, H. V. *Codices manuscripti operum Thomae de Aquino.* 3 vols. to date. Rome: Comissio Leonina, 1967–.

Driscoll, Michael S. "Penance in Transition: Popular Piety and Practice." In *Medieval Liturgy*, edited by Lizette Larson-Miller. New York: Garland, 1996.

Dronke, Peter. *Women Writers of the Middle Ages: A Critical Study of Texts from Perpetua to Marguerite Porete.* Cambridge: Cambridge University Press, 1984.

Economou, George D. *The Goddess Natura in Medieval Literature.* Cambridge, Mass.: Harvard University Press, 1972.

Edwards, Catharine. *The Politics of Immorality in Ancient Rome.* Cambridge: Cambridge University Press, 1993.

Encyclopaedia of Islam· New Edition Prepared by a Number of Leading Orientalists. Edited by H. A. R. Gibb et al. 7 vols. to date. Leiden: E. J. Brill, 1960–.

Encyclopedia of Homosexuality. Edited by Wayne R. Dynes et al. 2 vols. New York: Garland, 1990.

Espejo Muriel, Carlos. *El deseo negado. Aspectos de la problemática homosexual en la vida monástica (siglos III–VI d. C.).* Granada: Universidad de Granada, 1991.

Fábrega Grau, Angel. *Pasionario hispánico.* 2 vols. Madrid and Barcelona: CSIC, 1952.

Florez, Enrique. *España Sagrada Theatro geográphico-histórico de la iglesia de España.* 2d ed. Vol 23. Madrid, 1799

Foucault, Michel. *Histoire de la sexualité* Vol. 1: *La volonté de savoir.* Paris: NRF/Gallimard, 1976

Gaillard, Georges. *La sculpture romane espagnole de saint Isidore de Leon à saint Jacques de Compostela.* Paris: Paul Hartmann, 1946.

Galen. *Ars medica.* Edited by C. G. Kuhn. In *Galeni opera omnia.* 20 vols. Leipzig, 1821–1833. Vol. 1, pp. 305–412. Reprint, Hildesheim: G. Olms, 1965.

García Abad, Albano. *Leyendas Leonesas.* Madrid: Everest, 1984.

Geary, John S., ed *Historia del Conde Fernán González.* Madison, Wis.: Hispanic Seminary of Medieval Studies, 1987.

Ghisalberti, Fausto. "Medieval Biographies of Ovid." *Journal of the Warburg and Courtauld Institutes* 9 (1946): 10–59.

Glorieux, Palémon. *Aux origines de la Sorbonne.* Vol. 1: *Robert de Sorbon.* Études de philosophie médiévale, vol. 53. Paris: J. Vrin, 1966.

———. "La Somme 'Quoniam homines' d'Alain de Lille." *Archives d'histoire doctrinale et littéraire du moyen âge* 20 (1953): 113–364.

Glossa ordinaria. As in *Biblia latina cum glossa ordinaria . . . et interlineari.* Strasbourg: Adolf Rusch, 1480. Reprinted in facsimile under the editorship of Karlfried Froehlich and Margaret Gibson Turnhout: Brepols, 1992.

Grabmann, Martin. *Einfuhrung in die* Summa theologiae *des heiligen Thomas von Aquin.* 2d ed. Freiburg: Herder, 1928.

Gratian. *Decretum.* In *Corpus iuris canonici,* edited by Æ. L. Richter and Æ. Friedberg. Leipzig: Tauschnitz, 1922.

Green, Monica. "The *De genecia* attributed to Constantine the African." *Speculum* 62 (1987): 299–323.

Green, Richard Hamilton. "Alan of Lille's *De planctu Naturae.*" *Speculum* 31 (1956): 649–674.

Gregory the Great. *Moralia in Job.* Edited by Marc Adriaen. Corpus Christianorum Series Latina, vols. 143–143B. Turnhout: Brepols, 1979–1985.

———. *Registrum epistolarum.* Edited by Dag Norberg. Corpus Christianorum Series Latina, vols. 140–140A. Turnhout: Brepols, 1982.

———. *Regula pastoralis.* Text edited by Floribert Rommel. Sources Chrétiennes, vols. 381–382. Paris: Éditions du Cerf, 1992.

Hagele, Gunter. *Das Paenitentiale Vallicellianum I· Ein oberitalienischer Zweig der fruhmittelalterlichen kontinentalen Bußbucher: Uberlieferung, Verbreitung und Quellen.* Sigmaringen: Jan Thorbecke, 1984.

Haimo of Auxerre. *Expositio in epistolam ad Romanos.* In Migne *PL* 117:362 - 508.

Hallam, Paul. *The Book of Sodom.* London and New York: Verso, 1993.

Hankey, Wayne J. "The *De Trinitate* of St. Boethius and the Structure of the *Summa Theologiae* of St. Thomas Aquinas." In *Congresso internazionale di studi Boeziani (Pavia, 5–8 ottobre 1980) Atti,* edited by Luca Obertello, 367–375. Rome: Herder, 1981.

Hippocrates. *Aphorismata.* Edited by W. H. S. Jones. In his *Works,* vol. 4, pp. 97–221. Cambridge, Mass., and London: Harvard University Press, 1992.

Horace. *Epistulae.* In *Opera,* edited by D. R. Shackleton Bailey. Stuttgart: Teubner, 1985.

Hrotswitha. *Opera.* Edited by H. Homeyer. Munich, Paderborn, and Vienna: F. Schoningh, 1970.

Hudry, Françoise. "Prologus Alani *De planctu Nature.*" *Archives d'histoire doctrinale et littéraire du moyen âge* 55 (1988): 169–185.

Hunt, R. W. *Collected Papers on the History of Grammar in the Middle Ages.* Edited by G. L. Bursill-Hall. Amsterdam: John Benjamins, 1980.

Innocent III. *Vineam Domini Sabaoth* = *Epistola* 16.30. Migne *PL* 216:823d - 825c.

Isaac, Jean. *Le Peri hermeneias en Occident de Boèce à Saint Thomas: Histoire littéraire d'un traité d'Aristote.* Bibliothèque Thomiste, vol. 29. Paris: J. Vrin, 1953.

Isidore of Sevilla. *Sententiae.* In Migne *PL* 83:1203 - 1217.

Ivo of Chartres. *Decretum.* In Migne *PL* 161:47 - 1022.

Jacquart, Danielle, and Claude Thomasset. "Albert le Grand et les problèmes de la sexualité." *History and Philosophy of the Life Sciences* 3 (1981): 73–93.

———. *Sexuality and Medicine in the Middle Ages.* Princeton, N.J.: Princeton University Press, 1988.

Janini, José. *Manu,critos litúrgicos de las bibliotecas de España.* 2 vols. Burgos· Aldecoa, 1977–1980

Jerome *Commentaria in Esaiam.* Edited by Marc Adriaen. Corpus Christianorum Series Latina, vols. 73–73A. Turnhout: Brepols, 1963.

———. *Commentaria in Hieʒechielem* Edited by Francis Glorie. Corpus Christianorum Series Latina, vols 75–75A. Turnhout: Brepols, 1964.

——— *Epistulae* Edited by Isidor Hilberg Corpus Scriptorum Ecclesiasticorum Latinorum, vols 54–56 Vienna: Tempsky, 1910–1918.

Johannitius. *Isagoge* Text as in London, Wellcome Institute, MS 801A.

John of Lodi. *Vita Petri Damiani* In Migne *PL* 144:113 - 146.

Kaeppeli, Thomas *Scriptores ordinis praedicatorum medii aevi.* 4 vols. Rome: S. Sabina, 1970–1993.

Kirsch, Wolfgang "Hrotsvit von Gandersheim als Epikerin." *Mittellateinisches Jahrbuch* 24–25 (1989 - 1990). 215–224.

Kohler, Johannes. "Natur und Mensch in der Schrift 'De Planctu Naturae' des Alanus ab Insulis." In *Mensch und Natur im Mittelalter,* edited by Albert Zimmermann and Andreas Speer. 2 vols. Miscellanea Mediaevalia, vol. 21/1–2. Berlin and New York: W. de Gruyter, 1991.

Kottje, Raymund. *Die Bußbucher Halitgars von Cambrai und des Hrabanus Maurus Ihre Uberlieferung und ihre Quellen.* Beitrage zur Geschichte und Quellenkunde des Mittelalters, vol 8 Berlin and New York· W. de Gruyter, 1980

Kusche, Brigitte. "Zur 'Secreta Mulierum'-Forschung." *Janus* 62 (1975)· 103–123.

Lafont, Ghislain. *Structures et méthode dans la Somme théologique de S Thomas d'Aquin.* Paris. Desclée de Brouwer, 1961

Lasko, Peter. *Ars Sacra, 800–1200.* 2d ed New Haven and London: Yale University Press, 1994

Lateran IV Ecumenical Council. *Inter cetera.* In Alberigo, *Conciliorum oecumenicorum decreta,* pp. 239–240.

———. *Omnis utriusque sexus.* In Alberigo, *Conciliorum oecumenicorum decreta,* p. 245

Leclercq, Jean. *Otia monastica Études sur le vocabulaire de la contemplation au moyen âge.* Studia Anselmiana, vol. 51. Rome: Pontificia Universitas "San Anselmo," 1963.

——— *Saint Pierre Damien, Ermite et homme d'Église.* Uomini e dottrine, vol. 8. Rome: Storia e letteratura, 1960.

———. *Témoins de la spiritualité occidentale.* Paris. Éditions du Cerf, 1965.

Lemay, Helen Rodnite. "Some Thirteenth and Fourteenth Century Lectures on Female Sexuality." *International Journal of Women's Studies* 1 (1978): 391–400.

———, trans and ed. *Women's Secrets A Translation of Pseudo-Albertus Magnus's De Secretis Mulierum with Commentaries.* Albany: SUNY Press, 1992.

Little, Lester K. "The Pesonal Development of Peter Damian." In *Order and Innovation in the Middle Ages Essays in Honor of Joseph R. Strayer,* edited by William C Jordan, Bruce McNab, and Teofilo F. Ruiz, pp. 317–341 Princeton, N.J.: Princeton University Press, 1976

Lottin, Odon "Le traité d'Alain de Lille sur les vertus, les vices et les dons du Saint-Esprit." *Mediaeval Studies* 12 (1950): 20–56.

Lynch, Kathryn L. *The High Medieval Dream Vision. Poetry, Philosophy, and Literary Form.* Stanford, Calif.: Stanford University Press, 1988.

Mandonnet, Pierre "La *Summa de poenitentia mag. Pauli presb. S. Nicolai.*" In *Beitrage ʒur die Geschichte des Philosophie und Theologie des Mittelalters,* Supplementband 3, pp. 525–544. Münster: Aschendorff, 1935.

Martianus Capella. *De nuptiis Philologiae et Mercurii.* Edited by James Willis. Leipzig: Teubner, 1983.

Meersseman, G. *Introductio in opera omnia B. Alberti Magni O.P.* Bruges: Beytaert; Paris: Dillen, and Rome: Marietti, 1932.

Menéndez Pidal, Ramón, ed. *Primera crónica general de España.* Reprint, Madrid: Gredos, 1977

Mercken, H. Paul F., ed. *The Greek Commentaries on the Nicomachean Ethics of Aristotle.* Vol. 3. Corpus Latinum Commentariorum in Aristotelem Graecorum, vol. 6/3. Leuven: University Press, 1991.

Millet-Gérard, Dominique. *Chrétiens mozarabes et culture islamique dans l'Espagne des VIIIᵉ –IXᵉ siècles.* Paris: Études Augustiniennes, 1984.

Newhauser, Robert. *The Treatise on Vices and Virtues in Latin and the Vernacular.* Typologie des Sources du Moyen Âge Occidental, fasc. 68. Turnhout: Brepols, 1993.

Nicholas of Damascus. *De plantis: Five Translations.* Edited by H. J. Drossaart Lulofs and E. L. J Poortman. Amsterdam and New York: North Holland, 1989.

Nietzsche, Friedrich. *Samtliche Werke: Kritische Studienausgabe.* 2d ed. Edited by Giorgio Colli and Mazzino Montinari. Vols. 3 and 5. Munich· DTV; Berlin and New York: de Gruyter, 1988.

Nitzsche, Jane Chance. *The Genius Figure in Antiquity and the Middle Ages.* New York and London: Columbia University Press, 1975.

Ovid. *Metamorphoses.* Edited by William S. Anderson. Stuttgart: Teubner, 1993.

Palazzini, Pietro. "S. Pier Damiani e la polemica anticelibataria." *Divinitas* 14 (1970):127–133.

Paul of Hungary. *Summa de poenitentia.* In *Bibliotheca Casinensis seu codicum manuscriptorum qui in tabulario casinensi asservantur series . . . ,* vol. 4. Monte Cassino: Typographia Casinensis, 1880.

Payer, Pierre J. *Sex and the Penitentials.* Toronto: University of Toronto Press, 1984.

Peter Damian. *Book of Gomorrah: An Eleventh-Century Treatise against Clerical Homosexual Practices.* Translated by Pierre J. Payer. Waterloo, Canada: Wilfried Laurier University Press, 1982.

———. *Letters.* Vol. 2. Translated by Owen J. Blum. The Fathers of the Church: Mediaeval Continuation. Washington: Catholic University of America Press, 1990.

———. *Liber Gomorrhianus = Epistola* 31. In *Die Briefe des Petrus Damiani,* vol. 1, edited by Kurt Reindel. Monumenta Germaniae Historica: Die Briefe der deutschen Kaiserzeit, vol. 4. Munich: MGH, 1983.

———. *Vita Romualdi.* Edited by Giovanni Tabacco. Fonti per la storia d'Italia, vol. 94. Rome: Istituto Storico Italiano, 1957.

Peter Lombard. *Sententiae in IV libris distinctae.* Edited by members of the Collegium S. Bonaventurae Grottaferrata: CSB, 1981.

Peter of Poitiers. *Compilatio praesens.* Edited by Jean Longère. Corpus Christianorum Continuatio Mediaevalis, vol. 51. Turnhout: Brepols, 1980.

Petroff, Elizabeth Alvilda. *Body and Soul: Essays on Medieval Women and Mysticism.* New York: Oxford University Press, 1994.

Philippe, Marie-Dominique. "La lecture de la *Somme théologique.*" *Seminarium* 29 (1977): 898–915.

Phipps, Colin. "Romuald—Model Hermit: Eremitical Theory in Saint Peter Damian's *Vita beati Romualdi*, Chapters 16–27." In *Monks, Hermits and the Ascetic Tradition· Papers Read at the 1984 Summer Meeting and the 1985 Winter Meeting of the Ecclesiastical History Society*, edited by W. J. Sheils, pp. 65–77. [Oxford:] EHS/Basil Blackwell, 1985.

Pinborg, Jan. *Logik und Semantik im Mittelalter: Ein Uberblick*. Stuttgart: Frommann; Bad Canstatt: Holzboog, 1972.

Pliny. *Historia naturalis*. Edited by Ludwig von Jan and Karl F. T. Mayhoff. 6 vols. Stuttgart: Teubner, 1967–1970.

Prudentius. *Psychomachia*. In his *Works*, vol. 1. Edited and translated by H. J. Thomson. Loeb Classical Library. Cambridge, Mass.: Harvard University Press; London: William Heinemann, 1953.

Raymund of Peñafort. *Summa, textu sacrorum canonum, quos laudat, aucta et locupleta . . .* Paris: Anisson & Posuel, 1718.

Robert of Flamborough. *Liber poenitentialis*. Edited by J. J. Francis Firth. Studies and Texts, vol. 18. Toronto: PIMS, 1971.

Rodríguez Fernández, Celso. *La pasión de S. Pelayo: Edición crítica, con traducción y comentarios*. Monografías da Universidade de Santiago de Compostela, vol. 160. Santiago de Compostela: Universidade de Santiago de Compostela, 1991.

Roger Bacon. *Opera hactenus inedita*. Edited by Robert Steele. Fasc. 5. Oxford: Clarendon Press, 1920.

———. *Opus majus 7*. In *Rogeri Baconis Moralis Philosophia*. Edited by Ferdinand Delorme and Eugenio Massa. Zurich: Thesaurus Mundi, 1953.

Rosenthal, Franz. "Ar-Razî on the Hidden Illness." *Bulletin of the History of Medicine* 52 (1978): 45–60.

Ruello, Francis. "Les intentions pédagogiques et la méthode de saint Thomas d'Aquin dans la *Somme théologique*." *Revue du moyen âge latin* 1 (1945): 188–190.

Ryan, J. Joseph. *St. Peter Damiani and His Canonical Sources. A Preliminary Study in the Antecedents of the Gregorian Reform*. Studies and Texts, vol. 2. Toronto: PIMS, 1956.

Schmitz, Hermann Joseph. *Die Bußbucher und das kanonische Bußverfahren nach handschriftlichen Quellen dargestellt*. 2 vols. Graz: Akademische Druck- und Verlagsanstalt, 1958.

Sedgwick, Eve Kosovsky. *Epistemology of the Closet*. Berkeley: University of California Press, 1990.

———. "Queer Performativity: Henry James's *The Art of the Novel*." *GLQ* 1 (1993): 1–16.

———. *Tendencies*. Durham: Duke University Press, 1993.

Seneca. *Ad Helviam*. Edited by Hosius. 2d ed. Leipzig: Teubner, 1912.

Shaw, James R. "Scientific Empiricism in the Middle Ages: Albertus Magnus on Sexual Anatomy and Physiology." *Clio Medica* 10 (1975): 53–64.

Sidgwick, Henry. *Outlines of the History of Ethics for English Readers*. 5th ed. London: Macmillan & Co., 1902. Reprint, Indianapolis and Cambridge, Mass.: Hackett, 1988.

Siraisi, Nancy. "The Medical Learning of Albertus Magnus." In Weisheipl, ed., *Albertus Magnus and the Sciences*, pp. 379–404.

Thomas Aquinas. *Contra errores Graecorum*. In the Leonine *Opera omnia*, vol. 40.

———. *Opera omnia*. Edited by Roberto Busa. 7 vols. as supplement to the *Index Thomisticus*. Stuttgart: Frommann; Bad Canstatt: Holzboog, 1980. Cited here as "Busa *Opera omnia*."

———. *Opera omnia iussu impensaque Leonis XIII. P. M. edita* Edited by members of the Order of Preachers. Rome, 1882–. Imprint varies. Cited here as "Leonine *Opera omnia*."

——— *Quaestiones disputatae De malo*. In the Leonine *Opera omnia*, vol. 23

————. *Scriptum super libros Sententiarum.* Edited by Pierre Mandonnet and Maria Fabianus Moos. 4 vols. Paris: Lethielleux, 1929–1933.

————. *Sententia libri Ethicorum.* In the Leonine *Opera omnia,* vol. 47.

————. *Sententia libri Politicorum.* In the Leonine *Opera omnia,* vol. 48.

————. *Summa "contra Gentiles."* In *Liber de Veritate Catholicae Fidei contra errores Infidelium seu "Summa contra Gentiles,"* edited by Ceslao Pera, Pierre Marc, and Pietro Caramello. Turin and Rome: Marietti; Paris: Lethielleux, 1961–1967.

————. *Super ad Ephesios.* In the Busa *Opera omnia,* 6:445–465.

Tonneau, Jean. "Le passage de la *Prima Secundae* à la *Secunda Secundae.*" *Bulletin du Cercle Thomiste Saint-Nicolas de Caen* 69 (1975): 29–46, and 70 (1975): 21–31.

Torrell, Jean-Pierre. *Initiation à saint Thomas d'Aquin: Sa personne et son oeuvre.* Fribourg: Éditions universitaires, 1993.

Tugwell, Simon. *Albert and Thomas: Selected Writings.* New York: Paulist Press, 1988.

Vaquero, Mercedes. "La Devotio Moderna y la poesía del siglo XV: elementos hagiográficos en la *Vida rimada de Fernán González.*" In *Saints and their Authors: Studies in Medieval Hispanic Hagiography in Honor of John K. Walsh,* edited by Jane E. Connolly, Alan Deyermond, and Brian Dutton, pp. 107–119. Madison, Wis.: Hispanic Seminary of Medieval Studies, 1990.

Viarre, Simone. *La survie d'Ovide dans la littérature scientifique des XIIe et XIIIe siècles.* Publications du CESCM, vol. 4. Poitiers: CESCM/Université de Poitiers, 1966.

Vives, José. "Las 'Vitas sanctorum' del Cerratense." *Analecta sacra tarraconensia* 21 (1948): 157–176.

Vives, José, and Ángel Fábrega Grau. "Calendarios hispánicos anteriores al siglo XII." *Hispania Sacra* 2 (1949): 29–146.

Wasserschleben, F. W. Hermann. *Die Bußordnungen der abendlandischen Kirche.* Halle: Graeger, 1851. Reprint, Graz: Akademische Druck- und Verlagsanstalt, 1958.

Weisheipl, James A., ed. *Albertus Magnus and the Sciences: Commemorative Essays, 1980.* Studies and Texts, vol. 49. Toronto: PIMS, 1980.

————. *Friar Thomas d'Aquino: His Life, Thought, and Works.* Revised ed. Washington: Catholic University of America Press, 1983.

————. "The Life and Works of St. Albert the Great." In Weisheipl, ed., *Albertus Magnus and the Sciences,* pp. 13–51.

Wenzel, Siegfried. "The Seven Deadly Sins: Some Problems of Research." *Speculum* 43 (1968): 1–22.

Wierzbicka, Anna. *Semantics, Culture, and Cognition: Universal Human Concepts in Culture-Specific Configurations.* New York and Oxford: Oxford University Press, 1992.

William of Auvergne. *Guilielmi Alverni . . . opera omnia.* 2 vols. Paris: A. Pallard, 1674. Reprint, Frankfurt am Main: Minverva, 1962.

William of Auxerre. *Summa aurea.* Edited by Jean Ribaillier. 6 vols. to date. Spicilegium Bonaventurianum, vols. 16, 17, 18A, 18B, 19, 20. Paris: CNRS, 1980–.

William Peraldus. *Summae de vitiis et virtutibus.* Venice, 1497.

Ziolkowski, Jan. *Alan of Lille's Grammar of Sex.* Cambridge, Mass.: Mediaeval Academy of America, 1985.

Index

'Abd al-Rahmân III (Abdrahemen), 10–28
Achilles, 73–74
Adonis, 70, 81, 86
adultery, 31, 73, 96, 144
agapé, 174–175
Alan of Lille critique of natural ethics, 87; erudition, 67; and grammatical analogies, 79–80 as moral teacher, 92; motives for writing allegory, 87–91, *Plaint of Nature*, 69–91, 151, 167; *Summa "Quoniam homines,"* 90–91, 108, 141
Albert the Great. erudition, 114–115, 164; as expositor of Aristotle, 114; justifications for destruction of Sodom, 133–135, and purpose of genital organs, 130–133, 151, suppression of science, 115, 125–135, 164–165
Alexander of Hales: *Summa*, 164
al-Majusi, 'Alī ibn al-'Abbas, 116
al-Mansur (Almansor), 23
aluminati, 119–122
Ambrose of Milan, 34, 159–160, 173–175
Ancyra, Council of, 54, 90
animals. in analogies to human sex, 39, 124–125; in disanalogies, 55, 149–150; irregular copulations, 70
Antigamus, 77–78
Apollo, 74
Aristotle: and *Problems*, 120–123, and *Secret of Secrets*, 124–125, *History of Animals*, 131–133, *Metaphysics*, 124; *Nicomachean Ethics*, 88, 132, 149–150, 164; *Politics*, 150–151
ar-Razi, Abu Hatim, 122
Articella, 115–116
Augustine and adultery, 95–98; and need for grace, 153, *Confessions*, and sin against nature, 34–35, 148–149

Avicenna. *Metaphysics*, 124; *Canon of Medicine*, 115–123, 134

Bacchae, 13–14
Bacchus, 74, 89
Benjamites, 30–31
Bernard Silvestris, 67
bestiality, 104, 106, 124, 149–150
bisexuality, 82
blasphemy, 29, 32, 43
Boethius: *Consolation of Philosophy*, 14, 72–73, 80, 124
Bonaventure, 123
Boswell, John, 147
Burchard of Worms, 52–54, 56

cannibalism, 149–150
castration, 70
Ceres, 89
Cicero, 159, 173–175
Cistercians, 67
cleanliness, as principle in moral theology, 168
Cluniacs, 67
Colossians, Epistle to the, 168
confession, auricular: in canonical legislation, 92–93; and incitement to sin, 93, 113; invalid if between Sodomites, 47; proper order of, 107, scandalous matter in, 130
confessor character of, 92–93; dangers to, 93, 112, 165–166; unfaithful to experience of penitents, 165
Constantine, emperor, as legislator, 101
Constantine the African, 115–117
copulation· causes of, 117; effects of, 118; positions for, 131–132, 144–145

187